THE SCHNEIDER TROPHY RACES

By the Same Author

DOWN IN THE DRINK
THE SHIP-BUSTERS
STRIKE HARD, STRIKE SURE
THE THOUSAND PLAN
GREAT MYSTERIES OF THE AIR
AVIATOR EXTRAORDINARY
VERDICT ON A LOST FLYER

★

THE LAST BLUE MOUNTAIN

★

TEN GREAT INNINGS
TEN GREAT BOWLERS
TEST CRICKET: ENGLAND V AUSTRALIA
(with Irving Rosenwater)

Jacques Schneider

THE SCHNEIDER TROPHY RACES

Ralph Barker

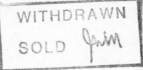

1971

CHATTO AND WINDUS
LONDON

PUBLISHED BY CHATTO AND WINDUS LTD
40 WILLIAM IV STREET LONDON W.C.2
CLARKE, IRWIN AND CO. LTD
TORONTO

ISBN 0 7011 1663 3

PRINTED IN GREAT BRITAIN BY
R. & R. CLARK LTD, BRANDON STREET, EDINBURGH

Contents

Illustrations and Maps

MAPS

Circuit maps, incorporated in the text at appropriate points, are provided for each race.

A 2

Acknowledgements

The copyright in the photographs is acknowledged as follows:

Frontispiece 1 (a), and (b), 2 (b), 8 (b), 12 (b)—Musée de L'Air

2 (a), 3 (a) and (b), 5 (b), 6 (a) and (c), 10 (a) and (b), 11 (a) and (b), 14 (a), 20, 21 (b), 23 (c), 29 (a)—Flight

5 (a), 6 (b), 12 (a)—Radio Times Hulton Picture Library

4, 21 (a)—Central Press

2 (c), 28 (a), 29 (a) and (c), 30—Royal Aeronautical Society

7 (a) and (b), 9 (a), 15 (c), 16 (a), 17 (b) and (c), 18 (a), 22 (b)—H. C. Kavelaars

8 (a), 9 (b), 13 (b), 19 (a) and (b), 24—Real Photographs

13 (a)—Syndication International

15 (b), 18 (b), 23 (a), 26 (c), 27—U.P.I.

14 (b), 15 (a), 16 (b)—Captain Hubert Broad

17 (a), 22 (a), 26 (a) and (b)—Thomas G. Foxworth

18 (a) (inset), 22 (a)—Franco Bugada

23 (b)—Air Commodore Sydney Smith

25 (a)—Mrs. A. H. Orlebar

25 (b)—The Aeroplane and Astronautics

28 (b)—P.A.-Reuter

The maps were produced by H. C. Kavelaars, and the references he used are noted on them.

INTRODUCTION

1 *The Vision of Jacques Schneider*

The man who began it all, Jacques Schneider, was a visionary who saw in the seaplane man's brightest hope for spanning the oceans and bringing the corners of the earth closer together. Born near Paris on 25th January 1879, he was the son of the owner of the Schneider armaments works at Le Creusôt, and he was trained as a mining engineer; but when aviation fever spread through France after the flying of Wilbur Wright at Le Mans in 1908 his mind turned in the reverse direction, and he became passionately interested in aviation. His fascination with the subject was broad: after joining the Aero Club of France in 1910 he gained his pilot's brevet in March 1911 and qualified as a pilot of free balloons a fortnight later, and in 1913 he broke the French altitude record in his balloon *Icare* with a height of 10,081 metres. These successes were achieved despite multiple arm fractures suffered while hydro-planing at Monte Carlo in 1910, which left him handicapped for life.

But for this accident Schneider might have gained greater fame as an aviator; but with his active career restricted he turned more and more to the organising of aviation events and competitions, and he was soon struck by the neglect of the seaplane as opposed to the landplane form. His concept of a special contest for seaplanes thus combined a vision of maritime aviation with a passion for speed; at the banquet following the fourth annual James Gordon Bennett race for landplanes on 5th December 1912 he presented the trophy which bears his name.

The trophy is a vessel of silver and bronze, mounted on a base of dark-veined marble, in which a nude winged figure representing speed is shown kissing a zephyr recumbent on a breaking wave. Into the breaking wave the heads of two other zephyrs are worked, also the head of Neptune, god of the sea. The symbolism—speed in the elements of sea and air—is clear. The trophy stands today in the Royal Aero Club in Pall Mall, but Schneider did not live to see it settle in its permanent home; he died at Beaulieu-sur-Mer, near Nice, not far from the Monaco course where the first Schneider race was run, on 1st May 1928, at the age of 49. He died in reduced circumstances and in relative obscurity, at a time when vast sums were being spent in quest of the trophy he presented.

Schneider's vision of a world traversed by seaplanes and flying-boats must have seemed, in the 1920s and 1930s, very likely to be fulfilled; long ocean cruises were accomplished in these years by most of the major air powers, led by America, Italy and Britain, and the first trans-ocean commercial routes were opened up by flying-boats. But by the end of the Second World War, concrete runways of suitable length, conveniently situated, were available in most parts of the world, and the efficiency and endurance of landplanes had greatly increased. When global air transport eventually became available to all, it was the landplane that provided it. And in the field of air defence, the seaplane had long since been eclipsed by the landplane. Nevertheless the contest for the Schneider Trophy, spanning as it did 18 years in all, from 1913 to 1931, had a far wider influence on aviation than mere advancement of the seaplane form, proving to be the strongest of all peacetime incentives to aviation progress. Especially was this true in the development of power and reliability in aircraft engines and in clean aircraft design.

2 The First Seaplanes

It was more than six years after the Wright Brothers made their famous flight at Kitty Hawk in December 1903 before anyone was successful in using water as a runway for powered flight. The man who succeeded was a Frenchman named Henri Fabre. Born at Marseilles in 1882, and still alive today, he studied the work of the French landplane pioneers before building his first hydro-aeroplane in 1909. On 28th March 1910, with no previous experience of flying, not even as a passenger, he made his first successful flight. Although lack of finance prevented him from continuing his experiments he must rank alongside the great American Glenn Curtiss as the progenitor of the seaplane.

Glenn Curtiss, winner of the first of all international air races—the James Gordon Bennett Cup—at Rheims in 1909, at a speed of 47 m.p.h., also began his hydro-aeroplane experiments in 1910, but it was not until January 1911 that he made his first successful flights. He progressed so rapidly, however, that by 1912 he was supplying a primitive form of flying-boat to the United States Navy. In later years his racing biplanes were to dominate the Schneider contest and very nearly win the trophy outright for America.

The first flight of a seaplane in Britain (it was a modified Avro landplane) was made at Barrow in November 1911; like Henri Fabre, the pilot, Commander Oliver Schwann, had never flown before. In the same month the Admiralty gave permission for four naval officers to learn to fly, and a naval arm of the Royal Flying Corps was formed in 1912. Horace and Eustace Short, already established at Rochester as boatbuilders, branched out into aviation and soon earned orders from the Admiralty, and a young man named Sopwith was building an amphibian at Kingston-on-Thames—a pusher biplane bolted on to a hull constructed by boatbuilder Sammy Saunders at Cowes. (The requirements of strength of construction combined with lightness made the boatbuilders the natural allies of the plane-makers.) France, Germany and Italy were building on similar lines.

Yet by far the majority of the entries at the early hydro-aeroplane meetings in Europe (they were not called seaplanes until Winston Churchill dubbed them such in 1913, after he became First Lord of the Admiralty) were hastily converted landplanes, and their instability and general unsuitability for water-work betrayed their origin. Pilots flew them gingerly, not daring to bank steeply because of the cumbersome floats, and spills of all kinds were frequent. The design of floats was primitive, and little attention was paid to the technique of hydro-planing. "The German hydro-aeroplane meeting at Heilingendamm," said a report of the period, "was in many respects a distinct farce, as it was some time before any of the competitors could rise from the water at all."

Two Curtiss biplane flying-boats took part in the first hydro-aeroplane meeting at Monaco in 1912, but although they took third and fourth places in the Grand Prix they were beaten for speed by the box-kite Farman biplanes mounted on floats. It did not seem likely that the flying-boat, with its greater weight and increased head resistance, would be able to compete for speed with the twin-float seaplane; but what the flying-boat lacked in speed and manoeuvrability it gained in robustness, and as the rules of the Schneider contest called for various tests of seaworthiness—designed to eliminate the freak machine constructed purely for speed—flying-boats played an important part in the races for some years.

3 *The Flying Flirt*

The full title of the Schneider contest was 'La Coupe d'Aviation Maritime Jacques Schneider'—the 'Schneider Cup' to the British and Americans and the 'Coppa Schneider' to the Italians; but it was not, of course, a cup at all. Yet the nations in pursuit of the sculptured trophy all recognised the sensuality of its design and the aggressive femininity of the winged figure representing speed, so that by the early 1920s, when France, Great Britain and Italy had all in turn possessed her, she had earned the soubriquet of the 'flying flirt'. Yet she was not by nature promiscuous, her lifespan being divided into four great loves. Her first love, as might be expected, was France, the boy next door. Then, after seeming likely to make her permanent home in Italy, she was swept off her feet by the Americans. Carried back three years later in brief triumph to Italy, she finally settled in England.

France, Italy, the United States, Great Britain: those are the four natural divisions of the Schneider Trophy story. Created by the French, and brought to maturity by the Americans, the flying flirt finally fell to the British. But of her four suitors the one who loved her best, the one who always came back to woo her, almost to the bitter end, was Italy.

PART I

THE *AFFAIRE* WITH THE FRENCH

1913
at Monaco

"The hydro-aeroplane has become a reality."

Aeronautics

THE Monaco Hydro-Aeroplane Meeting of 1913, run by the International Sporting Club of Monaco, was scheduled to last a fortnight, beginning on 3rd April and ending on the 17th after the first race for the new Schneider Trophy. The main event was the Grand Prix de Monaco, and this race and its preliminary tests and 88-kilometre cruise kept the pilots and their mechanics busy for most of the fortnight.

One word cropped up again and again in descriptions of the early hydro-aeroplane meetings: farce. Planes either failed to get off the water or crashed when they did. Of 16 entrants for the Grand Prix de Monaco, only seven finished the qualifying tests in one piece—or in few enough pieces to be stuck together again in time for the cruise that preceded the race. And thanks to the mistral, which soon after eight o'clock that morning began to blow with destructive force, the cruise itself was a travesty. Of the seven entrants, two failed to get away at all; two more were smashed irreparably at the first alighting point; a fifth broke its tail trying to taxi; and the remaining two, seeing the fate of the others, wisely sought the shelter of Beaulieu harbour. The race was annulled.

Because of the low take-off and alighting speeds of the time, these catastrophes were not attended by serious injury to the pilots. But a reminder that the new sport of seaplane racing could be dangerous was eventually vouchsafed in spectacular fashion to the crowd which gathered daily on the palm-fringed terraces in front of the famous Casino. A pilot named Gaudart, fully experienced and indeed one of the earliest French aviators, elected to give a display of flying despite persistent stability troubles with his machine, a biplane of the flying-boat type. His take-off presented a terrifying sight as the machine bounded out of the water and advanced in a series of violent oscillations. Ten feet above the water it reared up. Gaudart applied a correction, but the machine oscillated again before rearing up a second time, climbing steeply. After a momentary recovery it lifted its nose almost vertically, then pivoted round to the left and dived towards the Tir aux Pigeons—the pigeon-shooting ground below the Casino. The pilot shut off the motor, but the plane continued its dive, narrowly missing the spectators before hitting the sea nose first. There was a violent thud and plane and pilot disappeared, leaving nothing more than a frothy bubbling at the surface. Motor boats rushed to the scene and the plane floated just under the surface, but the body of the pilot had vanished.

* * *

The rules for the Schneider contest provided for eliminating trials on the basis of which each national team would be chosen; as with the Gordon Bennett landplane race, each competing nation was allowed to field a team of three. In addition to the trophy, which was to be awarded annually to the aero club making the winning entry, there was to be a prize of £1,000 for the winning pilot in each of the first three contests. Competition would be by international challenge, and any club affiliated to the Fédération Aéronautique Internationale (formed in Paris in 1905 and the recognised authority for regulating air competitions and certifying air records) would have the right to challenge the club holding the trophy. The holders must then organise the succeeding contest. The course was to be not less than 150 nautical miles, and any club winning the contest three times in five years would be deemed to have won the trophy outright.

Aspirants for the French team originally numbered eight, but the catastrophes of the first week narrowed the field down to three only— Maurice Prévost in a Deperdussin, Dr. Gabriel Espanet in a Nieuport, and Roland Garros in a Morane-Saulnier, so the team selected itself. Nevertheless when the time came for the eliminating trials on Friday 11th April, all three pilots presented themselves and all three prepared to fly the course.

The situation with regard to a challenger was somewhat Gilbertian. Representing America was a pilot of world renown named Charles Weymann; but he had been born at Port au Prince, Haiti, and he had been brought up in France. Stranger still he was flying a French machine—a Nieuport. How could he possibly be said to be representing America? Yet his challenge was taken perfectly seriously. No doubt the absence of any other foreign competitor made the challenge of Weymann and his Nieuport that much more acceptable.

The eliminating trials were run over two laps of the Grand Prix racing course, which was concentrated into a 10-kilometre circuit between Monte Carlo and Cape Martin, near Mentone. This would also be the course for the race itself. As a test of seaworthiness competitors were required to alight once and cover a distance of 500 metres in contact with the sea. On the day of the trials the sea was calmer, and all three Frenchmen successfully completed the test. Weymann, it seems, wisely avoided the risk of eliminating America's sole representative; there is no record that he flew the two trial laps.

Much the fastest time in the trials was recorded by Maurice Prévost in the Deperdussin. In February 1912 the landplane version of this machine had been the first aeroplane to exceed 100 m.p.h. on a straight course, putting the air conclusively ahead of anything yet achieved on road or rail; and in September the same year—seven months before the Monaco meeting—Deperdussins flown by Jules Vedrines and Prévost had come first and second respectively in the Gordon Bennett Cup in Chicago, establishing the type as the fastest in the world. But the substitution of floats, and a larger wing area to give increased lift, would inevitably affect performance.

The Deperdussin was the creation of a young French engineering genius named Louis Bécherau who had worked in French aviation from its earliest days and was still only 29 when he joined the Deperdussin company in 1909. Bécherau studied the monoplanes of Bleriot and Nieuport, with their enclosed fuselages, tractor airscrews, partly enclosed cockpits, and other aerodynamic refinements, and decided he could improve on them; he designed a cigar-shaped fuselage into which the popular Gnome engine, cowled to conform to the fuselage line, fitted neatly. His conception was of a mid-wing monoplane with a revolutionary shell-like or monocoque fuselage of his own invention; this was built up of wood-lattice girders covered with a 3-ply wood veneer. Strong wing bracing appeared at first to offer increased head resistance, but even in the floatplane version the streamlining was good. A small pontoon at the rear kept the tail clear of the water, the centre of gravity being rather far back.

The engine installed in Prévost's Deperdussin was a 160 h.p. 14-cylinder Gnome of the rotary type. The Gnome was the most advanced engine of its time and the most important single factor in France's world supremacy in aviation. The delay between the first flight of the Wright Brothers in 1903 and the achievements of the Rheims meeting of 1909—the real beginning of practical aviation—

was entirely due to the absence of a suitable power unit. Such a unit had to be light-weight but reliable, and it is not perhaps surprising that the answer should have come from the nation that had already gained the lead in the design of the motor-car. The invention that lent reliability to the new science of aviation was the rotary engine; the inventor was a Frenchman named Laurent Seguin.[1] The chief cause of engine failure up to 1909 had been overheating, but this problem was solved to a considerable degree in Seguin's rotary engine by fixing the crankshaft and making the radially-arranged cylinders rotate about its axis, giving far more efficient cooling. There were other advantages too: the revolving engine produced more even torque and ran more smoothly, and the weight-power ratio (about 3 lb per h.p.) was the best of its time. The engine was soon being produced under licence throughout the aviation world.

Another important factor in the success of the Deperdussin was the man who gave it its name. The dapper Armand Deperdussin was a strange mixture of shrewdness and reckless extravagance. Starting business as a shop assistant he made a fortune as a silk broker in the early stages of the Russo-Japanese war, selling at enormous profits when the war caused a shortage. Then in 1910, after meeting Louis Bécherau, he financed an aircraft construction business and a flying school, and soon he was entering his machines in every important contest and retaining some of the finest pilots in the world, regardless of expense. He had borne the cost of sending three of his machines to the United States to compete in the 1912 Gordon Bennett Cup, and for his patriotism—and his victory—he had been awarded the Legion of Honour.

The Deperdussin's chief rival at Monaco was the Nieuport—especially in the hands of Charles Weymann, who had won the Gordon Bennett Cup at Eastchurch, on the Isle of Sheppey, in a Nieuport in 1911. As the longer established machine the Nieuport could be expected to be the more reliable; and in addition the type, and Weymann with it, had flown many more hours in the hydro-aeroplane version than its chief rival. Opinion was divided as to which was the handier machine; but it was known that Weymann's Nieuport had been specially tuned up and held back for the Schneider race, and there was no doubt that it performed better on the water and showed smoother characteristics during take-off.

[1] Lawrence Hargrave, the Australian pioneer, actually built a model rotary engine in 1889.

Although Glenn Curtiss had won the first Gordon Bennett race in 1909 in a biplane, his speed had soon been bettered by the monoplanes of Louis Bleriot. It was a Bleriot, flown by an Englishman, Claude Grahame-White, which won the race in 1910. Then in 1911 had come the Nieuport, borrowing from Bleriot's ideas and experience but improving and streamlining the basic design. Edouard Nieuport, the designer, quickly fastened on to the monoplane as cheaper to build than the biplane because of its simplicity and faster than the biplane because of its reduced head resistance; and his machines, by careful attention to detail, set a new standard in aircraft design and proved an important advance on the Bleriot. The fate of Edouard Nieuport, however, was a tragic one; four months after his new monoplane won the Gordon Bennett in 1911 he was killed in a flying accident; he was the first successful designer to lose his life in this way.

Weymann's Nieuport was powered by a 100 h.p. Gnome engine, less powerful than that of the Deperdussin. But with a "straight" restricted to $2\frac{3}{4}$ miles and sharp cornering, manoeuvrability and the skill of the pilot were almost as important as speed. And whereas Prévost had added a maze of bracing struts to reinforce the under-carriage of his Deperdussin, and the floats themselves were primitive, the undercarriage of the Nieuport was cleaner in outline and more thought had gone into the design of the floats.

One of the problems of the seaplane lay in attaining sufficient speed against the drag of the water-surface to enable it to rise. This, to-gether with the lack of thrust at low speed of the fixed-pitch propellers of the time, was why, on a calm day, many seaplanes failed to take off at all. In rougher water they often bumped off, but this could cause damage. The ability to skim the surface with the minimum of drag was therefore invaluable. Many of the early seaplanes—including the Deperdussin—used flat-bottomed floats set back at an angle, toes sticking up and heels dug in. These were some help in getting the plane into a take-off attitude, but the extent of their stern wave betrayed the force that held the plane down on a take-off run as the water clung to the floats. A more sophisticated method, borrowed from experience of hydroplaning in boats, was to construct the floats on the 'step' principle, so that the water no longer clung to that part of the float behind the step. The floats of Weymann's Nieuport had a three-stepped keel, twelve inches wide, in accordance with this principle.

Perhaps the most accomplished flyer of the four engaged in the con-test was the handsome Frenchman Roland Garros, whose stunting over

Monte Carlo (but not in a floatplane) had thrilled the crowd earlier in the week. Because of his daring, adventurous character Garros was always prepared to take a calculated risk, and his well-tried Morane, with an 80 h.p. Gnome engine, was expected to finish the course. Yet he was likely to be beaten for speed by the other entrants.

What were these machines like to fly? Jules Vedrines, the 1912 Gordon Bennett winner, said he could fly his Deperdussin with the finger and thumb of his left hand, and the Nieuport was normally at least as positive and stable. But this assessment referred to the land-plane versions. Even the best designed floats of the period were imperfectly tested aerodynamically, and were thus almost an unknown phenomenon.

* * *

The mistral that had blown with such force earlier in the meeting had completely subsided by the morning of Wednesday 16th April, the day set aside for the contest for the Schneider Trophy, and the lumpy sea which had caused so many spills and disasters in the previous fortnight lay smooth and calm under a brilliant sun, with a gentle breeze from the south-west causing scarcely a ripple. The course started in front of the Tir aux Pigeons and after a very short leg of 240 metres headed 2¾ miles across the bay to Cape Martin, where there was a severe 165-degree hairpin bend, followed by another straight section of over two miles bringing competitors back to a position off Pointe de la Vielle and finally south-west for Monaco. The short leg at Monaco meant that pilots had two abrupt turning-points only 240 metres apart. The 10-kilometre course was to be flown 28 times, a total of 280 kilometres or 174 miles in all. To demonstrate seaworthiness the first five kilometres, or half the first lap, were to be covered on the water. The race regulations had been approved by the F.A.I.

Although it was a closed-circuit race and some of the turning-points were severe, the crowding and baulking at corners that were so often a dangerous feature of closed-circuit races were reduced to a minimum by starting the competitors at intervals, the pilots racing against time rather than individually against each other. For the pilots it was thus a speed contest pure and simple, like a golfer competing against par, and the continual distraction of a circuit milling with rival planes jockeying for position was mostly eliminated. This left pilots free to get the maximum performance out of their machines, and recklessness and opportunism took second place to flying skill. This impaired the contest

1913 AND 1914 SCHNEIDER TROPHY RACE COURSE

"FLIGHT" April 4, 1914

to some extent as a spectacle, but it had its compensations in the fascination of a regular comparison of lap times—boldly posted on a huge score-board at the Tir aux Pigeons—and in estimating the progress, prospects and ability of first one pilot and then another.

Competitors were allowed to start at any time after eight o'clock in the morning, and after drawing lots Maurice Prévost won the right to go first. To take advantage of the calm conditions the pilots were down at the harbour early, and after Prévost had signalled his readiness to go, the starting-bomb exploded overhead and Prévost opened the throttle gently and aimed his Deperdussin at the starting line. The time was eight minutes and 45 seconds past eight o'clock.

In the next few minutes Prévost completed the taxying test without difficulty and then opened the throttle fully. The clouds of spray that rose behind him settled into a smooth double wake as the floats surfaced, and at length the Deperdussin was away, levelling out at 50 feet and continuing round the circuit. Prévost's first lap, including the taxying, took 11¼ minutes, and before it was completed the starting-bomb exploded for Roland Garros and he too crossed the line in front of the Tir aux Pigeons and began his taxying test.

The Morane-Saulnier, however, proved difficult to handle. Whereas the Deperdussin, once the floats had properly surfaced, had skimmed the water well, the Morane bounced along jerkily, apparently impatient to get airborne. So much water was thrown up by this continual bouncing that the motor was drenched and eventually it stopped altogether. Garros could be seen signalling for a tow back to port, and although this was allowed by the race rules his time would count from his original start. A tow duly arrived and the engine was repaired, but by the time the Morane was ready for another try Garros had lost nearly an hour. It looked an impossible handicap, but the machine was brought out.

Meanwhile the remaining competitors, Gabriel Espanet and Charles Weymann in the two Nieuports, had crossed the starting-line— Espanet at 8.50 and Weymann at 9.14—and were chasing after Prévost, their times for their first few laps closely checked by the spectators. Espanet's skimming test took rather longer than Prévost's and at the end of the first lap he had lost half a minute on his compatriot, while Weymann taxied so cautiously and took so long to get going— despite a much smoother take-off when he finally opened the throttle— that his time for the first lap was by far the worst—18 minutes 21 seconds, or more than 7 minutes behind Prévost. His specially tuned

Nieuport was believed to be the fastest machine in the race, but he had left himself a lot of lee-way to catch up.

A better comparison between the chances of the three pilots came when their times were available for five laps: Prévost had taken 34 minutes 49 seconds, or just under 7 minutes per lap, and at this stage he was 1¼ minutes ahead of Espanet and 5¼ minutes up on Weymann. Thus while forging ahead of Espanet he was losing ground lap by lap on Weymann. For a time the three machines were flying practically together, and the superior speed of the Nieuports was apparent. But when it came to rounding the turning-points Prévost in the Deperdussin scored every time. The clever way in which he negotiated the shorter legs of the course, where the wind was first astern, then abeam, and then ahead, drew appreciative applause from the crowd, and he was making up much of the ground on the corners that he lost on the straight. Espanet and Weymann, for instance, both flew rather wide of the first buoy, were carried off their course by the beam wind on the short leg, and then lost further time in rounding the second buoy and lining up again for the straight. It seemed that Prévost's skilful handling could still win him the race.

The contrast with the handling and flying characteristics of the land-plane versions of these models, however, was all too apparent: none of the pilots dare fly their machines hard into the turning-points and bank steeply, as they would have done without the cumbersome floats.

Two more laps and Espanet was in trouble; his engine was misfiring, and he turned slowly out of the circuit and headed for the harbour. Meanwhile Roland Garros had completed his taxying tests, but seeing that Prévost and Weymann were still flying strongly he decided it was hopeless to continue and taxied in. The race thus became a straight contest between Frenchman and American.

Weymann had settled down now and was putting on the pressure; lapping at nearly 70 miles an hour against Prévost's 60, he was overhauling him steadily. After 10 laps he had cut Prévost's lead by half, and after 15 laps the two men were almost exactly level, Weymann being actually about 3 seconds in front. Weymann's best lap, timed at 71 miles an hour, was nearly half a minute better than Prévost's, but because of the distance Weymann lost on the turns the result was still in doubt.

Lap by lap, however, the greater speed of the Nieuport looked like being decisive. After 20 laps—200 of the 280 kilometres gone— Weymann led Prévost by more than three minutes and the race looked won. By this time Prévost's earlier start meant that he was about to complete his 28th circuit, and he planed down 500 metres short of the finishing line in accordance with the rules as he understood them and taxied in. His total time was given as 2 hours 50 minutes. Weymann had completed his 20th circuit in just under two hours, averaging exactly six minutes a circuit in spite of that ponderous first lap, so he only had to keep going at six minutes a circuit to win.

As Weymann's supporters—who included the President of the Aero Club of America—watched the Nieuport anxiously, listening to every nuance of sound from the engine, the preponderance of Frenchmen watching the race were dealt a further blow: Prévost, it was announced, should have flown, not taxied, over the finishing-line. This was clearly stipulated in the race regulations, and as Prévost had failed to observe them correctly he would be disqualified. Incredulity was followed by bitter controversy: some declared that Prévost's part in the race had ended when the finishing gun was fired and that any disqualification after that was illegal. Others blamed Prévost for not studying the rules more carefully. Prévost himself was too upset for rational reaction: when it was explained to him that all he had to do to qualify for second place was to go out straight away and fly over the finishing-line he refused. His time had been mounting up, he pointed out, ever since his false finish; it was useless to go out again, it was Weymann's race, he wasn't interested in second place.

While this drama was unfolding Weyman completed four more laps —only another four laps to go. But suddenly he was seen to put the nose of his Nieuport forward and plane down on to the water. Everyone expected that he would soon be off again, but there he lingered, tantalisingly still. The Nieuport had suffered a burst oil-pipe, and when it was towed back into the harbour it was discovered that the engine had been so starved of oil that it had been damaged. It would be impossible to repair it or change it that day.

As soon as Weymann planed down, word was sent at once to Roland Garros, and he brought his Morane-Saulnier out for the third time. He had to pass the navigability test all over again, which delayed him still further, but soon he was reeling off circuit after circuit with clock-like regularity, giving a display of precision flying that was high-lighted by his wonderful skill on the bends, quite the equal of any-thing shown by Prévost. But that competitor had been alerted as well, and his machine, too, was quickly brought out again. Soon he was circling the bay, and after flying deliberately over the line to enthusiastic cheers Prévost was eventually declared the winner. Those last 50 yards had cost him 58 minutes on his official time and had brought his average speed down from 61 to 45 miles an hour, but although Garros in his little Morane, only half as powerful as the Deperdussin, averaged over 60 miles an hour for much of the distance and successfully completed the course, the time he had lost at the beginning proved too great a handicap and Prévost was a clear winner.

The first contest for the Schneider Trophy thus ended in a fortuitous but well deserved victory for France. The popular Charlie Weymann did his best to hide his chagrin, and the most keenly disappointed spectator, it seems, was the President of the Aero Club of America, who had come specially armed with the Stars and Stripes to drape Weymann's plane. But even a win for Weymann would have been a French triumph, materially as well as morally, since both machine and engine were of French design and inspiration.

The contest had given Armand Deperdussin his last great victory; four months later, on 5th August 1913, he was arrested in his Paris flat on a fraud charge involving a total of over a million pounds. He confessed that the charges were true. Yet, in employing Louis Bécherau, and in entering his machines for international competitions in Europe and America, Armand Deperdussin had made a significant contribution to the advancement of aviation.[1] After the business collapsed, Louis Bleriot was quick to see that Bécherau's talents must not be wasted; taking over the grounds and sheds of the Deperdussin firm he founded the Société (Anonyme) Pour l'Aviation et ses Dérivés (the famous S.P.A.D. Company), and employed Bécherau as chief designer. The firm later became one of the most successful producers of machines of the first world war.

"As the Rheims meeting of 1909 marked the beginning of practical aviation, so the Monaco meeting, from April 3rd to 17th [1913], showed in one brief but intensely interesting fortnight that the hydro-aeroplane has become a reality." That verdict, expressed by the British magazine *Aeronautics*, would have been altogether too generous but for the success of the final race of the meeting, the first race for the Schneider Trophy.

[1] Deperdussin shot himself in a dingy hotel room in the Rue St. Lazare in Paris on 11th June 1924.

1914

at Monaco

"Mine's a small Bass."

C. Howard Pixton

FRANCE's overwhelming superiority in world aviation was amply confirmed in September at Rheims, when the first three places in the Gordon Bennett Cup went to French pilots flying French aeroplanes. England, the United States and Germany, realising that they were outclassed, withdrew their entries, and the only foreign challenger— a Belgian—flew a French machine. All four entries were powered by 160 h.p. Gnomes, but smart cornering by Maurice Prévost turned the race in his favour and he won at an average speed of 124·5 miles an hour. Under the inspiration of Bécherau the Deperdussin had now reached the ultimate in streamlining for its era, and as no engine had yet been produced to compare with the Gnome rotary, there seemed little prospect of any worthwhile challenge to French supremacy in the 1914 race for the Schneider.

There was, perhaps, one small flaw in French confidence. Louis Bleriot, one of the earliest prophets and pioneers of the monoplane form, had written frankly and courageously of aerodynamic and structural problems as early as 1911, and for a time he had withdrawn his machines from service for special strengthening. The thick, tapered-wing form of cantilever construction that later became almost universal for monoplanes had not yet been developed, and the wings of both monoplane and biplane were so lightly built that external wire bracing in both types was essential. The drag of this wire bracing was so high that the inherent aerodynamic advantages of the monoplane were to some extent obscured.

The biplane had, at that time, undoubted advantages in lift, structural strength, compactness and lightness; and aerodynamic knowledge being limited the tendency was towards the eclipse of the monoplane form, despite the wonderful performance of individual types. An analysis of aeroplane accidents showed that the monoplane was more frequently involved in crashes causing serious injury or death than the biplane, and although this was largely due to the preponderance of the type, there were instances of structural failure or suspected failure; and in any case the higher wing loadings of the monoplane made it more dangerous to fly, while the higher stalling speeds involved greater hazards on landing. The biplane, too, because of its greater mass, offered the pilot more protection; even when the plane crumpled up on impact the pilot often stepped out unhurt. The result was a somewhat panic-stricken revulsion from the monoplane form, and in September 1912 the British War Office actually banned the flying of monoplanes by the military wing of the R.F.C. Since any aircraft manufacturer who wanted to stay in business had to aim at a government contract, Britain became largely a builder of biplanes. A War Office report of 1913 held that the monoplane was *not* structurally inferior provided proper precautions were taken; but with the increasing stresses to which racing and military aircraft were being subjected, and with the state of constructional knowledge of the time, the more robust biplane began to be preferred.

One of the first to get a contract for building a military biplane was a young six-footer named T. O. M. Sopwith. Born in January 1888, Tommy Sopwith had been trained as an engineer; but before he was 20 he had become a competent balloonist, and after learning to fly at Brooklands in 1910 (Royal Aero Club Certificate No. 31), he won a £4,000 prize within a few weeks for a 169-mile flight from England to the Continent. In 1911 he embarked on a tour of the United States, taking his own aircraft and servicing team with him, and demonstrating to the Americans how far they had fallen behind Europe in aviation progress; and when he returned to England in 1912 he won the first Aerial Derby—despite an initial disqualification. One of his team in America had been a young marine engineer named Fred Sigrist, and now, renouncing the glamorous role of pioneer pilot, Sopwith turned to combining his practical experience of flying with his engineering skill.

With the money he had won in America, Sopwith established a workshop and flying school at Brooklands; he taught one of his young mechanics—the Australian Harry Hawker—to fly and appointed him test pilot; and from then on he concentrated on building aeroplanes instead of flying them. It was an evolutionary rather than a sudden process, but it led to the War Office contract and this led in turn to expansion: abandoning the aggregation of sheds which had become his 'factory' at Brooklands, he took over a disused roller-skating rink at

Kingston-on-Thames and there began to fulfil his first production order.

In his two years as a pilot Tommy Sopwith had formed the opinion that a biplane could be built capable of outpacing any monoplane of equal power; because of its basic characteristics the biplane could be built smaller and lighter than the monoplane, and the reduced dimensions brought down total resistance below that of the intrinsically cleaner monoplane type. In conjunction with Fred Sigrist and Harry Hawker—Sopwith gives 90% of the credit to Hawker—a single-bay biplane was designed which, although actually preceded by Geoffrey de Havilland's B.S.1 built at the Royal Aircraft Factory at Farnborough, is often regarded as the first fast single-seater scout, the ancestor of every fighter plane. Certainly it had an enormous influence on scout and fighter design. Of wooden construction, with wire bracing and canvas covering, it was 20' long and had a span of 25' 6", the upper wing being staggered about a foot in advance of the lower wing, with a gap of 4' 3". The cockpit, situated under the upper wing and immediately above the centre of the lower wing, was tiny, but in the original version it was just wide enough to accommodate pilot and a single passenger side by side.

Fred Sigrist, who was responsible for the detailed engineering, had originally intended the plane for racing and demonstration flying, and to this end he had reduced head resistance to a minimum and kept the loading as light as possible. Because of its compact and diminutive design—it was the first biplane in the world to be fitted with only one pair of inter-plane struts on either side—it was dubbed the 'Tabloid', and as the wing surface was about the same as that of the very much heavier monoplanes, the loading was consequently smaller and the flying characteristics better. The engine—Sopwith had chosen the 80 h.p. Gnome rotary—was almost wholly enclosed in the cowling, enhancing the neat appearance and streamlined effect, and early flight tests showed that no monoplane of the period would be able to match its rate of climb or its manoeuvrability.

On 29th November 1913 Harry Hawker flew a special trial for military observers at Farnborough, which resulted in the War Office order; and the same afternoon he thrilled a display crowd at Hendon with his spectacular handling of the new machine. A maximum speed of 92 miles an hour was achieved at the trial, and the machine climbed to 1,200 feet in sixty seconds. Almost as remarkable was the slow stalling speed of 36·9 miles an hour, giving a speed range of 55·1. The all-round excellence of the design was immediately recognised, and the machine was hailed as the most satisfactory aeroplane likely to be built for a long time.

With his background of competitive flying, Sopwith was quick to recognise the publicity value of success in the more important sporting events, and he earmarked one of the first production models of the Tabloid for modification as a seaplane and entered it in the Schneider contest for 1914, due to be run at Monaco on 18th April. He was aware, though, that the French monoplanes were using twice the horse-power of the Gnome installed in the Tabloid, and he made a special trip to Paris to see the Seguin brothers, makers of the Gnome engines, in quest of more power. He was not interested in the 160 h.p. twin-row Gnome engine—it was far too big and heavy for the little Tabloid—but he had heard of a new 100 h.p. engine which involved very little addition in weight. This was the 'Monosoupape', so called because of its single-valve design; it differed from other Gnome engines in that it dispensed with inlet valves. This engine was to become the best-known of all rotary engines, and in March 1914 Sopwith became the first man to import one to England. He brought it back by train and boat in his luggage.

The Monosoupape had nine cylinders against the 14 of the 160 h.p. Gnome; it developed 104 h.p. at 1,200 revolutions a minute, and consumed about 10 gallons of petrol an hour and rather more than two gallons of oil. Its total weight of 260 lb represented a weight-power ratio of only 2·5 lb per h.p., and Sopwith was satisfied that with this engine the Tabloid would do well at Monaco.

Early in 1914 Harry Hawker went to Australia to demonstrate the land version of the Tabloid there, in the hope of attracting further orders, and Sopwith engaged an experienced test pilot named C. Howard Pixton to continue the test flying programme and to fly the Tabloid in the Schneider race. Pixton, a gentle, unassuming fellow with a slight but rather engaging idiosyncrasy of speech, had joined A. V. Roe as a working pupil in 1910 and qualified as a pilot (Certificate No. 50), in the following year. From then on he entered nearly all the Brooklands competitions and won most of them, and after touring Europe demonstrating and testing aeroplanes he had a period with what was to become the Bristol Aeroplane Company before joining Tommy Sopwith. Not perhaps the most excitable of men, he was one of the outstanding flyers of his time—factors which may not have been unrelated.

The first requirement was to construct a suitable undercarriage. Sopwith had already built the first British flying-boat/amphibian (the Bat Boat), and he was employing a young carpenter named Syd Burgoine, son of a Kingston boatbuilder. Between them they produced a design for a central main float with two wing-tip floats for balance; this, they thought, would be stronger and more stable than the alternative of twin floats or pontoons. Working against time they had the first seaplane version of the Tabloid ready for its water tests towards the end of March. Removing the wings, they transported the machine by road to the river Hamble, near Southampton, and by 31st March the Tabloid had been reassembled and everything was ready for the trials.

Howard Pixton—Picky, as he was known—had meanwhile caught a chill, and all day Tuesday 31st March he was confined to his bed. He was not feeling much better next morning, but any further delay would almost certainly have meant that the Tabloid would not be ready in time. Thus the first trials actually fell on 1st April—an inauspicious date for what proved an inauspicious start.

The pallor of Picky's complexion that morning was accentuated by his dark hair with side parting, brushed straight over to hide incipient baldness, and the small military moustache that he sported, with waxed ends. The point from which they planned to launch the Tabloid was a high-water jetty at the mouth of the Hamble river, so they had to wait for the tide to come in. When the water rose to within six inches of the jetty, Pixton climbed into the cockpit and started the engine, and Sopwith and his team pushed the machine off the end of the jetty. But the main float had been fitted too far aft, and when Pixton started to taxi, the machine cartwheeled and sank. Pixton was thrown into the water, but in spite of his chill and his cumbersome flying clothing he struggled back to the jetty. The Tabloid, upside down in the water, was already out of reach, and soon it had drifted out into midstream. It was late in the day before the handling party could get a rope to it, but eventually they pulled it up on to the beach, where they left it for the night, returning to their hotel in Southampton in some dejection. Sopwith called for champagne that night to cheer them up.

When they got down to the Hamble next morning the Tabloid presented an alarming sight. The receding tide had left it stranded and it had tilted on to the nose of its float and its propeller boss, with its tail high in the air. The sodden, buckled machine was immediately dismantled and taken back to Kingston. Not only would it have to be partly rebuilt before the race, which was now little more than a fortnight off, but the undercarriage would have to be re-designed.

Fred Sigrist and his team worked day and night to restore the airframe, but time was too short for a complete re-design of the undercarriage. Burgoine, however, achieved a more conventional arrangement this time by sawing the single main float in half along its centre line; the inboard side of each half was filled in and two small pontoon-type floats, rather box-like in appearance, were produced. Each float was attached to the fuselage by two struts. Two supporting cross-bars were fitted, and the whole structure was wire-braced. The wing-tip floats were discarded, a tail float was added, and a small triangular fixed fin was installed forward of the rudder.

There was no time to go back to Hamble, so the rebuilt Tabloid was taken down to the river just below Kingston Bridge for tests at five o'clock on the morning of 7th April. Permission to fly the machine off the Thames had not been applied for, which explained the early hour. But by the time the machine was rigged up and ready to fly it was 9.30, and although the launching was successful it did not escape the vigilance of officials of the Thames Conservancy Board. In the face of their vehement objections only floating tests were made. But Sopwith's men were nothing if not resourceful. Victor Mahl, Sopwith's chief mechanic, a dapper little fellow with plenty of bombast, hated anyone to get the better of him. It occurred to him that the jurisdiction of the Thames Conservancy Board did not extend below Teddington Lock, where control passed to the Port of London Authority. Next morning, 8th April, at an equally surreptitious hour, the Tabloid was transported to Ham and launched opposite Glover's Island.

Pixton was at the controls, and after testing the plane's behaviour on the water he headed up river and opened the throttle. At that point the Thames Conservancy Board men arrived, but they were too late. "Beat you to it this time," crowed Mahl. The re-designed floats climbed on top of the water nicely on the take-off run, and although the engine had not fully recovered from its immersion and was misfiring intermittently, and the reach was too short for full acceleration, Pixton estimated that a speed of over 80 miles an hour was achieved. The Tabloid still looked to have a chance at Monaco, and preparations were made at once for its despatch. The race was now only ten days away.

Sopwith went to Monaco himself to supervise the preparations, taking mechanic Victor Mahl with him to tune the engine, and boat-builder Burgoine in case of further trouble with the floats. He got possession of the Tabloid at Monaco on Thursday 16th April, two days before the race, and he and his team soon had her out of the packing case and into the tent that had been erected for their use. Next morning the wings were fitted and all parts re-assembled, and the machine was ready for flying except for the engine, which had still not recovered from its ducking at Hamble. It was badly rusted externally and the salt was still sweating out of it.

All day long Sopwith and Mahl worked on the engine, watched with tolerant amusement by the French, who ridiculed the idea of a tiny biplane, the smallest and lowest-powered machine in the race, competing successfully with the speedy, streamlined monoplanes that had carried all before them in the racing events of previous months. Stories that the Tabloid in its landplane form had achieved speeds in excess of 90 miles per hour were simply not credited.

The eliminating trials to decide the French team had already been held when Sopwith and his party arrived, and among the contestants was Maurice Prévost in the Deperdussin with which he had won the 1913 Gordon Bennett at an average speed of 124 miles an hour. Fitted with floats and a new 200 h.p. 18-cylinder Gnome engine, it was one of the fastest and most beautifully streamlined machines of its time. But on the day of the trials there was a high wind and a choppy sea. Prévost's new engine failed to develop sufficient power to get him off the water, and of the eight contestants only Gabriel Espanet in a 160 h.p. Nieuport completed the four-lap course—at an average speed of 62 miles an hour. Roland Garros, who six months earlier had become the first man to fly the Mediterranean, completed two laps on a 160 h.p. Morane-Saulnier, and Pierre Levasseur also completed two laps on his 160 h.p. Nieuport. These two pilots joined Espanet in the official team, leaving Prévost and three other pilots—two in Deperdussins and one in a Morane—as reserves. The elimination of Prévost was a disappointment, but no one imagined it would make any difference to the destination of the trophy.

Apart from Weymann in another Nieuport, powered by an 18-cylinder 160 h.p. Le Rhône rotary, the foreign challenge was not taken seriously. The German Ernst Stoeffler, in an Aviatik 'Arrow' with a Benz engine, did not have the speed of the Nieuports. Switzerland's entry—an F.B.A. flying-boat with a 100 h.p. Gnome Monosoupape, like the Tabloid—would only be a credible challenger if rough weather wrecked the floatplanes, and the second American entry—a rickety old Curtiss biplane pusher flying-boat, with baggy surface fabric that badly needed renewing and with piano-wire bracing —was openly laughed at. Indeed the jeers of the other competitors and their followers so shamed the pilot, William Thaw, of Pittsburgh, that when he was offered another mount—a Deperdussin with a 160 h.p. Le Rhône—he accepted. A second British entrant, Lord Carbery, was also flying a French machine—a Morane—and the only man who took much interest in the Tabloid was Charlie Weymann: he visited Sopwith in the assembly tent and seemed impressed.

Saturday 18th April was the day allotted for the race, but as yet the Tabloid had not flown since its brief trial on the Thames a week earlier. Working late into Friday night, Sopwith and his team had the plane ready, but a rough sea ruled out all hope of flying next day and the race was postponed until Sunday.

At five o'clock on Sunday morning Sopwith had the Tabloid out of its tent and loaded with fuel and oil for a two-hour flight; this was not quite a full load but it was sufficient for a satisfactory trial. The plane was launched and for the first time the French had an opportunity of appreciating the compactness of its outline. More conspicuous at first, however, was the clumsy appearance of the makeshift floats and the peculiar 'sit' of the fuselage, the tailplane barely kept afloat by the aft pontoon, the elevators almost drooping into the water. Pixton then taxied out towards the mouth of the awkward little harbour that had been allotted to the planes. Heading into a light on-shore wind, he surprised the spectators by getting airborne in a run of no more than a hundred feet from the moment he opened up, in striking contrast to the earlier performance of the monoplanes, whose take-offs had been painfully sluggish. Eight minutes later, after some prettily banked turns and an impressively fast run—though the actual speed was difficult to judge as there were no other machines in the circuit—he landed neatly and taxied to the bottom of the slipway almost clear of the water. The French still remained sceptical, but there was no more ridicule.

The test had revealed one fault: the large diameter, medium-pitch propeller was causing the engine to over-rev. With a disregard for partisanship that was to become typical of these contests, the Gnome experts were soon in attendance, and their advice was that 1,350 revolutions per minute, which was the recorded speed of the engine with the existing propeller, was too much for a race that was expected to last over two hours. A smaller propeller of coarser pitch was accordingly substituted. The only other important modification was to the fuel system: here Sopwith and Mahl were working in the dark as there had been no time for consumption or speed tests, and therefore the time it would take to complete the necessary 28 laps could only be roughly estimated. The existing tank held 24 gallons—about 2 hours 20 minutes' flying—but this gave too small a margin; so an additional tank holding approximately six gallons was lashed in beside the pilot's seat and connected to the main tank. Also, as a precautionary measure, a heavier pair of stay wires was spliced in on the float chassis, the original wires having stretched during the test flight. Fortunately the wind breezed up after the early morning flight tests and a further 24-hour postponement gave time for these changes to be made.

The circuit marked out for the race was exactly the same as the previous year, the course again being concentrated into the bay between Monaco and Cape Martin, with the 165° hairpin bend at the Cape Martin end and two turning-points in Monaco harbour only 240 metres apart. (See page 23.) The morning of Monday 20th April looked favourable and it was announced that the race would be run. Competitors were informed that they could start at any time after 8 a.m. and before sunset at 6.47, but the south-east wind was expected to freshen later and most of the pilots were out practising for an early start.

Two competitors had suffered mishaps the previous day and were apparently out of the race—Lord Carbery in his Morane and Ernst Stoeffler in the Aviatik—but Lord Carbery was successful in borrowing a Deperdussin from one of the French reserves (not Prévost, he was still hoping to compete). Carbery was out on the water soon after first light and airborne for about an hour. Weymann took his Nieuport out soon afterwards, and the Swiss flying-boat got airborne at 6.15, the pilot, Burri, getting a special cheer because of his exploits flying for Bulgaria in the Balkan war. At 6.30 the Tabloid was launched, and within two or three minutes Pixton was taxying out towards the harbour mouth. His take-off run was rather longer than the previous day, and the machine didn't seem quite so fast in the air, but this was put down to the coarser pitch of the propeller and the additional weight of the fuel. After a final familiarisation flight round the course Pixton beached the Tabloid in the main harbour in front of the Hotel Bristol, where the Sopwith party were staying. No further modifications proved to be necessary, but the Tabloid had still done so little flying since its immersion at Hamble that Sopwith and Mahl were intent on giving the engine a final check before the race.

The rules this year obliged each competitor to make two alightings and take-offs during the first lap, but since the throttle could be opened again immediately after touch-down, these alightings approximated to a landplane's circuits and bumps and offered little proof of seaworthiness except in rough conditions. At eight o'clock, when the starting-bomb was exploded, the sea was fairly smooth, and although it was rippled in places it was much to the liking of the floatplane pilots and gave little encouragement to Burri, piloting the only flying-boat in the race.

First away were the favourites, the two French-entered Nieuports, Levasseur just after eight o'clock and Espanet half a minute later; Levasseur crossed the starting-line somewhat sedately and took 200 yards to get off, but Espanet was going all out as he crossed the line and was soon airborne. Levasseur's caution, however, paid off after he had turned off Cape Martin and descended for his two alightings; he accomplished them neatly in the space allotted, while Espanet overran the line after his first alighting and was obliged to turn back and execute his second one separately. Thus although Levasseur flew his first lap at a slower pace he completed it in under 9 minutes against Espanet's $9\frac{1}{4}$.

Meanwhile Burri in the F.B.A. had amused and excited the crowd on the terraces above the Tir aux Pigeons by a long, porpoising take-off, beginning with a series of hops and finally bounding and ricocheting into the air. His alightings on his first lap, after each of which he bounced into the air again with the buoyancy of a football, were equally entertaining, and by doing no more than breast his hull into the waves he lost very little speed and completed his first lap in $6\frac{1}{4}$ minutes, easily the best so far. This put him in the lead for the moment, but the Nieuports had the speed to overtake him readily enough as the race went on.

Delayed while Sopwith and Mahl made the final touches to the engine, Pixton finally took off a quarter of an hour after the two Nieuports at 8.16. Opening the throttle, he was accelerating rapidly as he crossed the starting-line, and his floats actually left the water only 50 or 60 feet beyond it. There was a moment when the machine faltered, the floats bounced once on the water, and then the little biplane was climbing strongly away, heading into wind down the long leg of the course towards Cape Martin. At the sharp turn Pixton banked steeply; then on the way back he had to do his two bumps. With very little reduction in speed he came down low and his floats kissed the water twice; they were hardly bumps, but the two separate touches were unmistakable and were all that was required to satisfy the judges. It was a beautiful piece of flying and the Tabloid seemed to be slowed by the contact hardly at all. Then as he took the square turns in front of the crowd at the Tir aux Pigeons Pixton was watched in astonishment and admiration; monoplanes with floats were still being handled gingerly, and no waterplane had been seen banking like this before, not at Monaco or anywhere else. The Sopwith biplane was obviously much faster and more manoeuvrable than the monoplanes, and when Pixton's time for the first lap was announced the crowd whistled with astonishment. It had taken him only 4 minutes 27 seconds, half the best French time, and although the Nieuports were now lapping more smartly it seemed that the Sopwith would win if its engine held out.

When Pixton completed his second lap in 4 minutes 10 seconds, half a minute better than Espanet's average from the second lap onwards, with Levasseur even further behind, the news caused a sensation. The Sopwith would run away with it. And for the next few circuits Pixton, still flying in thrilling fashion and never seeming to miss the pylons by more than inches, lapped with almost clockwork regularity in even better time: 4 minutes 5 seconds, 4·08, 4·04, 4·06, and then 4·09 steadily for three consecutive laps, while Espanet was rarely doing better than 4·40. Pixton in fact was lapping 15 miles an hour faster than Espanet, and although both Espanet and Levasseur opened right out as the race progressed in an effort to keep up with the Tabloid, increasing their speed by nearly five miles an hour, Pixton kept going steadily at nearly 90 miles an hour and the two Frenchmen fell further behind. After ten laps Pixton was more than 10 minutes up on Espanet and 13 minutes up on Levasseur, and although Burri in the F.B.A. was going well he was another 3 minutes behind the French second string.

With the Sopwith securely established as the best machine aerodynamically, to the amazement of the French, the result now depended on mechanical durability. In choosing the 100 h.p. Monosoupape Sopwith had gone first and foremost for reliability, and his judgment found early confirmation in the experience of Lord Carbery, who failed to get off again after his alighting tests in his borrowed 160 h.p. Deperdussin, due to mechanical trouble. His engine kept popping and banging, and although he managed to make a fresh start after being towed in he was down again after two laps, his engine wrecked.

By the half-way stage both Espanet and Levasseur were having trouble with their engines. The rear banks of the twin-row Gnomes were prone to overheating, and under the strain of chasing the

Tabloid the trouble was affecting them now. The lap times of both the Nieuports fell away, and after 16 laps Espanet was forced to come down. Levasseur kept on for a time, but after 17 laps he too alighted. In both cases the trouble was seized pistons. Pixton and Burri were thus left with the race to themselves.

Charlie Weymann and Roland Garros, who had been watching the lap times recorded by the Sopwith with dismay, both refused to start, deciding to see first if Pixton could complete the course. But on its 15th lap the engine of the Tabloid began to misfire. Pixton had not even got as far as Espanet and Levasseur. Burri was still chasing him, and if he faltered seriously the French would put up another contender, and Weymann too would be ready to start.

Pixton's time in his 16th lap fell to 4·22; then in his 17th to 4·31; and in his 18th to 4·40. The Monosoupape was missing on one cylinder, and there was no telling what further trouble might develop. The fault had brought Pixton's lap times down to the level of Espanet's and threatened to put him out of the race altogether.

For six agonising laps the drama went on. Sopwith had pushed 28 drawing pins into the dashboard in front of Pixton as a primitive form of lap-counter, and one by one Pixton tore them off, wondering each time whether he would get round again. But at last the Gnome began to settle down on its eight good cylinders, and Pixton's times improved. Indeed he began to recapture the precision of earlier laps. Fears of a breakdown receded and finally disappeared in heady triumph as Pixton went through from his 22nd to his 27th and penultimate lap with a variation between laps of no more than 1¾ seconds.

Throughout the final lap the Sopwith was applauded, and when Pixton crossed the finishing-line there was no mistaking the enthusiasm of the predominantly French crowd. An elapsed time of just 13 seconds more than two hours gave Pixton and the Tabloid an average speed of 86·78 miles an hour for the Schneider course, beating Prévost's true average of the previous year by 25 miles an hour. And with the finishing-line safely behind him Pixton kept going for two more laps— by pre-arrangement with Sopwith—to set up a new floatplane record of 86·6 miles an hour over a measured 300 kilometres.

The excitement was still not quite over. Burri had run out of petrol on his 23rd lap and had alighted to refuel; he came down in very rough water, the weather being nothing like so placid as earlier, and although the flying-boat coped with this well enough the conditions looked dangerous for floatplanes. Pixton got down smoothly, but immediately afterwards his machine disappeared in a trough—only to reappear apparently undamaged. Pixton decided to wait for a tow rather than attempt to taxi in, and while he was waiting for Mahl to come out a big sea damaged his elevator. But no further damage was sustained and the Tabloid was safely towed in.

At this point Weymann and Garros accepted defeat, and the race seemed over—apart from Burri's marathon attempt to claim second place. But then it was whispered that, with the withdrawal of Roland Garros, Maurice Prévost intended to take his place as third string for France to try to beat Pixton's time. There was tremendous excitement as his chocolate Deperdussin was launched; but almost at once the engine failed and he was forced to retire. Levasseur came out late in the afternoon on Weymann's Nieuport to try to complete the course and gain third place, Burri having finished in an elapsed time of 3 hours 24 minutes, but after nine laps he had to retire a second time with engine trouble.

Significant as the Tabloid's victory was, it did not mean the complete eclipse of the French. The British had captured the Schneider Trophy, but they had done it with a French engine, a debt that Sopwith himself was the first to acknowledge. The Gnome Monosoupape, he said afterwards, was the greatest single contribution of the era to aviation progress. It was to become the most ubiquitous rotary engine of the war.

* * *

The victory of Tommy Sopwith's despised biplane was to have a traumatic effect on the minds of aeroplane designers of the period. Hitherto the monoplane, with certain reservations as to its safety, had been the established favourite for speed and manoeuvrability; now a biplane had been produced that could beat the monoplane at its own game. Of revolutionary design, and representing an entirely new standard in aeroplane construction, the Sopwith Tabloid upended contemporary theories and delivered a massive shock to the accepted conventions of the aviation world. British designers, not unnaturally, followed Sopwith's lead, and when the French government copied Britain's example by putting restrictions on the monoplane for France's military programme, her designers were forced to turn to the biplane. Had the war not intervened it is probable that the monoplane would have recovered from this setback, but in wartime speed, although important, was not the only factor. Some useful load over and above pilot and fuel was necessary, and a low landing speed that would give the average pilot room to operate safely from restricted bases, and a rapid rate of climb and a good ceiling, were mandatory. Under these conditions the structural advantages of the biplane outweighed the superior streamlining of the monoplane, and with growing experience in design and more powerful engines, the speed of the military biplane soon equalled and surpassed that of the pre-war racing monoplane. An unfortunate result was that for many years the development of the monoplane was neglected.

The lack of Press coverage of this outstanding British victory drew cynical comment from the aviation magazines. But Sopwith himself did not forget to pay a deserved tribute to the War Office. "The building of this aircraft," he said, "was due largely to the support of the authorities in helping us forward with orders. The actual machine which won was the direct outcome of a machine built practically to the specification of General Henderson."[1] It was the first production aircraft to go into service as a single-seater scout with the British flying services, and although not itself produced in quantity it had illustrious successors in the Camel, the Pup and the Snipe. The official war history had this to say of it: "When the Sopwith Tabloid was first produced, it was unfavourably reported on by the pilots who flew it, and at once fell into disrepute throughout the squadrons. The fact is that the pilots of that time were not good enough for the machine; if they had stuck to it, and learnt its ways, they would soon have sworn by it, as, later in the war, they swore by the Sopwith Camel."[2]

The victory celebrations that followed in Monaco produced another British triumph, also largely unsung. When Jacques Schneider invited the victorious British pilot to celebrate his win in traditional fashion that evening in the Sporting Club, 'Picky' must have known that he had one of the finest cellars in Europe at his behest. Everywhere the champagne was flowing, but 'Picky' rejected it all. "Thanks very much," he said, in that slightly muffled voice of his, "but mine's a small Bass."

[1] Brigadier-General Sir David Henderson, Director of Military Aeronautics.
[2] *War in the Air*, Vol. 1, Sir Walter Raleigh (O.U.P.).

PART II
ATTACHMENT IN ITALY

1919

at Bournemouth

"We claim to have won the Cup and the pilot's prize . . ."

Royal Aero Club of Italy

THE long sandy shore of Bournemouth Bay held that curious tranquil stillness and silence that comes only with a low mist that dampens the sand and smooths the surface of the sea into glass. The beach that would otherwise have been thronged with people was deserted, disturbed only by the faint lapping of the sea; the boatmen stood about in disconsolate groups, and even the gulls were inanimate. The pier was an amputated finger, more than half of its length obliterated, and the two super-dreadnoughts that were anchored a mile off the pier—*Barham* and *Malaya*—were invisible. The landmarks that delineated the shape and limits of the bay were completely obscured.

The date was 10th September 1919, the day fixed for the first Schneider Trophy contest for five years. The course had been laid out in Bournemouth Bay. It was a superb arena. From the gallery of the high cliffs to the dress circle of the raised promenade and the raked pit of the beach, the view of a great spectacle would be uninterrupted if only the mist would clear. The competitors were due to fly down the coast from their anchorages at Cowes during the morning; they would land in the shallows and taxi up to the beach, where the multitude could inspect them. Then, when the race began, each contestant would be given the starting-signal from the *Ombra*, the Royal Aero Club yacht anchored off the pier.

The pilots would take off and head almost due south out to sea, past Poole and Sandbanks and Studland Bay and on towards Swanage. In Swanage Bay they would round the first mark boat before heading back diagonally across Bournemouth Bay to Hengistbury Head. There they would round the second mark boat—known as the Christchurch mark boat—before completing the triangle by running back along the coast to Bournemouth Pier. The circuit, 20 nautical miles in length, would be flown ten times, making a total distance of 200 nautical miles.

Nodding their heads sagely, the boatmen predicted that the mist in the bay would clear before midday. And indeed by eleven o'clock the outline of the pier at Boscombe a mile along the beach was faintly visible, although not yet quite in focus, a pale reflection of the darker etching now limned by the piles and struts of Bournemouth Pier. The warships at anchor, too, were glimpsed as insubstantial wraiths and then as great masses of metal hovering in the mist. To the east, Hengistbury Head was emerging from its shroud; but although the breeze could now be felt on the face, the Old Harry Rocks, on the foreland which abutted to block the view of Swanage Bay, were still invisible.

The war had brought a progress and expansion in aviation unimagined when the last Schneider race had been flown in 1914. One of the biggest advances was in power units. With the materials then available the rotary engine was limited to 150-200 h.p., and it had other disadvantages in terms of power utilisation and fuel and oil consumption. When the war began the R.F.C. and R.N.A.S. didn't have a single aircraft powered by a British engine between them; but under the stimulus of wartime needs, economical water-cooled engines were soon produced which developed twice as much power as the rotary engine, with a longer life, and often without any great disadvantage in power-weight ratios. Thus the rotary engine had been almost entirely superseded by the war's end.

Most British engineers, among them men like Henry Royce and Montague Napier, had always preferred water-cooled to air-cooled engines, and after studying the methods of the leading continental engine-makers Royce evolved the first successful V-shaped 12-cylinder aero engine in 1915, the famous Eagle. This was virtually the engine that had gone into the Silver Ghost motor-car before the war, with its stroke increased from $4\frac{1}{2}$ inches to 6. Royce had refused to be pushed into increasing the bore, which remained at 6 inches. Nevertheless a cylinder that had originally produced only 11 horse-power was eventually persuaded to give 30, and in June 1919, three months before the Schneider race at Bournemouth, two Eagle engines, each producing 360 h.p., had powered the Vickers 'Vimy' flown by Alcock and Brown in the first non-stop heavier-than-air crossing of the Atlantic.

But reliable as Royce's engines were, they were comparatively heavy. And after the war, with Rolls-Royce tooled up for the Eagle and concentrating on that as their principal aero engine, they were suddenly left behind by Montague Napier, who took the bold decision of abandoning the making of cars in the post-war depression years and starting an assembly line for an aero engine that had been designed for him by a gifted engineer named A. J. Rowledge. Napier had begun to make aero engines to an official specification in 1915, but he soon determined to make his own engines, and the Napier 'Lion' was designed by Rowledge in 1916. It was a 12-cylinder water-cooled engine of the 'W' or 'broad arrow' type; it came too late to play much part in the war, but it packed 450 h.p. into a compact shape and had the best power-weight ratio of any aero engine produced up to that time.[1] It was to become in its various forms the outstanding British aero engine of the twenties, and around it the post-war Royal Air Force was virtually reconstituted. It powered the winner of four Aerial Derbies and two Schneider Trophy contests, and its first big success came in the Aerial Derby of 1919, when it performed better than any other engine, British or French.

Britain thus started firm favourites for the 1919 Schneider race. But although the ebb of national demand had left the European aircraft industry almost stranded, the desire to get back to normal times was intense, and when the F.A.I. called on the Royal Aero Club of Great Britain at the end of May 1919 to organise the next race in September, entries were promised from France, Italy, Spain, the United States and Belgium. But this was short notice to prepare for such an event, and many constructors were unable to get their selected machines ready in time. Spain, the United States and Belgium subsequently withdrew, and Britain was the only competitor obliged to hold eliminating trials to choose a team. France planned to enter a team of three, but Italy would be represented by a lone Savoia flying-boat. Thus Britain's chances were further enhanced.

Early in August it was announced that the race would be held on Wednesday 10th September at Bournemouth. This was good news for spectators, but it presented difficulties for the competitors and for race organisation. There were no slipways or sheds at Bournemouth, and competitors would have to fly down from Cowes on the day of the race and presumably park on the beach. Messrs. C. E. Saunders Ltd. offered their premises at Cowes for the accommodation of competing machines before and after the race.

Four British machines took part in the eliminating trials, three sea-

[1] The cylinders were arranged in three banks of four, with an angle of 60 degrees between the vertical bank and each lateral bank.

planes and a flying-boat. All were biplanes and all were specially built for the occasion. They were:

A Sopwith seaplane with a 450 h.p. Cosmos Jupiter radial engine designed by Roy Fedden. The machine was not so very different in conception from that of the original Tabloid, but it was expected to prove the fastest of the four. The pilot was Harry Hawker.

A Fairey III seaplane with a Napier Lion engine, which was expected to run the Sopwith close for speed. The pilot was Vincent Nicholl.

An Avro 539 seaplane with a 240 h.p. Siddeley Puma engine. This was a small, neat, stubby machine of conventional construction. The pilot was H. A. Hamersley.

A Supermarine Sea Lion flying-boat, built on the lines of the same firm's Baby fighter (which had been produced too late for the war), but specially modified for racing by a young designer named R.J. Mitchell. The pilot was Basil D. Hobbs.

When the preliminary trials were held on 8th September, the Sea Lion showed a slight edge on the Avro 539 and the latter was eliminated.

Compared with the technological advancement of landplanes, seaplane development during the war had been relatively stagnant. In spite of a growing belief that aeroplanes which could use the sea as a landing area would prove convenient and cheap to operate, at the end of the war the only small high-speed seaplane that the R.A.F. possessed in any quantity was the original Sopwith Schneider, admittedly with a more powerful engine. Thus after 5½ years the Schneider Trophy was still principally attracting high-speed landplanes on floats.

The French team struck trouble from the start. They planned to enter two Nieuports and a Spad-Herbémont, the latter named after the chief designer of the Spad company, André Herbémont, formerly an associate of Bécherau with Deperdussin. The Nieuports were standard single-bay biplanes derived from the military type 29-C-1 and fitted with floats. This was the type on which the Corsican Lieutenant Jean Casale—a famous wartime combat pilot and one of the pilots nominated for the race—had set up new height and speed records earlier that summer. In its seaplane form, powered by a 300 h.p. Hispano-Suiza, it was credited with being capable of a speed of 150 m.p.h.[1] But both the

---

[1] The Hispano-Suiza engine, originally of Spanish design, was later built under licence in France, Italy, Britain and America.

1 (a)   Maurice Prévost in his Deperdussin

1 (b)   Weymann's Nieuport, showing stepped floats. (Inset) Charles T. Weymann

2 (a)   T. O. M. Sopwith

2 (b)   Ernest Burri
in his F.B.A. flying-boat

2 (c)   The Sopwith Tabloid at Monaco

3 (a)   The Trophy

3 (b)   Jacques Schneider (centre) congratulating Howard Pixton after his 1914 victory, with Victor Mahl extreme right

4
The
Fairey IIIA
on
Bournemouth
Beach, 1919

5 (a)   Sadi Lecointe in his Spad, showing sawn-off wing-tip

5 (b)   Henri Biard and the Supermarine Sea Lion I

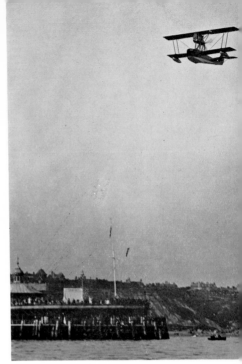

6 (a)   Sadi Lecointe and
Lt. Jean Casale

6 (b)   Jannello and his
Savoia S.13 over
Bournemouth Pier

6 (c)   Sgt. Guido Jannello (right)
with Lawrence Santoni

7 (a)   A standard Savoia S.12 of the type which won the 1920 contest

7 (b)   The Macchi M.7 which won in 1921

8 (a) The Supermarine Sea Lion II against the background of Naples Bay

8 (b) The Savoia S.51, an unlucky loser at Naples

Nieuports were damaged in trial flights on the Seine. Determined efforts finally produced two newly modified machines, and Casale was the first to leave Paris. But when he reached Cowes Roads in failing light on 7th September he judged that the surface was too rough for a safe alighting, and he sought shelter inside the estuary of the Medina river. As he alighted he struck a buoy. Casale was picked up and the Nieuport was salved, but the damage was extensive and looked impossible to repair in two days. In any case the French had no facilities for doing so. Next day, Monday, 8th September, Henri Malard left Paris in the other Nieuport, but there was no further news of him. He was believed to be held up at Le Havre with engine trouble.

The spirit of the races was now exemplified by Sammy Saunders and his employees at Cowes. As soon as his men arrived on Monday morning he put them to work. The Nieuport was towed into the sheds, the wings were completely rebuilt, new undercarriage struts were fashioned, and repairs to the fuselage and tail unit were effected. In the course of their labours they virtually re-erected the entire machine. Nieuports sent a spare engine and new floats over from France, and after toiling for 48 hours almost at a stretch the Saunders men had the machine ready by the morning of the race.

The arrival of the second Nieuport was still awaited. When it was discovered that it had not reached Le Havre the Air Ministry put a call through to Paris. Yes, Malard had left Paris on Monday. He was known to have set out to cross the Channel, but from that point he had vanished. The Royal Aero Club pleaded with the Admiralty to organise a search; they remembered all too well how Gustav Hamel had disappeared in the Channel on his way to the 1914 Aerial Derby. But Malard had been luckier; in perfect weather he had clung to his half-submerged Nieuport for 24 hours, and he had been picked up in mid-Channel.

Meanwhile the Spad company wisely transported their entry by sea, and it arrived safely at Cowes. Again it was a standard type, built in the monocoque style pioneered by Bécherau, and although not a new machine it was speedy. Like the Nieuport, it had recently set up new height and speed records. But after a preliminary trial at Cowes, Herbémont, who had travelled over with the plane, decided that he would get more speed with less surface, and he directed the amputation of parts of each upper plane. The engine was a 340 h.p. Hispano-Suiza, and the pilot was the famous Spad veteran Sadi Lecointe (French certificate No. 431, 3rd March 1911).

With the French challenge so seriously handicapped it was fortunate
that the Italian challenge, about which there had been considerable
doubts, should have materialised. The Italian aviation industry, of
little account up to 1913, had achieved tremendous progress and
expansion during the war, the impetus coming at first from the manufacture of proved French types under licence and then, with the support
of an engineering industry that quickly adapted itself from motor-car
to aero engines, settling down to original design. The needs of war
inevitably favoured fighter types, but bomber aircraft were also built.
Another type that Italy specialised in was the flying-boat, so they were
well equipped to challenge for the Schneider Trophy.

The actual challenge came from the Savoia company (Societa
Idrovolanti Alta Italia), whose founder and president, D. Lawrence
(or Lorenzo) Santoni, had been an early pioneer in British aviation: he
was the first to establish a British factory for the building of a foreign
plane under licence—the British Deperdussin Syndicate of 1911. Then
in 1913 he opened a factory on the outskirts of Milan, originally for the
building of French aircraft for the Italian government under licence,
and it soon became one of the biggest aircraft factories in the world.
His Schneider entry, a specially built S.13 flying-boat, had been produced in a fortnight and then transported by rail across France to
reach Britain in time for the race. It was a sleek reconnaissance and
bombing machine, strong and manoeuvrable, and it was reputed to
attain the speed of the swiftest scouts. Normally it was a two-seater,
but the model built for the race accommodated the pilot only, and like
the Spad it had had its wing area reduced to increase its speed. The
engine was a 250 h.p. Isotta-Fraschini, and although this was the
least powerful in the race it ran so sweetly that the S.13 was confidently
expected to do well. Guido Jannello, the blond pilot, was a sergeant in
the Italian Air Force.

During the morning the Royal Aero Club yacht *Ombra* anchored off
Bournemouth Pier, marking the starting and finishing point. There
were some 170 members on board, and there was also a Club enclosure
on the end of the pier. At midday the Corporation staff cleared the
pier, after which the price of admission was doubled—from 6d to a
shilling.

By this time the Old Harry Rocks were visible, the sun was breaking
through, and the beach was filling up. It promised to be a warm
September afternoon, there was still very little breeze, and the sea
was as smooth as a mill-pond except in the shallows, which were dotted

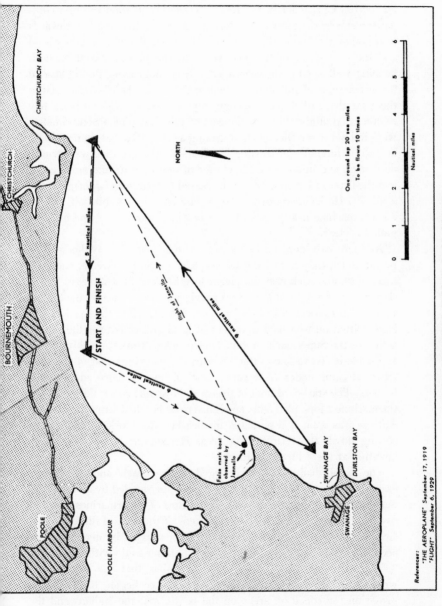

1919 SCHNEIDER TROPHY RACE COURSE

with bathers. Heads were turned in the direction of Hengistbury Head and across Christchurch Bay to the Needles, and soon the first competitor emerged from Cowes Roads and sped across the bay towards Bournemouth. The outlines of the Fairey seaplane were recognised and the first cheer of the day went up; the pilot, Vincent Nicholl, keeping well out to sea, veered away from Bournemouth and headed for Swanage, evidently taking a look at the course. He disappeared into the mist that still filled Swanage Bay, but reappeared within a few minutes and alighted just to the east of the pier. The absence of slipways did not deter Nicholl from seeking a safe anchorage on the beach; he had no intention of trusting his floats any longer than was strictly necessary, and in any case the clutter of motor boats and small craft, and the litter of bathers, greatly increased the danger of damage in the shallows. He had arranged to be met by Dick Fairey himself, and he ran his machine neatly up on to the beach, where Fairey and his men pulled it clear.

At 12.20 two more machines were seen approaching as though in a private race; they turned out to be the Spad and the Savoia, and they raced neck and neck past the pier before heading for Swanage. When they returned to alight there was nearly a double disaster; the Savoia was forced to swerve to avoid a rowing boat, while the Spad would have drifted on to a boat at anchor after alighting but for the timely action of the Supermarine motor launch, which took it quickly in tow and made it fast to one of the Supermarine moorings east of the pier, where it came under close surveillance from the more adventurous bathers. The starboard float of the Spad, however, was leaking, giving the machine a lop-sided look, and it had to be beached for repairs. More damage was done as it mounted the beach. After working all night at cutting down the Spad's wing area, Herbémont broke down with vexation at these further setbacks.

The Savoia had also been dragged up the beach, and although it escaped the fate of the Spad it was quickly surrounded by an admiring but alarmingly inquisitive crowd. James Bird of Supermarines motored over to the committee boat to tell them of the lack of direction and facilities for the foreign machines and was stunned by his reception: according to a committee-man, it was "nothing to do with him".

The race organisers, apparently assuming that the competitors would be content to ride anchor until the race began, had made no provision for roped-off areas on the beach, and the Italians and the French soon found themselves seriously hampered by sightseers. The

other competitors suffered in the same way, the only exception being
Vincent Nicholl, who escaped through the prescience of Dick Fairey.
Fairey had argued that the whole fabric of British society depended on
unwritten laws of property and land tenure. Police and officials were
powerless to hold back a determined crowd; but drive a few stakes into
the ground and connect them up with a rope and the public would
instinctively respect the resultant enclosure. Fairey had sent a lorry-
load of posts and wire down to Bournemouth, and as soon as Nicholl's
machine was beached the Fairey gang came down, stuck the posts in
the sand, and unrolled their wire. It was the only plane that was un-
harried.

Next to approach, at what seemed a promising pace, was the Supermarine; like the others, the pilot went off for a look at the course.
Then came Hamersley in the Avro; although eliminated from the
race he had undertaken to trace the course for foreign entrants who
might otherwise be confused by some detail or mistake a turning-
point. The mark boats, clearly painted red and white, were already
positioned at both the Hengistbury and Swanage turning-points, and a
third mark boat, acting as reserve, was anchored off the course in
Studland Bay.

Then the fastest machine to show itself so far was seen to be approaching. To the crowd's delight it was Hawker, and he was firmly
established as favourite. He made a perfect touch-down, and seeing the
huge crowd on the beach east of the pier he taxied round to the Poole
side and beached his Sopwith there. He was soon surrounded just the
same.

The scene on the beach had become one of utter confusion. There
was no organisation of any kind, and while 170 fortunate members of
the Royal Aero Club ate a superb lunch on board the *Ombra* the pilots
and their ground teams went hungry. But for the thoughtful consideration of the Saunders company they would have starved. As it was,
Britain's reputation for hospitality and courtesy was to some extent
redeemed by the personal efforts of the Saunders team, who somehow
found food for the French and the Italians and formed some sort of
guard for their machines, as well as commandeering planks to make
temporary launching slips. Even so, the lack of communication between
yacht and beach threatened to be disastrous, and the folly of separating
the storage and servicing centre at Cowes from the assembly and
starting-point became abundantly clear.

The race was due to start at 2.30, and although soon after two o'clock the fog began to roll in again from seaward, the competitors began to make ready. They had been told originally that they were to start at one-minute intervals on a signal from the *Ombra*; but these arrangements had been changed that morning without any reference to the pilots, most of whom knew the revised details only vaguely. By 2.30 the fog was almost as bad as it had been earlier, visibility was down to 400 yards, and a postponement was inevitable. Yet somehow the Nieuport got through from Cowes, arriving at a speed that proclaimed it a worthy rival of the Sopwith. If only the fog would clear.

The decision was taken to postpone the race until six o'clock, but even this news filtered through only slowly, causing further confusion. The local boatmen shook their heads when they heard it—the mist, they said, having once returned, would not clear properly now. Yet soon after four o'clock there was a sudden and distinct improvement, so much so that the race committee changed their minds again and decided to run the race as soon as possible. A launch went round telling the competitors that the race would start in 15 minutes. James Bird, who had long experience of flying and sailing in the bay, at once protested to the race committee that conditions were still dangerous and that with the weather as it was there was no chance of the fog at Swanage lifting; but his advice was ignored.

The French, believing that they had at least until six o'clock, were busily repairing their floats; they protested that they could not possibly be ready in time. Soon afterwards another launch came round with the news that the race would start not in 15 minutes but in half an hour. Some of the competitors rushed to get started, others determined to take their time. The beach became a tornado of sand and flying hats as engines were started and revved. Nobody knew for certain what was happening, but by 4.45 the Fairey seaplane, drawn No. 1, was cruising about east of the pier, apparently waiting for the starting-signal.

The revised instructions were that the red flag would be raised five minutes before each machine was due to start; at the end of 4 minutes 45 seconds it would be dipped as a warning, and after five minutes it would be raised again as the actual starting signal. This was to be repeated for each machine. But when the red flag dropped the Fairey pilot not surprisingly took off. The time was 4.50.

The Nieuport was due off next, but it wasn't ready. Hawker was No. 3, but he was still sitting about on the beach. The Supermarine, however, was in position awaiting its turn, and the pilot, Basil Hobbs, although badly baulked by rowing-boats which had been allowed to

stray on to the course—there was nothing and no one to stop them—
managed to get off safely.

The frantic efforts of the French to get their machines repaired had
meanwhile ended in failure; in both cases the cause was damage to the
floats. The Nieuport and the Spad were non-starters, but the Sopwith
and the Savoia had at last started up, and Hawker was in position near
the starting-line. The starter seemed undecided, and Hawker,
anxious not to expose his floats for long, and fearing that his plugs
might soot up with the engine throttled down, concluded that he had
better make up the starter's mind for him. He opened the throttle and
roared away.

The Fairey, the Supermarine and the Sopwith were thus all somewhere on their first lap, at the end of which they would be required to
make two alightings between the two piers before continuing. The
Fairey, at least, ought to have showed up by now, but there was no
sign of her. Meanwhile Jannello in the Savoia had manoeuvred into
position, carried out the revised starting procedure correctly—the only
competitor to do so—and pulled away confidently, the sole overseas
challenger left in the race.

The field had been cut down to four, but there was a general feeling
of relief that there was to be a race at all, and excitement mounted as
the crowd awaited the arrival of the Fairey. But the local boatmen were
still shaking their heads pessimistically over the likely conditions in
Swanage Bay. The Royal Aero Club's inexperience, manifest all day
and culminating in the bungled start, had misled them into running the
race without so much as sending someone for a trial run round the
course. Several aircraft, including the Avro, were circling the pier that
afternoon and could have done it, but the rump of the competition
entry was left to explore the conditions in the race itself.

First to penetrate Swanage Bay, as expected, was Vincent Nicholl in
the Fairey. At 100 feet he flattened off into a gentle descent, but he
didn't get a glimpse of the sea until he was less than 50 feet up. He
came down low over the water and flew on through the mist, certain
that he must be somewhere near the mark boat. Suddenly the masts of
what he took to be a yacht—it was the mark boat—loomed out of the
fog right in front of him and he pulled up instantly. In the same
moment another machine flashed by on his left. He emerged into clear
air again above the fog and decided against any further attempt. It was
far too dangerous. Returning to Bournemouth, he found a clear stretch
of water, alighted, and beached his machine. "Conditions aren't good

enough," he told Dick Fairey. "The fog in Swanage Bay is impenetrable. I couldn't see the mark boat and I'm quite sure he couldn't see me."

Engines were heard again within a minute or so and people looked for the Supermarine; but it was Hawker in the Sopwith. He flew straight in, alighted in the shallows, skilfully avoided sundry bathers, and with a final burst of engine skidded to a halt on the sands. That was two of the four surviving competitors out of it; surely the Royal Aero Club would now abandon the race.

A heated argument was in full swing on the *Ombra*. On the one hand was the experience of Nicholl and Hawker, on the other was the fact that Hobbs and Jannello had not yet returned. The committee decided to let the race continue for the moment. Indeed they had no option when Jannello was seen approaching from Hengistbury Head on the competition course at the end of his first lap. He alighted near Boscombe Pier, got off again smoothly and touched down for a second time just short of Bournemouth Pier to comply with the rules for proving navigability and seaworthiness.

The continued absence of the Supermarine made everyone uneasy, but there was Jannello to show that the circuit could be flown. Seeing the Fairey and the Sopwith pulled up on the beach, Jannello hesitated; he thought the race had been abandoned. But after further argument amongst the race officials he was waved on. He took off again and headed for Swanage.

When Hobbs reached Swanage Bay on his first lap he found, like Nicholl and Hawker before him, that the fog was dense. A momentary glimpse of the Fairey flashing past him on an opposite course did not encourage him, but he decided to see if visibility was any better near the surface. There was no improvement when he descended, by which time he was unsure of his position and feared that he might be in danger of flying into the cliffs. With a flying-boat hull underneath him he was not worried about alighting, and he put down somewhere in the region of where he thought the mark boat must be, in the hope of locating it and fixing his position. After taxying about for several minutes he decided to return to Bournemouth to orientate himself and then make a fresh attempt to find the mark boat. Just as he was getting airborne he felt a terrific jolt beneath him; almost certainly he had hit something and damaged his hull. The sooner he was out of the fog of Swanage Bay the better, and as he had sufficient speed to continue he headed for Bournemouth.

Keeping a check on his course from the top of the cliffs and the Purbeck Hills, Hobbs circled Swanage Bay a second time, satisfying himself that he must have rounded the mark boat. He couldn't see it, but quite possibly they would see him. He then steered for Hengistbury Head on a compass course and soon came out of the fog. After rounding the Christchurch mark boat he ran back along the coast towards Bournemouth, preparing to make his two alightings.

Knowing that his hull was probably damaged Hobbs took especial care to descend smoothly, and his touch-down was perfect. But the hull—which had been ripped clean open—immediately filled with water, and the flying-boat turned over with its tail in the air. Hobbs was thrown clear, and the motor launch at the touch-down point soon picked him up, but it was some time before his machine was salvaged.

That left only the Italian Jannello; and he, in contrast to the bewilderments of the others, was lapping with maddening regularity, making it look the simplest thing in the world. As a pilot in the Italian Air Force Jannello was the only serving airman in the race, and the manner of his start and his exemplary handling of his machine suggested a disciplined approach. Many of the spectators had left, wearying of a long day in which even the little that had happened was often beyond their comprehension (there was nothing remotely resembling a public address system); but those that remained began to take a real interest in Jannello. Although the race had proved to be a one-man show the crowd had a name to conjure with.

Because the two required alightings reduced the average speed of the first lap, competitors were allowed to fly eleven laps and take their last ten as an attempt on the seaplane speed record over 200 nautical miles; and this Jannello had elected to do. His lap times of just under 10 minutes each were giving him a good average speed; but as lap succeeded lap, one man—not one of the official time-keepers—began to doubt whether Jannello was in fact flying the full course. Everyone else assumed that because the laps were consistent the Italian must be rounding the mark boats consistently too. The exception—it was Tommy Sopwith—was an exceptional judge of pace. He began to check Jannello's times for each lap, and by the ninth lap he had concluded that they were faster than his own estimate of the probable speed of the aircraft warranted. If Jannello was completing the full course he was averaging over 140 miles an hour. Sopwith put his top speed at not much above 120. One lap, indeed, seemed exceptionally fast on paper to everyone and was obviously suspect; but Sopwith doubted them all.

Jannello completed his eleventh and final lap to prolonged applause; but Lawrence Santoni went out in a motor boat to meet him when he alighted, and he asked Jannello to fly an additional lap to make sure of covering the full distance. Jannello was doubtful whether he had enough petrol left to do it, but Santoni pressed him and he consented.

Off went Jannello again in the direction of Swanage, but ten minutes passed and he failed to reappear. Soon it was clear that something had gone wrong. Twenty minutes passed, and then half an hour, and still there was no Jannello. The crowd, impatient to give him an ovation, lingered disappointedly. Darkness was falling and concern for Jannello grew, but the launches that had been patrolling the course had gone home when Jannello touched down after completing eleven laps and no one was available to go and look for him. The Christchurch mark boat, which had returned earlier with the news that Jannello had rounded it correctly ten times but not eleven (which probably accounted for the very fast lap), had also motored off.

Meanwhile on board the yacht *Ombra* confusion was turning to chaos. The yacht crew announced that they must hurry back to Cowes for fear of getting fog-bound in the Solent as night fell. When the Aero Club officials had digested this they asked to be landed on Bournemouth Pier—they could hardly abandon the scene with the result still unconfirmed and the winner missing. But most of the guests on the *Ombra*—French, Italians and Press—had left all their belongings at Cowes and had to get back there. "Thus," wrote C. G. Grey of *The Aeroplane*, "one perceived the true beauty of the Committee's scheme of having one headquarters at Cowes, another on the yacht, and another at Bournemouth."

At last the ubiquitous Saunders boat was traced, and the crew at once agreed to take Santoni and his team out in search of Jannello. It transpired that, as Jannello had feared, he had run out of petrol.

After the Savoia had been towed in and beached at Bournemouth the Saunders boat took the whole Italian party back to Cowes, overtaking the *Ombra* on the way. The race officials had meanwhile established a fourth headquarters at the Branksome Towers Hotel, Bournemouth, and a telephone call to that establishment produced the final sensation. The Swanage mark boat had returned with the news that they had never seen Jannello at all. The Italian had been disqualified and the race declared void.

When Jannello heard this he was at first dumbfounded, then voluble. He had seen the mark boat clearly each time. It had been exactly like the one positioned at the Christchurch end. He had rounded it without question, and they must have seen him. Someone had made a mistake. An official map of the course was produced and Jannello was invited to indicate the position of the mark boat he had rounded. Without hesitation he stabbed his finger at the map: it alighted on a point in Studland Bay.

It began to dawn on people what had happened. The reserve mark boat had been anchored off the course in Studland Bay, and Jannello had understandably mistaken it in the foggy conditions for the true one. Either he had thought he was in Swange Bay, or he had assumed that the race committee had altered the course. The Italians immediately lodged a protest, and the general opinion was that it was well justified and that the race should be awarded to Jannello.

First, Jannello had completed eleven circuits, at least equivalent to the full distance, during which he had recognised and rounded a mark boat at the Swanage end of the course exactly similar to the boat at the Christchurch end. Second, observation from below may have been obscured by the mist. Third, if Jannello had rounded the wrong boat, the error was due to faulty organisation for which the Italians could not be blamed. The Italians also protested against the way the race had been managed and against the absence of proper notification to the pilots of the change in the time and order of starting. "We say we complied with all the rules and conditions . . . and we claim to have won the Cup and the pilot's prize. . . ."

The theme of perfidious Albion echoed at home and abroad. Everyone felt the race should have gone to Italy. "This would have been more in accordance with British spirit, and less reminiscent of the kind of thing we have so often professed to deplore in foreign sporting events," said *Aeronautics*, hinting at a particularly unpleasant form of hypocrisy. And the general view in Paris was very much in favour of the prize going to Jannello. "Our English friends," said one French writer, "have not yet regained their customary skill as organisers or sportsmen." There was even a charge that the reserve mark boat had been ambiguously placed on purpose, and foreign pilots maliciously deceived. The Avro pilot who had undertaken to point out the course before the race, said another report, had gone round the reserve mark boat in Studland Bay. "It is openly said that this was purposely done by the Avro."

The committee of the Royal Aero Club, determined to make amends, met on 22nd September and unanimously decided to recommend that the trophy should be awarded to Italy and the prize to Jannello, and when this was announced there seems to have been no dissentient voice. Yet such a recommendation was perhaps unfair to those pilots who had attempted to fly the correct course and found it impossible. This, no doubt, was the view of the F.A.I. when it met in Brussels on 24th October and rejected the recommendation. As a concession to the Italians, however, and perhaps as a rebuke to the organising club, the Royal Aero Club of Italy was asked to organise the race for the following year.

1920-1921
at Venice

"This great speed contest!"
Italian irony

IF 1919 perpetuated the farce which had so often characterised the early hydro-aeroplane meetings, 1920 and 1921 degenerated into fiasco. In all three contests an Italian pilot finished alone, and had it not been for the refusal of the F.A.I. to award the 1919 race to Italy—a decision that was universally unpopular at the time—the Schneider Trophy would have become Italian property in September 1921.

During the war years British aircraft had been the equal of any, and the French, too, had maintained their position in the forefront of aviation. The inevitable retrenchment of the early post-war years, however, and uncertainty about future government policy, had a depressing effect in both countries, and with Germany restricted by the terms of the armistice treaties, Italy, having been awarded the right to stage the 1920 contest, looked in a strong position to retain the trophy. Their advantage was two-fold: they had greater experience in building flying-boats, and, more important, they would be on their own ground. The 1920 race for the Gordon Bennett Cup, to be run at Étampes shortly after the Schneider, drew many foreign entries, but this was a landplane race, and Étampes was not so far away as Italy. Without government support the financial burden of entering a team for a seaplane race at a venue as distant as Venice, the circuit chosen by the Italians, was prohibitive. The Americans, it is true, planned to send four aircraft to compete in the Gordon Bennett, but they had never shown much interest in the Schneider, Charlie Weymann notwithstanding.

Britain's future in aviation, it was often argued, would be closely related to the development of the seaplane, and her inability to compete in these years was widely deplored. The inhibiting factor was money, and in an attempt to attract British entries the Royal Aero Club offered prizes of £250, £150 and £100 for the first three British machines to finish; but this failed to stimulate the manufacturers. "In the present indeterminate state of the industry," said the magazine *Flight*, "when the Government cannot make up its mind whether or not it has an aerial policy, there is, on the face of things, scant encouragement for firms . . . to spend money and trouble in the evolution of craft best suitable for bringing the Cup back to England." But the writer believed that another factor was involved, of more lasting importance than the sporting viewpoint: it was essential to make a good showing so that when maritime nations placed orders for aircraft, Britain's had been demonstrated to be the best. This was to be a recurring theme.

The Italians had succeeded in getting the contest rules revised so that all entries were obliged to carry 300 kilograms of unusable ballast as a commercial weight, a requirement that greatly favoured the rugged but graceful flying-boat type in which they specialised. They mustered a formidable list of entries, all of the biplane flying-boat bomber-reconnaissance type, as follows:

Savoia 19 (tractor type, 550 h.p. Ansaldo), built exclusively for the race, which Jannello was to fly.

Savoia 12 (pusher type, 550 h.p. Ansaldo), a bomber developed for racing.

Macchi 19 (tractor type, 680 h.p. Fiat), a two-seater, developed from the M.7 and specially built for the new payload regulations.

Macchi 12 (pusher type, 430 h.p. Ansaldo), an armed reconnaissance type built in 1918.[1]

A French entry—a Spad-Herbémont on floats, with Jean Casale named as pilot—was withdrawn at the last moment, partly through transport difficulties due to labour unrest in Italy; and these same troubles, coupled with design and mechanical faults in the S.19 and the M.19, and unfavourable weather, finally reduced the field to one exceptionally seaworthy contestant—the S.12, with Lieutenant Luigi Bologna of the Italian Navy as pilot. Bologna completed the seaworthiness and navigability tests on 18th September, and two days later, after storms had caused a postponement, he successfully covered the full course, despite continuing bad weather, and was declared the winner. Taking his time, he covered the 200 nautical miles of the course in 2 hours 11 minutes, an average speed of 107·22 miles an hour.

A week later, at Étampes, the race for the Gordon Bennett Cup

[1] Nieuport-Macchi, as it was originally known, was founded by Guilio Macchi in 1912 for the manufacture of Nieuport designs under licence.

1920 SCHNEIDER TROPHY RACE COURSE

"FLIGHT" September 2, 1920

attracted a much more representative entry; the winner was Sadi Lecointe in a Nieuport, at an average speed of 168·5 m.p.h. This was France's third consecutive victory, and with it they gained permanent possession of the Cup. With the passing of what had become recognised as the race for the world landplane speed championship, the only international speed race left of any standing was the Schneider, so a revival of interest in seaplane racing seemed likely. Another pointer for the future was the manner of Sadi Lecointe's victory: he had trained assiduously for the race, flying his Nieuport over the course time and time again until he knew every inch of it.

* * *

The recrudescence of seaplane racing that had seemed indicated in 1920 failed to materialise in 1921. From being for a short period a keenly contested event amongst European countries, the race for the Schneider Trophy degenerated into a one-man show. Britain's financial situation was still depressed, and the doctrine that competitions of this kind were a tonic to commercial aviation found few adherents. Britain still claimed to have the finest seaplanes in the world, but they were not inclined to put this boast to the test. That the Royal Aero Club and the Society of British Aircraft Constructors between them ought to have been able to finance a worthy entry was freely asserted; but despite a full discussion of the problem between the racing committee of the Club and S.B.A.C. representatives as early as 29th November 1920, nothing materialised except a squabble with the Aero Club of France over race regulations. The requirement to carry 300 kilos of dead weight ballast was eventually dropped and the contest reverted to a speed race pure and simple, but to discourage freak machines a watertightness test was introduced under which entrants had to remain afloat fully loaded for six hours after a more searching navigability test. This provision necessitated a fairly seaworthy type of seaplane in which strength and weight of landing structure could not be wholly sacrificed for speed. It did of course favour the flying-boats, but it was a wholly reasonable precaution against the domination of the contest by freak machines, and it remained in force up to and including the 1929 race.

Because of the mounting costs of race organisation and the frequency of withdrawals, each entrant was required to deposit a guarantee of 5,000 fr. in addition to the nominal entry fee: the deposit was returnable if the entrant competed. This provision was calculated to

NORTH

CANALE TRE PO

PORTO DI LIDO

Naval
Air Station
San Andrea

VENEZIA

LAGUNA
DI·LIDO

LIDO DI

Excelsior Hotel

START AND FINISH

Malamocco
light

VENETA

ALBERONI

PORTO DI MALAMOCCO

LAGUNA

ADRIATIC SEA

One round lap approx. 24,6 km

- - - Navigability test ·
——— Speed course

To be flown 16 times

0 1 2 3 4 5
Kilometres

1921 SCHNEIDER TROPHY RACE COURSE

Source: MUSEO AERONAUTICO
CAPRONI DI TALIEDO - Rome

deter haphazard or ill-considered entries, and it achieved its object depressingly well: when entries closed on 15th May 1921 the only foreign challenger was the ubiquitous Sadi Lecointe. He was to fly a specially-built Nieuport-Delage, subsidised by the State and powered by a 300 h.p. Hispano-Suiza. Britain was leaving it to France.

That the Italians were determined to win for the second year running was shown by the strength of their entry for the eliminating tests, which were again held, like the race itself, at Venice. 16 machines in all were nominated. They were:

5 Macchi 7s.

2 Macchi 18s. These were an attempt at standardising the various types of Macchi flying-boat.

1 Macchi 19—the one specially built for the previous year.

6 Savoia 13s—standard machines of the type flown by Jannello at Bournemouth.

1 Savoia 21⎫
1 Savoia 22⎭ Both specially built for the race.

The S.21 was a small and unusually proportioned single-seat flying-boat with the upper wing much shorter than the lower, which was itself only 20 feet; during its trials, with Jannello at the controls, it attained a speed of 160 m.p.h. The S.22, in contrast, was twin-engined, one tractor one pusher, but it crashed on an early test flight to a total loss. Interest in the race was further subtracted when the little S.21 was withdrawn through the illness of Jannello, the only pilot trained to fly it, and the two Macchi 18s were also withdrawn. Only nine of the 16 Italian entries actually took part in the team trials.

Arturo Zannetti in the Macchi 19—with mechanic Pedetti—finished an easy first, but all six Savoia 13s were surprisingly eliminated, and second and third places went to Piero Corgnolino and Giovanni de Briganti in Macchi 7s. This type was the earliest and clumsiest of the Italian military flying-boats, and although successful in its time its top speed was no more than 130 m.p.h.

The race itself, which was run on 11th August, was again a sad disappointment. The Nieuport-Delage, with the most powerful engine in the race next to the Macchi 19, failed to pass the navigability test; when Sadi Lecointe attempted his first alighting the float chassis buckled and collapsed. The Macchi 19, designed to meet the load-carrying requirements of the previous year and hitherto thought to be hopelessly handicapped, started favourite, but after showing a useful turn of speed on the opening laps it suffered a crankshaft failure and caught fire. Zanetti put the machine down safely and he and Pedetti escaped unhurt, but they were out of the race.

That left the two outdated Macchi 7s. For 15 of the 16 laps Corgnolino confirmed his placing in the team trials by leading de Briganti, but after two hours' flying and when only two kilometres from the finish he ran out of fuel. The outpaced de Briganti, in the slowest machine in the race, had already finished, and he thus became the winner of what was ironically described as "this great speed contest" at an average speed of 118 miles an hour.

For the Italian aircraft designers the race provided a bitter lesson: they had over-reached themselves. For all the novelty and variety of their specially designed racers, only one such machine—and that last year's—had made the Italian team, and even that had not stood up as well as the old warhorse the Macchi 7. Yet the designers were less at fault than the engineers. The majority of the withdrawals were due to engine trouble, generally caused by ill-judged efforts to increase power.

1922

at Naples

A Young Man named Mitchell

"How would you like to fly in the Schneider Trophy race this year?"

The speaker was Hubert Scott-Paine, Managing Director of Supermarines. The man addressed was his chief test pilot, Henri Biard. Scott-Paine, an early aviation pioneer, had turned almost at once to the design and construction fields; he had managed Supermarines at Woolston, Southampton since 1914. Biard, now 30, had qualified as a pilot in 1912 and had subsequently become an instructor; he had joined Supermarines in 1919. His reply to Scott-Paine's question was enthusiastic. "I'd give anything for the chance." But Biard could scarcely believe that his boss was serious. For three years Italy had monopolised the trophy and there seemed not the slightest hope of dislodging them now, certainly not without financial help from the government, which in the prevailing economic situation was unlikely to be forthcoming. Popular though a British challenge might be, it had little hope of saving the trophy. For Supermarines to mount such a challenge on their own was likely to prove a costly and ignominious failure.

Scott-Paine led Biard along to one of the building sheds, and there, out of sight of prying eyes and under construction in absolute secrecy, was what Biard described some months later as "one of the finest little flying-boats I have ever seen". Yet he can scarcely have believed in it as a likely Schneider challenger at this stage. Re-modelled from a six-year-old amphibian hull, it was the reverse of revolutionary in design. The removal of the amphibian gear had lightened it, and the wing area had been reduced, but the machine retained the solid appearance and characteristics of the Supermarine entry of 1919, and indeed it was almost indistinguishable from it at first glance, the only obvious differences being in the bow of the hull and in the design of the tail fin and rudder. This close relationship with the 1919 entry was recognised in the plane's nomenclature: it was christened 'Sea Lion II'.

Construction was virtually the same, and with the typical pusher-biplane outline, plus wing struts and wire bracing, and with its massive vee-bottomed hull, it bore little resemblance to the popular conception of a racing aeroplane. In design and vintage, in fact, it more or less corresponded with the outdated Macchi 7, the derided winner of the race of the previous year, and it did not compare with the latest Italian flying-boats.

Whatever Biard's misgivings may have been, however, it was clear to him that Scott-Paine sincerely believed that this old aeroplane could be converted into a successful racer. It was certainly small—28 feet in wing-span, 25 feet long—and despite its cumbersome appearance it proved in practice to be exceptionally manoeuvrable. Whether it could compete with the latest Italian racers seemed problematical, but Scott-Paine, who was financing the entry, was optimistic, and among those who agreed with him were H. T. Vane, Managing Director of Napiers, who had promised to supply the engine—a 450 h.p. Lion—and the directors of Shell and Wakefield, who were supplying the petrol and oil. Their confidence may well have been based principally on a young man who had joined Supermarines as a draughtsman in 1916 and who was master-minding the conversion; his name was R. J. Mitchell.

The 1922 contest was to be staged over a triangular course of 200 nautical miles in Naples Bay, the Venetians having been forced to surrender their two-year monopoly; the race regulations were the same as in 1921. Unlike Britain, both France and Italy had government support for their entries. France was to be represented by two C.A.M.S. 36 military flying-boats with 300 h.p. Hispano-Suiza engines; both machines had been considerably modified to make them suitable for racing, and tractor power units had been substituted for the pusher type of the standard machine.[1] Meanwhile Italy, intent on winning the trophy outright, were again producing two new racers, both built by the Savoia company to the design of Alessandro Marchetti. This company, however, was still dogged by misfortune. In 1919 it had been the disqualification of Jannello; but for that infuriating mistake the trophy would have belonged to Italy already. In 1920 the new S.19 could not be got to the starting-line, and in 1921 Jannello had been unlucky for a third time when he was prevented by illness from flying the S.21, in which he was reputed to have reached 160 m.p.h. in practice. In the same year the S.22 was written off before the race. The

[1] The full title of the firm was Chantiers Aéro Maritime de la Seine, and the managing director was Lawrence Santoni, of Deperdussin and Savoia fame.

1922 race again began badly for them when one of the two new Marchetti designs—the S.50 floatplane—crashed on test and killed the pilot.

Despite these misfortunes the Savoia company still represented Italy's main hope of winning the trophy outright, through the second Marchetti design, the S.51 flying-boat. This was a single-seat sesquiplane or one-and-a-half plane in which the lower plane was little more than an outrigger for carrying the balanced side floats; the span of the upper plane was 32′ 9″ and the lower 13′ 1″. The sesquiplane form was an attempted compromise between the biplane and the monoplane: it had the biplane's structural compactness without the wing-to-wing interference associated with the biplane form. The loveliest of the racing flying-boats so far produced, and the most original machine in the race, the S.51 had a sleek, slender hull specially designed to reduce head resistance and drag, and it was powered by the well-tried 300 h.p. Hispano-Suiza. The pilot, Alessandro Passaleva, was to have flown one of the scratched Macchi 18s in the previous year. Supporting this unusual machine were an M.17 flying-boat, derived from the M.7 and to be flown by Zanetti, and an M.7 to be flown by Corgnolino; both were powered by 260 h.p. Isotta-Fraschinis. The M.17 had been specially renovated following the accident to the M.19 in the previous year, and it had an impressive record at seaplane meetings.

The race was originally scheduled for the second half of August, but for administrative reasons the Italians brought the date forward to 12th August, which meant a week or ten days less in which to prepare. They had no right to do this, but no protest seems to have been made. The Supermarine machine was still unfinished when this news came through, and the factory worked day and night to complete it. "In a fever of expectation", Biard wrote afterwards, "we wheeled her out of the sheds." The engine started with a roar, and as Biard opened the throttle the machine planed forward and climbed easily off the water. But 200 feet above the Docks the engine suddenly cut out and Biard found himself gliding down towards a forest of funnels. Somehow he picked out a clear patch of water and put the machine down safely, and the fault was diagnosed.

It was after sunset next day before the trials could be continued, but this time there was no false start. For once the instrument that commanded most attention was the speed register; although Sea Lion II was basically a well-tried aircraft, after the many modifications and improvements that had been made its speed was an unknown quantity.

If Mitchell's calculations were wrong, it would be a waste of time travelling to Italy. Scott-Paine had set Mitchell a target of 160 miles an hour to beat the Italians, and as Biard watched the speed reach 120, then 130, then 140, then 150, he knew he was handling the fastest flying-boat yet built in England, and just possibly in France and Italy as well. There was no loss of manoeuvrability either: Sea Lion II could be rolled and looped. The days that followed were taken up by further modifications and adjustments, and by tests which confirmed the machine's speed and handiness. Then it was dismantled, and team and packing-cases sailed from Southampton on the *Philomel*.

At Naples the Supermarine team had two principal pre-contest tasks: first was to unpack and reassemble the machine and test it thoroughly under the changed temperatures of the Mediterranean; second was to find out as much as possible about the performance of the Italian entries. The first of these tasks nearly ended in disaster when Biard, beguiled by the temptation to have a peep at Vesuvius, flew over the top of the apparently quiescent crater and was hoisted another 2,000 feet by an outsize thermal; and the second, too, had its pitfalls, notably in the alert counter-espionage practised by the Italians. All three contest teams, British, French and Italian, were based at a small air station about four miles from Naples, and it was easier for the Italians, in familiar surroundings, to evaluate the single British entry and the two identical French entries, than for visitors to make an accurate assessment of the assortment of Italian planes on view. The Macchi 7, of course, was well known, and to a lesser extent the M.17; but the S.51 was a mystery. Biard determined to be equally mysterious about Sea Lion II, or at least to deceive the Italians as far as possible about its true capability. Whenever he took his machine into the air he noticed that a little knot of Italian pilots, engineers and designers was always there to observe his every manoeuvre and to time his practice circuits by stop-watch, so he resolved never to let his new Napier Lion out fully when in sight of Naples Bay. In his practice circuits he took the corners with excessive caution, even clumsily, and he avoided giving any indication of the machine's reserves of speed and man-oeuvrability. To what extent the Italians were deceived is uncertain; but published figures in Italian aviation magazines show that Sea Lion II was credited with a top speed of 150 m.p.h., about equal with the Macchi 17, while the S.51 was assessed as 20 kilometres per hour faster. Even allowing a top speed of 160 m.p.h. for Sea Lion II, how-ever, the S.51 was the faster machine, and all the experts forecast an

Italian victory, the betting strongly favouring the Italians. Of the French very little was seen.

On Saturday 12th August, the day of the preliminary tests, the two French flying-boats were withdrawn after one of them had capsized during trials. This left three Italian planes and one British. The leading Italian machine, the S.51, also developed seaworthiness troubles: during the navigability tests she sustained damage which, although comparatively minor, resulted in her capsizing during the six-hour mooring-out test. She was righted by her crew, but this was against the race regulations, and had a protest been lodged she must have been disqualified, leaving Sea Lion II as the likely winner. But such a sporting atmosphere pervaded the contest in this period that no protest was made, and next day the judges allowed the S.51 to line up for the race. "We did not want to beat the fastest of the Italian planes on a disqualification," said Scott-Paine afterwards. Whether he would have acted so tolerantly had he known that, barring accidents, the S.51 was virtually certain to win is perhaps another matter.

The triangular course began with a short base leg running south-south-west along the coast from Naples and followed with the two longer sides of the triangle, roughly equal in length, the first crossing the bay to Torre del Greco and the second returning across the bay north-west to Naples. The fine natural harbour of the bay gave the competitors good protection from the open sea, and the background of hills and mountains, dominated on the eastern shore by Vesuvius, made a picturesque setting. 13 circuits were to be flown, of roughly $15\frac{1}{2}$ nautical miles each. The turning-points were marked by captive balloons.

Intense heat from the sun, shining clear in a vivid blue sky, dictated a starting-time of four o'clock in the afternoon, but even at that hour Biard discarded his flying clothing and dressed for the race in grey flannels and shirt-sleeves. He had drawn the right to be first away, and he settled himself in the tiny cockpit of Sea Lion II and waited for the starting-signal, watching the Italian trio moving into position behind him. He was glad of the chance to get away first, before there was any threat of being impeded by other aircraft. Then at 4.6 the signal was given and he taxied over the starting-line and climbed away down the coast towards the first pylon.

As it might be several laps before all the Italians joined him in the circuit, and particularly as the S.51 would be last away, Biard had resolved to go flat out from the beginning and to hold the throttle

OTTOVIANO
NAPOLI
START AND FINISH
A
B
C
D
Vesúvio
+ 1270 m
+ 1186 m
road
road
road
Cabo di Posillipo
Isola di Nisida
TORRE DEL GRECO
BOSCOTRECASE
POMPEI
NORTH
GOLFO DI NAPOLI
One round lap about 28.5 kilometres
To be flown 13 times
0
2
4
6
8
10
Kilometres

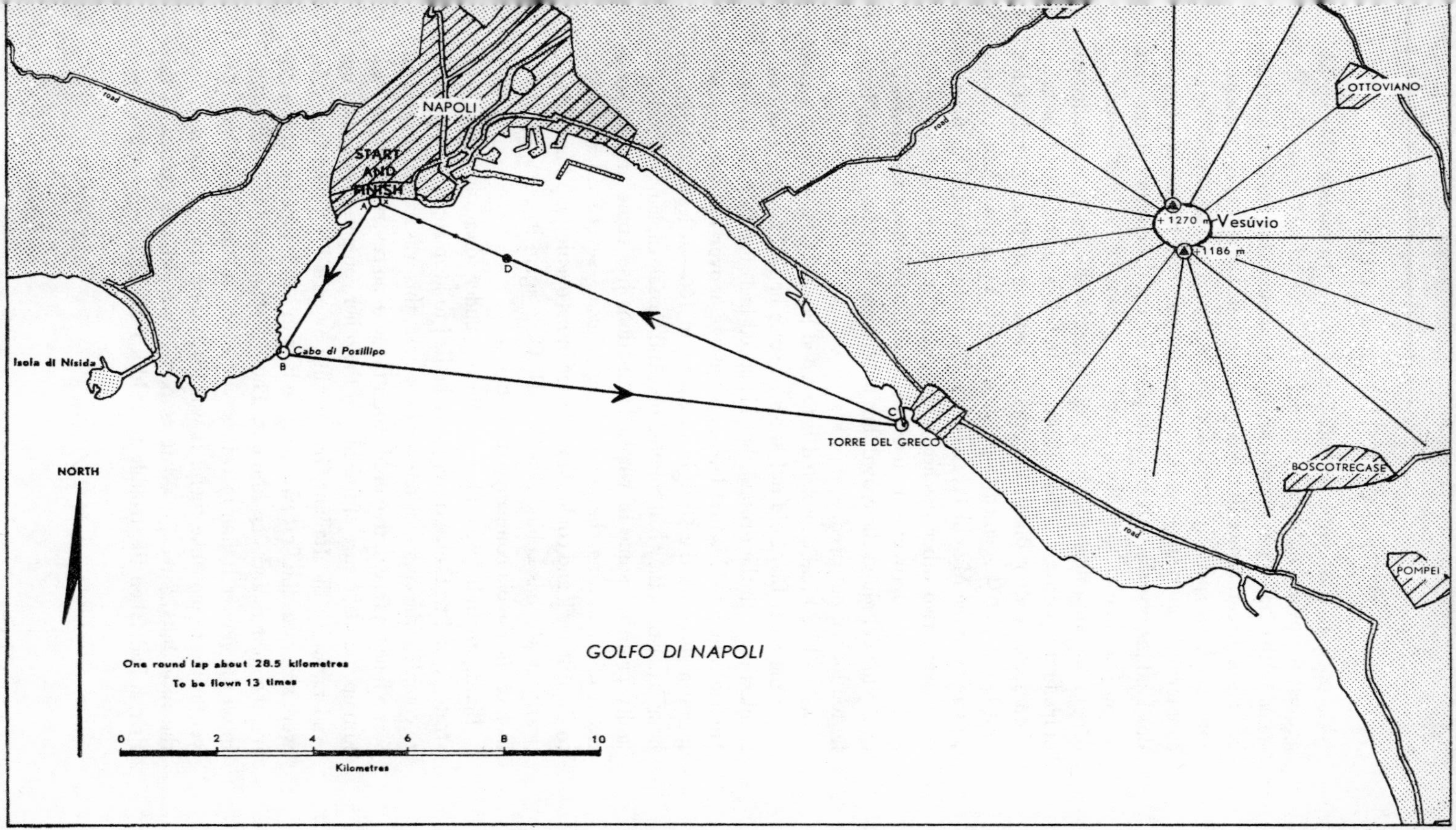

1922 SCHNEIDER TROPHY RACE COURSE

"AVIATION", August 1922
"L'AIR", August 5, 1922

wide open at least until he had had a chance to measure his speed against the other contestants. If he found after a few circuits that the speed of the Italians was inferior, he could nurse his engine then. He had absolute confidence in the Napier Lion, he knew that the carburettors had been specially tuned for the temperatures he would be encountering, and in any case he felt that for the front runner in a race of this kind his was the only sensible plan. He cut the corners on the first lap so fine that as he banked round the pylons he realised he was in danger of taking them too close; but his aggressive flying was reflected in his first lap time of 7′ 10″. It proved to be his fastest lap of the race.

45 seconds after Biard, Corgnolino took off in the Macchi 7; his first lap of 8′39$\frac{1}{5}$″ seemed to pose no threat. 4$\frac{1}{2}$ minutes later Zanetti was away in the Macchi 17, so before Biard had completed his first lap there were two other machines in the circuit. Zanetti's first lap of 8′2$\frac{3}{5}$″ was an improvement on the M.7 and his technique and virtuosity as a pilot delighted the crowd, but unless the M.17 had a lot in hand he too looked outpaced.

Before Biard had completed his second lap, at 4.17, Passaleva was off in the S.51. Biard did not know it, since he had no means of communication with the ground, but his speed had surprised the Italians. He had completed his first lap at an average of over 150 m.p.h., which meant a speed on the straight in excess of 160—at least 10 miles an hour faster than they had counted on. And Passaleva, handicapped by a faulty propeller some of whose laminations had come unstuck as a result of its wetting the previous day, causing severe vibration, had to throttle back and could do no better in his opening lap than 7′31$\frac{4}{5}$″, nearly 22 seconds behind Sea Lion II. Once again it seemed that the luck of the Savoia company was out.

Biard, though, was also labouring under disadvantages, both strategic and tactical. Strategically he had to keep something in hand to complete the course whatever happened; this was essential since he was a lone representative of his country, with no reserve plane to back him up and make sure of finishing if the other competitors cracked up. And tactically the Italians, by starting at carefully timed intervals, were able after the first two or three laps to bunch together approaching the corners and shut him out. Thus he soon found himself closing in on the slower Italian machines, and even catching up on the S.51, yet unable to overtake them. It was frustrating and it could cost him the race, but he recognised it as perfectly legitimate tactics; if the British had taken the trouble to field a team of three, as they were entitled to do, they could have made things just as awkward for the Italians.

Biard decided to make the best of it. He could not attempt to steer outside the Italians because that would lose him too much time. The same thing applied in lesser measure to climbing over the top, while to come through on the inside would almost certainly end in disqualification as the Italians moved in front of him and forced him to cut the pylons too fine. On one corner he thought he saw a chance to get through but the gap was instantly closed, and he realised there was no alternative but to fly close up behind the Italians and climb over the top. The speed lost in the climb, however, made it uncertain whether his subsequent dive would take him clear.

He crept up behind the three Italian flying-boats until he was bumped and jolted by the blast from their exhausts and the turbulence of their slipstream. Then he opened the throttle wide and pulled the nose up. As he levelled off above the Italian pilots he could see their goggled faces staring up at him, while they too opened up to baulk him yet again. Now he was diving for the next pylon about a mile away; he had to get there ahead of the Italians. Fearful that his tailplane might strike one of their machines and cause a hideous accident, he hurtled down towards the pylon, wondering as he did so whether the wings of Sea Lion II would stand the strain. Then the white balloon was just below him on the left and he flung the plane round the turning-point like a fighter, the Italians in their turn rocking in his slipstream.

For seven laps Biard kept going full out, his times wonderfully consistent, his worst lap in this sequence being $7'12\frac{3}{5}''$. In this period he built up a lead which he hoped would be unassailable. Yet Passaleva's times were improving, and Biard's sixth lap was only six seconds better than Passaleva's corresponding lap—his fourth. Then Biard began to ease off, fearful of overtaxing his engine, and the distance between the two planes remained exactly the same as they went round in precisely the same time. Biard's times deteriorated still further over his last four laps, twice being only a fraction under $7\frac{1}{2}$ minutes, and Passaleva was now going definitely the faster of the two. Would Passaleva's propeller hold together, and could he make up the time Biard had purloined on those thrilling early laps?

Even to the Italians it looked as though Passaleva, at his present rate of progress, would have too much to do to catch up. Certainly Zanetti and Corgnolino, although both flying good races, were out of it except for their nuisance value. Zanetti's best lap was just under

8 minutes and Corgnolino's just under $8\frac{1}{4}$. Biard finished the course in a total of 1 hour 34 minutes $51\frac{3}{5}$ seconds, and by then it seemed that barring miracles the race would be his.

Passaleva went on improving his times until the end, his last lap proving his fastest of all. But it was still six seconds slower than Biard's exhilarating first lap, and although he had gained 20 seconds on Biard in his last three laps it was not enough to put him in front. Biard was a clear winner, by 2 minutes $2\frac{3}{5}$ seconds; and Zanetti and Corgnolino were left even further behind.

The damage sustained by the S.51 in the navigability trials had cost Italy the race and with it permanent possession of the trophy; despite the handicap under which this graceful machine had laboured it still averaged 143·5 m.p.h. against the Supermarine's 145·7, and four months later, on 22nd December, the same machine set up a new world seaplane record of 174·08 m.p.h. on a straight run. This was far in excess of anything ever achieved by Sea Lion II and proved the Savoia's basic superiority beyond doubt.

Somewhat fortuitously, an obsolescent airframe skilfully cleaned up by Mitchell and brilliantly flown by Biard had proved equal to the task in hand; but the major credit was due to the Napier Lion. What might it achieve when housed within a true racing design? The Italians, too, could profess confidence in the result of future races; their turn would come again. And since the trophy could be won outright by three wins in five years, they still carried the biggest threat for 1923.

That was how it seemed after the race of August 1922. But a new contestant was about to enter the lists. The Yanks were coming.

PART III
A YANKEE LOVER

1923

at Cowes

"We've got you whipped."

Lt. David Rittenhouse, U.S. Navy

WHEN the war ended, America suffered the same slump in her aviation industry as had befallen manufacturers in Europe. But compared with that of her Allies, American war production of combat planes had been negligible, and when the Armistice was signed in November 1918 there were less than 200 American-built aircraft at the front, all built under licence from original British designs, and all obsolete. American engineers did have one major wartime success— the 400 h.p. water-cooled Liberty engine, the most powerful of all the engines that saw service during the war; but for several years afterwards, fighting aircraft in the United States were of such low performance that they were little more than single-seater training planes.

Many of the wartime builders of aircraft in America—as in Europe —reverted after the war to motor-car production or to general engineering, and only a handful of companies continued to build aircraft. One which retained its pioneering role was the Curtiss Company, which by 1923 had established itself at Garden City, Long Island, New York. It was they who had built, to an order from the U.S. Navy, the four huge flying-boats designated Navy-Curtiss, three of which attempted the first crossing of the Atlantic by heavier-than-air machine in May 1919. Powered by four Liberty engines, they cruised at 80-85 miles per hour, and although two of them met with mishaps and failed to complete the crossing, the third, piloted by Lieutenant-Commander A. C. Read, safely reached Plymouth via the Azores and Lisbon.[1]

Another factor inhibiting progress was the huge government stock of war-surplus engines; yet the complete absence of American-built pursuit planes forced American constructors to design afresh if

---

[1] Hawker and Mackenzie-Grieve were forced down in mid-Atlantic while the American attempt was in progress, but in the following month Alcock and Brown made their non-stop crossing.

they were to enter the post-war racing and sporting field. Thus for the 1920 Gordon Bennett Cup at Étampes there were only three entries built to a new racing design, and all were American. Two of them were monoplanes, and they proved to be the fastest machines in the race, but they lacked the mechanical perfection of the more conventional European biplanes, and they could not prevent Sadi Lecointe in his Nieuport from achieving the victory that wound up the contest.

Fortunately a new stimulus to progress and competition was about to be provided. The three Pulitzer brothers, Ralph, Joseph Jnr. and Herbert, owners of the *New York World* and the *St. Louis Post-Dispatch*, had gained the approval of the U.S. Army and Navy for the inauguration of an international speed race to be known as the Pulitzer Trophy, with cash prizes for the winners. The first race for the new trophy was run on Thanksgiving Day, 25th November 1920, and it was won by an Army Captain named Corliss Mosely in a Verville biplane with a 638 h.p. Packard engine at an average circuit speed of 156·5 m.p.h. This plane, one of America's three new but unsuccessful designs for the Gordon Bennett two months earlier, had undergone various minor modifications since then.

Other less superficial pressures were operating to stimulate American participation in air racing and air competitions generally. First was the appointment of General William ('Billy') Mitchell as Assistant Chief of the Army Air Service; his battle for a separate air force did much to make the services air-minded, and when the Navy Bureau of Aeronautics was created under Rear Admiral William A. Moffett, a healthy rivalry grew up between the Navy and Army air services and the pilots of each service. This rivalry acted as a tonic to the aircraft industry, and despite a parsimonious attitude by Congress, sufficient money was allocated for the construction of a number of racing aeroplanes.

Early in 1921 the U.S. Navy contracted with the Curtiss Aeroplane and Motor Company for the design and production of two small pursuit-type biplanes, the ultimate object being to encourage the development of military fighters and to use them as test beds for new engines. The design of this machine, designated CR-1 (for Curtiss Racer—1), was finalised at the beginning of June. Mostly of wooden construction, the monocoque fuselage was covered with a 2-ply spruce veneer, and the wings, of multi-spar design, also had a 2-ply covering. The ailerons and tail surfaces were fabric-covered. The resulting structure was strong, rigid and light, with excellent contour stiffness and superb finish. The engine was a specially built direct-drive version of the 12-cylinder water-cooled Curtiss C-12; redesignated CD-12 (Curtiss Direct-drive-12), it was fitted with high-compression cylinder heads and dual carburettors. Cooled by external Lamblin-type radiators, it produced 405 h.p. at 2,000 revolutions per minute. With this engine the Curtiss company achieved an enormous reduction in weight for a given power output, getting the ratio down to $1\frac{1}{2}$ lb per horse-power.

The prototype CR-1, A-6080, was completed on 1st August 1921, and the second machine, A-6081, was finished a week later. Both were test flown during the month by the company's chief test pilot, Bert Acosta. The second race for the Pulitzer Trophy was due to be held at Omaha on 3rd November, and when the Army Air Service decided, apparently for financial reasons, not to compete, and when the Navy Department baulked in turn at the expense and the possible loss of new machines, the Curtiss company succeeded in pulling a few strings and borrowing one of the new racers back from the Navy so as to enter the contest themselves. Brilliantly flown by Bert Acosta, A-6081 finished first at an average speed of 176·7 miles per hour.

Fortified by this success the advocates of air power, led by Billy Mitchell, succeeded in extracting further funds from Congress for development purposes, and American aircraft manufacturers, spurred on by the prospect of orders, threw their energies into the design of new machines for the 1922 Pulitzer. Twelve brand new aircraft, representing six new designs, were built for this event, and the result was a remarkable triumph for the Curtiss company, despite a rude setback in the early stages. Several months before the race they submitted new designs to the Navy Department which embodied many improvements resulting from the experience of the previous year, but the Navy, reluctant to order new aircraft to compete with the ones they already had, turned them down. After seeking a private sponsor in vain the Curtiss company were about to file their designs away when the Army stepped in. Working day and night the company built two machines designated R-6 to an Army contract; these aircraft, developed from the CR-1 but of smaller size, were designed around a brand new wet-sleeve aluminium monoblock Curtiss engine, the D-12, the world's first wet-sleeve engine and one of the truly great aero engines of aviation history. Evolved by Arthur Nutt from a long line of water-cooled engines, the D-12 weighed only 671 lb dry, gave 430 h.p. initially at 2,250 r.p.m., and after passing its 50-hour test in May 1922 it achieved the sales breakthrough that the company were looking for.

Skin-type radiators built into the wings, taking advantage of the areas exposed to the airstream to provide surfaces for water cooling, replaced the old external type, and although the wings had to be strengthened to accommodate them, the reduction in drag gave a speed increase of over 10 m.p.h.[1] The two R-6s finished first and second in the 1922 Pulitzer, and the two Navy racers of the previous year were beaten into third and fourth places. America was ready for any foreign challenge, and as such a challenge had dropped out of the Pulitzer, it was inevitable that they should look further afield.

The main purpose of the American government was to gain prestige for American aviation; from this it was thought that valuable commercial results would flow. The secondary purpose was to stimulate aeronautical research and experimental design. Research workers would be given an incentive to new endeavour with a definite object in view, while designers would be brought into more intimate relationship with the research side and encouraged to extract more benefit from it, as well as being spurred to devise and develop new ideas of their own. The stimulus would not be restricted to aircraft manufacturers, but would extend to the makers of engines, propellers and all aircraft accessories. These patriotic and commercial objectives, it was confidently expected, would eventually result in a marked improvement in ordinary service aircraft.

The policy of the Naval Bureau of Aeronautics became to train pilots and develop fighting methods and tactics in less advanced machines of moderate speed, and to depend on competitions as a stimulus to the production of high-speed types. The development of fast seaworthy fighters, a type that it seemed the U.S. Navy might need in great numbers in time of war, would be stimulated, it was argued, by entry for the Schneider Trophy, and accordingly the Navy decided to equip four seaplanes for the 1923 contest, which was to be held in Britain at Cowes on 28th September. The planes chosen were the two original racers built for the Navy in 1921, the second prototype of a new Navy racer built by the Wright Aeroplane Company, designated NW-2, and a spare machine of comparatively low power for practice purposes, built by the Naval Aircraft Factory at Philadelphia. (The government was also believed to have ordered a fast flying-boat from Curtiss as an insurance against sea conditions unfavourable to floatplanes, but the

[1] This type of radiator was a Curtiss development, and consisted of a network of pipings, lying flush with the wing surface, through which the water cooling the engine was run.

machine was never built.) The two Curtiss racers were given new D-12 engines of 465 h.p., flush wing radiators, and metal propellers.[1]

Although untested as seaplanes the two CR-3s, as they were now redesignated, were approaching their peak as landplanes and they were regarded as the cleanest and most streamlined aircraft ever built; as conventional biplanes with a docile landing speed they were also easy to fly. The NW-2 had been built to a requirement drawn up by the design section of the Navy's Bureau of Aeronautics, and it had a fuselage of welded tubular steel and a steel framework for its tail surfaces, but it also proved fast and easy to handle. Somehow, however, it earned itself the name of "mystery racer", and a crash due to lubrication troubles destroyed the first prototype. Powered by a 700 h.p. Wright T-2 12-cylinder engine, it was the only American entry that could be genuinely called a new type; like the Curtiss racers it was untried as a floatplane. This was the situation when, on 26th February 1923, the National Aeronautic Association (which had succeeded the Aero Club of America in the previous year) entered a team of three for the Schneider race on behalf of the Navy.

The American pilots were selected in June. The team leader was to be Lieutenant Frank W. 'Spig' Wead; he would also fill the role of reserve pilot.[2] The pilots were Lieutenants David Rittenhouse, Rutledge Irvine and A. W. 'Jake' Gorton, all of the U.S. Navy; they were six-footers to a man. "They've picked the biggest guys in the Navy," complained the Curtiss designers, thinking about the tiny cockpits the pilots would have to squeeze into. "Why can't they send us some normal-size people?" All three were hand-picked test pilots serving at the naval air station at Anacostia, Port Washington, Long Island, with Jake Gorton, winner of the 1922 Curtiss Marine Trophy on floats, possibly having the edge. This had been the first big race the Navy had taken seriously, foreshadowing the decision to enter the Schneider.

As a result of his victory Gorton was offered the choice of mounts, and as both the Wright and Navy engineers were confident that the NW-2 would prove to be the fastest machine in the world, Gorton agreed when it was suggested that this should be his choice. Gorton,

---

[1] The efficiency of wooden propellers fell off drastically and drag soared as the tip speed of the blades approached that of sound, but with the introduction of metal propellers, developed by an American scientist named Dr. S. A. Reed, tip speeds could be increased and performance improved.

[2] Wead was later portrayed by John Wayne in the 1957 M.G.M. film 'Wings of Eagles'.

still only 26, had seen service on the Western Front in the French ambulance corps before joining the U.S. Navy.

The pilots reported straight away for special training at Anacostia, practising turns and water work on standard service seaplanes. Then in July they left to make individual tests of the actual race machines, Gorton going to the Naval Aircraft Factory at Philadelphia, on the Delaware River, and Rittenhouse and Irvine to the nearby Curtiss factory at Long Island. Gorton made his first flight in the NW-2 on 23rd July and the first of the Curtiss racers was air-tested on the same day. Although Gorton found the NW-2 somewhat sensitive on the controls he had clocked over 180 m.p.h. on a timed run before the machine was given a new engine and crated for transport to Britain. His timed run was kept secret. Meanwhile on 30th July Rutledge Irvine was reported to have set up an unofficial seaplane record of 175·3 m.p.h. in one of the CR-3s.

On 18th August the American team, pilots and ground crews, embarked on the *Leviathan* for England, the machines being sent separately by cruiser. They would thus have a full month in which to practise over the race circuit and acclimatise to English conditions. This was typical of the entire American organisation for the race; the Navy were responsible for the American challenge and they were conducting it like a naval operation.

There was still room for friendly rivalry between the American pilots themselves: this had been building up from the start. Both sets of pilots—Gorton on the one hand and Rittenhouse and Irvine on the other—had been secretive about the performance of their machines, but the general impression had been that the NW-2, if it could stay the course, would win. On board the *Leviathan*, Rittenhouse determined to find out what the Curtiss racers were up against. "Hey Jake," he said, "did you really do 180 in that crate of yours?" Gorton, a big, warm, spontaneous man not much given to concealment, admitted that he had actually squeezed 181 out of it. "Hell Jake," said Rittenhouse, "we've got you whipped." The speeds achieved by the Curtiss machines had been better, and their secret had been better kept. "Irvine is doing 197," Rittenhouse told Gorton, "and I'm doing 201." Their speeds had been given out as around 175 to avoid publicity and to deceive their competitors in Europe.

For Gorton this news was exasperating; he had allowed himself to be misled into choosing the slower machine. But with all that power to play with in the huge Wright engine, it ought to be possible to im-

prove performance yet. Over a bottle of Scotch with his team captain—
as Gorton has since related—the decision was reached that the best
chance was to reset the pitch of the three-bladed metal propeller and
run the engine at maximum revolutions—about 2,250 per minute.[1]
But would the engine stand it? Wead agreed to cable the Wright
company to put a T-2 on the test block and run it at maximum revs for
a durability trial; meanwhile they would make their own tests with the
actual machine when they got to Cowes.

Britain, France and Italy had also entered the contest, so for the
first time it would be truly international. There was talk at one time of
a cross-Channel circuit, with turning-points off the French and English
coasts, but the frailty and caprice of racing machines of the time ruled
out such a spectacle. The lesson of Bournemouth 1919 had been learnt,
Sammy Saunders offered his sheds again and Cowes was the unanimous
choice.

Britain's hopes of retaining the trophy lay principally with Supermarines; Sea Lion II, the winner in 1922, had been bought by the Air
Ministry, but it had been lent back to Supermarines to compete in the
race. It had been cleaned up and improved in several ways, new wings
had been fitted, greatly cut down, the lines of the bottom of the hull had
been replanned to offer less wind resistance, and the Lion engine had
been boosted from 450 to 550 h.p., so there was some justification for
designating it "Sea Lion III". A lap speed in excess of 160 m.p.h. was
hoped for; but none of this could disguise the fact that essentially it
was the same machine as last year.

American claims that 175 m.p.h. had been reached by their aircraft
were discounted in many quarters; American brashness was a standing
joke in Britain, and few people in that country knew of the progress
made in air racing in the United States in the previous three years.
Thus the visible confidence displayed by the American team when they
got to Britain was dismissed as Yank swank. How, it was asked,
would the elongated floats of the American seaplanes, almost as long
as the fuselages themselves, cope with the variable conditions in the
Solent? The planes exhibited a tendency to porpoise at the best of
times, and although the American pilots kept this under control it was
an obvious hazard on take-off. If the weather was at all rough it was
thought that the Curtiss racers might capsize.

[1] Thomas G. Foxworth tells the story in "The Wright Navy Racers, Part 2",
Historical Aviation Album, Vol. IV, produced by Paul R. Matt, Temple City,
California, March 1967.

Those closer to the world of aviation, however, took a less sceptical view; and aviation writers had been complaining for months of Britain's unpreparedness to meet the American challenge. Compared with the American method of the buying of machines under government contract and the entering of a full Service team with government support, and against a French government promise to give substantial financial assistance to the builders of any French aircraft which completed the course, the Air Ministry's offer to buy the winning plane (less the engine) for £3,000 provided it was British designed, owned and built and had not won the race before sounded derisory. Agitation in the House of Commons when these conditions were known met with scant reward. The government, while regretting its inability to give further assistance, hid behind the fact that Britain had won in 1922 without government help and might presumably be expected to do so again. In vain was it urged that, if the trophy went to America, very considerable expenditure would have to be incurred if Britain were to participate again.

The government's niggardly and short-sighted attitude was compared unfavourably with American enterprise. "They are sending over four machines," said *Flight*, "with four of their best pilots, and, after a period of trial and testing extending over a month or more, they will select from them the team of three to represent the United States." The government were again urged to give adequate help before it was too late, if only in the interests of trade. It was not reasonable to suppose that Britain's neglected aircraft industry could repel such a highly organised challenge without government aid.

No further help, however, was forthcoming, and although the industry did eventually muster a team of three, they did not all get to the starting-line. Of the three, the only one that ranked as a seaplane (as opposed to a flying-boat) was a Sopwith-Hawker, a diminutive biplane which in its landplane form had finished second in the Aerial Derby six weeks earlier. Powered by a 500 h.p. Bristol Jupiter II radial engine, it had averaged 164·5 m.p.h. Modifications to the fuselage and engine cowling to reduce heat resistance were carried out specially for the race, but its last flight as a landplane before conversion ended in disaster and the entry was withdrawn.

The third entry came from the firm of Blackburn Aircraft at Brough; according to Robert Blackburn, he and his co-directors had debated whether they should pay a dividend in 1923 or enter for the Schneider. As the race was to be in England, and in view of the prestige that success would bring to the company, they decided on the latter, and in March 1923 they announced that a small, fast, single-seat flying-boat was being made ready. The shareholders probably suffered no great disappointment, as the new racing machine was improvised out of very little, and indeed its origins went back more than five years, to a war-time Admiralty requirement for a single-seat flying-boat fighter. Before this project was shelved at the end of the war a racing-type hull of slender design had been completed, built to the same specifications as the Supermarine Baby fighter which had sired the Sea King amphibian and the Sea Lion, and this was the hull around which the new machine was designed. It was a narrow-gap, single-bay sesquiplane. The engine, with tractor propeller, rested on the upper wing, and the power unit chosen was the latest Napier Lion—the actual engine which, fitted into the Gloster 'Bamel', had won the Aerial Derby that year at 192·4 m.p.h. It was reputed to be the fastest of all the British entries, but like the American NW-2 it was something of a mystery ship, and although Blackburn's chief test pilot, Reg Kenworthy, asked for the machine to be ready by the beginning of August, it was not until early September, three weeks before the race, that it was finally launched. Immediately it left the Brough slipway it was caught by a combination of cross-wind and tide, and after dipping its starboard wing-tip float into the water it slowly turned turtle and sank. Kenworthy thought this would be the end of the matter, but Robert Blackburn was determined to get the machine—now styled the 'Pellet' —to the starting-line, and it was stripped down and repaired, larger wing-tip floats were fitted, and the engine was sent back to Napiers for the removal of the viscous Humber mud. It was not until Sunday 23rd September that the plane was ready, and with no time for further trials at Brough it was crated and despatched by rail to Southampton for assembly in Fairey's yard at Hamble.

The French team provisionally consisted of five aircraft including reserves, representing three different constructors. First string was a new flying-boat, the C.A.M.S. 38. This was a development of the C.A.M.S. 36, sleeker and with a reduced wing area, and it reverted to the pusher type of propulsion, leaving room for a cockpit forward of the wings clear of visual obstruction. The engine was a 360 h.p. Hispano-Suiza. One of the C.A.M.S. 36 machines modified for the previous year was also given a new 360 h.p. Hispano-Suiza and entered as a reserve.

As an insurance against bad weather the French also planned to have

two Latham L1 flying-boats on hand in case of need: these machines, of
sturdy hull construction and with two engines mounted in tandem,
would be outclassed for speed, but if the 'fair weather' ships were
eliminated during the navigability and mooring-out tests, as many
people expected, the Lathams might well fly over unopposed. The
fifth French machine was to be a Blanchard-Bleriot, designated C-1,
with a 450 h.p. Jupiter engine built in France under licence.

In Italy, all efforts to persuade the Air Ministry to help financially
proved fruitless, but the private entry of the S.51 seemed likely until it
was learned that the Savoia company, seeking increased power, could
find no suitable racing engine. Shortly before the race the Italian
government announced that they were "not prepared to finance the
sending of a team".

All this time the Americans, using Sammy Saunders' yard at Cowes,
were testing their machines, getting accustomed to water conditions in
the Solent, and familiarising themselves with the circuit and the race
regulations. The way they went about their preparations, the strength
and efficiency of their ground team (there were seven mechanics plus
representatives of the Curtiss and Wright Companies), and the scale
of their equipment and accessories, impressed everyone, and interest in
the American machines, and particularly in Gorton's 'mystery racer',
grew. The reputation of the NW-2 had travelled ahead of it, and
stories of its tremendous speed had lost nothing in crossing the
Atlantic. While the results of the engine-test by Wright's in America
were awaited, little was seen of the machine in the air, but the race
number—No. 5—boldly painted on the fuselage and rudder, suggested
to onlookers that it was a certain starter. Gorton, impatient to put the
new blade setting to the test, did in fact take the plane out for a preliminary run, and in an unofficial speed trial over the course he averaged
204 m.p.h., better than any of the times achieved by the Curtiss racers;
but after this brief test the NW-2 was hidden away, and the figures of
its timed run were not divulged, not even to the other members of the
U.S. team. The pilots of the Curtiss racers, too, were content for the
British to believe that their top speed was around 175 m.p.h.

When the result of the test-bed trial made by the Wright Aeroplane
Company reached 'Spig' Wead, he decided that the risk they were
considering ought to be taken: the T-2 engine had run for five hours at
2,250 revs per minute before blowing up. So far Gorton's engine had
been run for little more than half an hour, and since the race and the
navigability test combined would last less than two hours, there was a

safe margin. Wead and Gorton discussed the news over another drink, and the decision was taken to nurse the NW-2 beforehand but to run it flat out in the race. Gorton continued to practise on the reserve machine; but a few days before the race Wead, nervous perhaps of a failure during the contest which might upset the whole team, ruled that Gorton must make at least one further handling and proving flight at full throttle over the race circuit, of a duration of about half an hour.

Four days before the race, on Monday 24th September, the NW-2 was brought out of the Saunders sheds and Jake Gorton climbed into the cockpit. The huge Wright engine pulled the machine off the water with ridiculous ease, and after getting the feel of the controls again Gorton turned on to the contest circuit, opening the throttle until the rev counter climbed to 2,250. The circuit, with its turning-points and landmarks, was now thoroughly familiar to Gorton and he joined it at the starting-line at Cowes and headed east past Spithead towards Selsey Bill. He covered this leg, a distance of 18½ nautical miles and the longest in the race, at 200 m.p.h. indicated, then turned to port round the white cross that had been marked on the hillside just north of Selsey Bill. Now, with the wind behind him, he hurtled low across the water towards Southsea Pier at a ground speed of over 220 m.p.h.

Everything was going perfectly, the trial had been a success, and after passing Southsea he aimed to continue to the finishing-line at Cowes before preparing to alight. But at that moment, without any warning, the engine blew up in his face. He ducked as rocker-box covers and other odd bits of metal flashed past him, and in the next second the NW-2 hit the water, its forward speed unchecked right up to the impact. Gorton was catapulted out of the cockpit at something near 200 m.p.h., yet he came to in the water fully conscious and apparently unhurt. He swam over to the wreckage and clung to it for several minutes until a small fishing vessel picked him up and returned him, somewhat more sedately, to the South Parade Pier at Southsea, where he was given 'restoratives', according to the euphemism of the time.

The Americans, confident that the T-2 must run for at least five hours, thought at first that the propeller had broken up and punctured the floats, but after they had towed the wreck back to Southsea it was clear what had happened—even without the colourful description eagerly given by Gorton. The propeller story, however, provided a plausible excuse, and they stuck to it. No hint of the true cause of the crash was allowed to leak out.

Even so, the dramatic exit of the American 'mystery racer' inevitably encouraged hopes of a British victory. That was one Yankee challenger out of it. What about the others? The Curtiss racers might have a good record as landplanes in America, but they had yet to prove themselves as seaplanes. In spite of their workmanlike showing at practice, many still believed that a good lop in the Solent on race-day would ruin their chances. And as for their reputed performance in the air, Britain's immense wartime lead over America in aviation lent complacency to all judgments.

There was further encouragement for the British next day when the Blackburn Pellet turned up at the Fairey sheds at Hamble. On 26th September, the day before the preliminary tests, the Pellet was launched for a second time, with the game Kenworthy still at the controls. She shipped a lot of water on the take-off run, but the take-off itself was smooth enough. Once in the air, however, the Pellet proved extremely nose-heavy, and Kenworthy had to exert all his strength to prevent the machine from diving. Nevertheless he headed across the Solent towards Cowes. He had barely passed the R.A.F. base at Calshot when the water in the engine cooling system began to boil. He made a successful forced alighting on the sea south of Calshot, and after drifting about for over an hour he was taken in tow by a Saunders motor-boat, which took him to Cowes. During this 4-mile tow the Pellet seemed stable and seaworthy, but there was a lot of work to be done if she was to be got ready to fly next day. The Saunders team once again took charge, the wing radiators were by-passed and a large Lamblin radiator was fitted under the nacelle, a two-bladed metal airscrew was fitted instead of the wooden original (which had been damaged by spray during the take-off from the Hamble river), and adjustments were made which it was hoped would improve the centre-of-gravity problem. With the chief American challenger out of it, the belated and somewhat undignified arrival of the Pellet still looked an important gain for Britain.

The French team, too, were suffering various misfortunes. The C.A.M.S. and Latham flying-boats were to have been transported across the Channel on two French naval vessels, but the vessel that was to have carried the two C.A.M.S. broke down. The C.A.M.S. machines were then transferred to the ship that was to have carried the Lathams, and the two Latham pilots, Duhamel and Benoist, flew their machines over on the evening of 25th September, 36 hours before the navigability trials. All that day there was a full gale blowing with tremendous seas—the sort of weather the Latham pilots had been praying for, but not for crossing the Channel. Benoist's machine, suffering engine trouble when almost in sight of Cowes and driven back to Little-hampton by the powerful sou-westerly, was forced to come down in shallow water just outside the harbour. Damaged by the surf, she was virtually pulled to pieces by the clumsy enthusiasm of the natives in their attempts at rescue, and she had to be withdrawn from the race. The other Latham reached Cowes safely—a winning percentage, per-haps, if the rough weather continued. The two C.A.M.S. flying-boats were already there, but the Blanchard-Bleriot with the French-built Jupiter engine had proved too slow, and a second machine, fitted with a boosted Jupiter giving 550 h.p., had crashed after a mid-air collision.

The Americans themselves were doubtful of their chances when they saw the sea conditions of 25th September; and one report said that "all England was praying for a wind, a lop, and an extra strong tide race up the Solent", suggesting a parallel with an earlier invasion. But this time English prayers went unanswered; or perhaps the Americans prayed more fervently. Anyway by the morning of 27th September, the day of the navigability trials, the storm had blown itself out and the surface was the sort upon which any racing freak affixed to floats might have survived.

Just before the tests began the U.S.S. *Pittsburgh* anchored off Cowes, to dominate the skyline and give moral support to the American team. The Americans said it was there "to see fair play". Any British resent-ment at the presence of this huge warship was allayed by the hospitality dispensed on board, against the warm background of a saxophone band.

The French were represented by the sloop *Verdun* and a sub-chaser. The British Navy was absent.

The navigability tests took the same form as in the two previous contests—taxying over the starting-line at Cowes (an imaginary line drawn between two mark boats which also served as the finishing-line); ascending and alighting; taxying over two half-mile stretches at a minimum speed of 12 m.p.h.; flying round the circuit; and finally alighting and taxying across the finishing-line. Machines would then be towed away for the six-hour mooring-out test; no repairs could be effected until this test was successfully completed.

The belief that the tendency of the Curtiss racers to 'porpoise' on the take-off run might get out of hand was not borne out at the trials; in the flat calm that prevailed they took a long time to get off, and they threw out a bow wave as big as a destroyer, but the pilots had practised in all kinds of conditions and their take-off when it came was nicely controlled. The aptitude of seaplanes for water work could not be expected to compare with that of flying-boats, but they got through their trials without incident and were towed to their moorings. The Americans did suffer one casualty nevertheless; the reserve machine, which Wead had intended to fly to make up the team, sheared its starting gear with a backfire and thereafter refused to start by ordinary prop-swinging. That left Rittenhouse and Irvine in the two CR-3s to carry the American standard.

The French flying-boats, as expected, manoeuvred in impressive style and looked thoroughly at home on the water, though the C.A.M.S. 36 got airborne prematurely and dropped back on the water with a resounding smack, bouncing four times before climbing away. The most sensational take-off, however, was provided by the home team. After the Supermarine had performed in most ladylike manner and shown a turn of speed which some thought superior to the Americans, Kenworthy came out in the Pellet. His first trial on the Humber had ended in a ducking, and on his only outing since then he had been forced down in Southampton Water. He was coming absolutely fresh, in a strange machine, to a series of tests specifically designed to probe the weaknesses of both machine and man. But he waved confidently to his wife and friends, who were watching from a nearby launch, before heading for the starting-line.

It seemed to spectators that Kenworthy opened up his engine hurriedly, in contrast to his relaxed take-off from Hamble the previous evening; and he was in fact baulked at the beginning of his run by a small rowing boat which appeared likely to cross his path, forcing him to open his throttle more quickly than he had intended. The result was far more spectacular than the most violent porpoising. The Pellet began to buck like a bronco. It left the water in a stalled attitude and thumped back twice with frightening force before tipping over to starboard. The starboard wing-tip float touched the water, and the machine took one final leap before diving almost vertically and turning turtle.

Kenworthy found himself pinned upside down in the cockpit several feet below the surface, his head on the floor and his feet pointing to the cockpit opening, which he could dimly see. Air trapped in the cockpit was giving him a tiny breathing space in which to assess his position and recover to some extent from the shock, but his seat belt had become twisted and he could find no way of levering himself clear. By this time the cockpit was completely flooded, but he held his nose and finally

1923 SCHNEIDER TROPHY RACE COURSE

Nautical miles
0 1 2 3 4 5

Kilometres
0 1 2 3 4 5

One round lap 37.2 nautical miles
(68.80 kilometres)
To be flown 5 times

"FLIGHT" September 27, 1923

NORTH

White Windmill

SELSEY

Left turn round white cross

WEST WITTERING

EAST WITTERING

10.23 nautical miles
18,946 km

HAYLING ISLAND

18.52 nautical miles
34,299 km

SOUTHSEA

Pier

PORTSMOUTH

Mark boat to be passed
on north side

Spit Fort

SPITHEAD

Horse Sand
Fort

Nomans Fort

GOSPORT

8.45 nautical miles
15,649 km

Pier

Calshot Castle

SOUTHAMPTON WATER

Left turn round mark boats No. 1 and 2

START AND FINISH
Mark boat No. 1

Mark boat No. 2

SOLENT

ISLE OF WIGHT

COWES

struggled free. Those on board the motor launch, including his wife, had almost given up hope when he finally bobbed to the surface; according to the race stop-watch he had been under water for 61 seconds.

Once again Britain's hopes would be carried by a single plane.

28th September, the day of the race, began with bright sunshine and a calm sea; but in spite of this the Supermarine was still thought to have a good chance and the betting was about evens, with the French hardly considered as likely winners. During the morning the wind freshened, but approaching 11 o'clock, when the race was due to start, there was nothing in the conditions to alarm anyone. Thousands of spectators were lining the promenade, the piers were packed, and several large yachts and launches dotted the Cowes anchorage. Even the British Navy turned up at last, though its representation was restricted to a modest 'P' boat.

The competitors were to start in national groups, each nation being given a span of 15 minutes. The Americans had drawn the right to go first, at 11 o'clock, followed by the Supermarine at 11.15 and the French at 11.30. There was one curious feature about the start: competitors had to cross the starting-line on the water, and the wind was sufficiently strong to oblige them to cross this line in a westerly direction, their backs to the circuit, and take off towards Bournemouth before turning through 180 degrees and coming back to the starting-line to join the circuit. This would inevitably make each competitor's first lap time an unusually slow one.

Four minutes before they were due to start, Irvine and Rittenhouse taxied out from the Saunders sheds and got into position a mile or so beyond the starting-line. Then, when the one-minute cone was hoisted on the starter's barge, they began to taxi towards the line, accelerating so that they were only a few hundred yards short of the line when the cone was dropped for the start. Now, as the little racers leaped for the line, the pilots held them firmly on the water so as to taxi across the line in accordance with the rules. Irvine was the first across, and a second or two later came Rittenhouse; once past the line, both machines sat up on the heels of their floats in a long skidding movement before finally leaving the water. Then, by pre-arrangement, Irvine turned right and came back to round the outer mark boat while Rittenhouse turned left over the Royal Yacht Squadron. Soon both disappeared at high speed down-wind towards Selsey.

Spectators at Selsey picked them out first at about 11.05 as they passed Horse Sand Fort, ten miles distant. They increased in size rapidly as they winged eastward, and as they roared round the white cross on Selsey Bill Rittenhouse, with slightly the faster machine (by about four miles an hour), was just in the lead. They turned very wide, seeming to lose considerable ground, but they had proved at practice that a wide turn incurred less penalty than a steep bank, in which rudder sensitivity, induced skids and induced drag from the floats entailed a speed drop that was not easily made up. Rittenhouse was opening up his lead as they disappeared towards Southsea Pier.

While they were on the circuit Biard had come out in Sea Lion III, and there was general astonishment when, just as he was about to begin his take-off run, the two American seaplanes thundered in from Southsea and began to swing round the mark boats at the end of their first lap. No one had expected them to arrive before Biard's take-off; a circuit in 15 minutes meant an average speed of 170 m.p.h., and this first circuit had been artificially slowed by the circumstances of the start. At this rate the Americans would finish far ahead of everyone.

Biard for the moment knew little or nothing of this; he was concentrating on his take-off. Getting the extensively modified Sea Lion III off the water was a knack he had mastered, but it entailed letting the engine out fully at once and climbing away from a phenomenally short run. He got off just as Irvine rounded the mark boat, which may have confused him; anyway he took off so sharply that no one in the judges' barge seemed certain whether he had crossed the starting-line on the water, as he was supposed to do, or not. Perhaps the judges were themselves confused. Anyway to make sure there were no accusations of favouritism they disqualified him.

Meanwhile Biard, although unaware of his disqualification, was assessing his chances as slim. He hurriedly joined the circuit and chased after the Americans with the throttle fully open, but he judged at once that his speed was inferior. He tried every trick he knew to coax the machine along and to catch up on the turning-points, but he still lost ground. At the end of his first lap the timekeepers confirmed his impression: he was two minutes slower than Rittenhouse.

Misfortune dogged the French team to the end. At 11.30, when their entries were due to start, only the C.A.M.S. 38, with Lieutenant de Vaisseau Hurel as pilot, actually crossed the starting-line. The C.A.M.S. 36 somehow collided with a moored yacht on the way out to the course, damaging its hull, and although "the damage was slight—especially to the yacht", as one report put it, it was enough to put the more brittle flying-boat out of the race. Then one of the tandem

engines of the Latham developed magneto trouble and that too was
out. Hurel in the C.A.M.S. 38 took nearly twenty minutes over his
first lap, and on his second lap he was forced to alight with engine
trouble off Selsey Bill. Thus of all the many entrants for the race only
three were actually contesting it—and one of those had been disqualified.

A frantic James Bird, newly-appointed Managing Director of
Supermarines, was trying to get the disqualification cancelled, and
soon a written report had gone from the observers on the starting-line
to the judges' barge confirming that Sea Lion III had touched the
water as it crossed the line. The argument went on for days, but the
judges promptly reversed their decision, and Britain—just in case it
made any difference—was back in the race.

Once the speed of the Curtiss racers was realised there was never
any doubt about the result, provided they could keep going. And that
was something about which the Americans, whose generally modest
approach to the race had been imperfectly understood, had always
expressed absolute confidence. Indeed, so far from faltering, the American planes improved their times lap by lap—except in one instance—
throughout the race. Biard at least did the same, and his average speed
over his fifth and final lap exceeded 160 m.p.h., which would have won
any previous Schneider race by a margin. But Rittenhouse in a final
hectic lap averaged 181·1, and with a race average of 177·38 m.p.h. he
was a clear winner over his stable companion Irvine, who averaged
173·46. Biard's 157·17, 12 m.p.h. faster than in 1922, left him a bad
third.

Those who had been close to the Americans during their training
were not much surprised at the result, but to others it caused a
sensation. America was as far ahead of Europe in aeronautical design
as Europe had been ahead of America in 1914, when the old Curtiss
biplane flying-boat had been laughed off the Monaco course. How
completely even the aviation experts were taken in by their own
exaggerated notions of American brashness is best illustrated by the
graph published by one British aviation magazine just before the race,
designed for the easy determining by spectators of individual progress
lap by lap. The graph began at 150 and ended at 170. Every American
lap except Irvine's first went off the graph at the top.

The fame of the little Curtiss racer was now internationally
established. The winner was the same basic machine that had won the
Pulitzer as a landplane in 1921, piloted by Bert Acosta, and which had

finished fourth in the 1922 Pulitzer, piloted by Al Williams. Now, with pontoons added, and with integral radiators, a metal propeller, and a more powerful engine, it had captured the Schneider, travelling faster than when winning the 1921 Pulitzer with a wheel undercarriage. European aviation circles might bemoan their lack of government support, but it was not just a question of money. Design, reduction of frontal area, absence of projecting gadgets, workmanship, finish—all approached perfection for their time. No other engine of the same power would go into a similar racing fuselage with nothing sticking out except the airscrew boss and the stub ends of the exhaust pipes.

In organisation, too, and in attention to detail, the Americans had proved themselves second to none. As one magazine put it, "even to the steerable landing trolleys, and the waders which the men wore, everything was essentially built for the job". There were some, indeed, who protested that the Americans had been guilty of over-organisation, and who affected to see something slightly repugnant in the manner of their victory. "British habits do not support the idea of entering a team organised by the State for a sporting event," said *The Times* loftily, "and the Government control of such a team would be resented." After the way in which the British government had been reproached for failing to give the contest its unstinted support, this smacked very much of sour grapes.

The Times itself admitted that to send a team to the United States in 1924 would cost £25,000, and they did not suggest where the money was coming from. It had been freely predicted before the race that if the Americans carried off the trophy it would never be brought back to England, and indeed it now seemed certain that the Americans would monopolise the contest for the foreseeable future. There was nothing to stop them from winning it outright.

Perhaps in this assessment the British under-estimated the senti-mental attachment to the trophy of the Italians. Certainly the Italians were relieved that the British had been denied a second victory, which would have carried with it the threat of an outright triumph in 1924. Now, under the three wins in five years rule, the only nation that could win the trophy outright in 1924 was Italy.

The Italians noted with satisfaction that the British had been taught a lesson they themselves were careful to absorb for the future. "The clean-cut American victory caused a great impression," was one Italian comment, "particularly in certain circles which were prone to believe that on the other side of the Atlantic everything is exaggerated."

D

1924

at Baltimore

"Warmest appreciation of this sporting action."
Royal Aero Club of Great Britain

EIGHT days after their victory at Cowes, the United States Navy took the first two places in the 1923 Pulitzer Trophy at St. Louis with two new Curtiss biplanes specially ordered and built for the race, improved versions of the victorious CR-3. These two machines, designated R2C-1, were slightly smaller than the CR-3 in wing-span and considerably smaller in fuselage length, and their top wings were flush with the fuselage. They also incorporated all the improvements made to the CR-3 before its entry for the Schneider—the new Curtiss D-12 engines, Curtiss-Reed metal propellers, and flush wing radiators. The winning Pulitzer pilot, Lieutenant Alford J. Williams, maintained an average speed of 243·67 in one of the two new racers, and after his machine, A-6692, had been put into storage, the Navy detailed the Curtiss company to modify it as a seaplane for the 1924 Schneider. The lead opened up by the Americans at Cowes was thus dramatically increased, and the prospect of a European challenger overhauling the holders within twelve months was correspondingly reduced. Nevertheless Britain, France and Italy all entered for the next contest, which was scheduled to be held by the Flying Club of Baltimore at Bay Shore Park, facing Chesapeake Bay, on 24th and 25th October 1924.

It was not long before all three European challengers were showing signs of distress. In Italy, the rehabilitation of the aircraft industry under Mussolini, who had seized power in 1922, was only just getting under way. Two Curtiss D-12 engines were ordered by General A. Guidoni, Director of Aircraft Construction, so that Fiats could make a study of them, and Guidoni also designed a new racer specifically for the Schneider, using one of these engines. But this aircraft, constructed by C.R.D.A. (Cant.), sank twice during trials and never flew.[1] The other engine was lent to the Piaggio company for their projected monoplane Pc.3, but this too was unsuccessful. In May the French

[1] Cantiere riuniti dell'Adriatico.

withdrew. And in June the British Royal Aero Club put out an appeal
for funds, "it being quite obvious that we cannot expect any help from
the Air Ministry." Despite the impressive American victory this
department remained opposed to State-organised teams; they felt they
had played their part by ordering two new experimental high performance racing machines, a flying-boat from Supermarines and a
floatplane from Glosters. If the performance of these planes proved to
be materially above that of the Americans at Cowes in 1923, the Air
Ministry would be prepared to lend them back to the manufacturers to
allow them to compete under private arrangements at Baltimore.

In contrast to the half-baked preparations in Europe, American
plans for the race were firm, and they took the same trouble with their
training and organisation as in 1923. The team was again a naval one,
and the seriousness with which they approached their task was underlined when the U.S. Navy decided not to enter the Pulitzer that year,
leaving it to the Army Air Service and concentrating all their effort on
the Schneider.

By the first week in September the pilots were practising from the
Naval Aircraft Factory at Philadelphia on the Delaware river. The
two Curtiss racers that had finished first and second at Cowes were
flight-tested by Lieutenants George T. Cuddihy and Ralph A. Ofstie,
who had been named for the team. Cuddihy did a run of 197 m.p.h. in
Rittenhouse's plane, Ofstie did 190 in Irvine's. Only one of these
machines—Cuddihy's, A-6081—was expected to take part in the race.
The American first string was to be the R2C-1—A-6692—which had
been specially preserved for the purpose, and the pilot would be last
year's winner, David Rittenhouse. When this machine was taken out
of storage, and after the engineering data under which it had been
constructed had been thoroughly overhauled, it was found perfectly
possible to fit substantial twin pontoons instead of landing gear without alteration to either fuselage or wings, though wind tunnel tests
with the pontoons showed that larger control surfaces were necessary,
and these were added. Fuel capacity was increased by putting tanks in
the pontoons. When Rittenhouse arrived at the Curtiss hangars at
Port Washington, Long Island on 27th September the machine—
designated R2C-2 as a seaplane—was ready, and he took it into the air
for its first acceptance trial. Without any preliminary testing he
attained an average speed over a measured course of 227·5 m.p.h.,
30 miles an hour better than the CR-3.

The American team was to be completed by a Navy Wright

machine developed from the 'Mystery' racer of the previous year, designated F2W-2 (the landplane version was F2W-1), and powered by a Wright T-3 engine which at its maximum racing output developed 750 h.p. After its conversion to a seaplane the F2W-2 was shipped to the Naval Aircraft Factory at Philadelphia for trials. Jake Gorton was again chosen as pilot, an honour he accepted with a certain cynicism, but the designers confidently expected a top speed of around 235 m.p.h. In early attempts at take-off Gorton found the rudder area insufficient to keep the machine straight against the twisting power of the engine, and a slightly larger rudder was fitted. This enabled him to get the plane up on to the step; but when he took off for the first time, only a fortnight before the race, the power of the engine and a tendency to tail-heaviness took him straight up and the next thing he knew he was at 5,000 feet. He had never trusted the plane and he was furious with himself now for going up in it at all, but he decided to alight as soon as he could. He managed the approach nicely, but a wrongly installed vent spurted a jet of hot steam from the top wing radiator into his face as he levelled off, and he bounced on the water at 140 m.p.h., rolled on to his back when he opened the throttle, and hit the water upside down. "When you think you're going to drown you can exert superhuman strength," he said afterwards. "I ripped the entire rudder bar from the floor of the cockpit and got my only injury—a bruised ankle." Gorton was picked up by a passing tug-boat. "Do you have a drink on here?" he asked. Whatever Gorton's luck with aeroplanes he had a natural homing instinct for a bottle of Scotch; they gave him a pint of whisky and took him ashore. His crash brought the Wright effort in racing aircraft to an end. All four of their Navy Racers had come to grief, two as landplanes and two as seaplanes.

The Curtiss machines, however, continued to perform well, plans for the accommodation of visiting machines at Bay Shore Park were laid, and it was clear that despite the loss of the F2W-2 the Americans were ready to mount a worthy defence of the trophy.

Of the two British designs in preparation for the race, Supermarines' was the less far advanced. To meet the Air Ministry order for a racing flying-boat Mitchell had designed a craft with a Rolls-Royce 'Condor' engine in the hull and a geared drive to the propeller; but difficulties were experienced with the shaft driving and gearing, and the machine, to be called the 'Sea Urchin', was never completed. The design was eventually scrapped, and Mitchell turned afterwards to a monoplane design on floats; but while Supermarines struggled and

finally aborted, the Gloster Aircraft Company, still thinking in terms
of the biplane, were building on past experience and producing a likely
challenger. Back in 1920 they had acquired, through a take-over, the
services of a designer with a reputation for high-speed aircraft in
H. P. Folland, once assistant to Geoffrey de Havilland in the early days
at Farnborough and the man who had fashioned the famous wartime
S.E.5. From a number of earlier designs, Folland had evolved a compact little biplane, conceived and built in only four weeks and powered
by a Napier Lion, which came to be nicknamed the Bamel. Less than a
month after its first flight it won the 1921 Aerial Derby at 163·3 miles
an hour, and with extensive airframe modifications and increased
power it carried off the 1922 and 1923 Aerial Derbies as well, after
which it was sold to the R.A.F. Its winning speed in the 1923 race—
the last of its kind—was 192·4 m.p.h., and it is a matter for lasting
regret and speculation that this machine was not fitted with floats and
entered for the 1923 Schneider. But putting such hypotheses aside,
here was an aircraft which, suitably developed, might stand up to the
Curtiss racers; and thus was born the Gloster II, very similar in
appearance to the Gloster I or Bamel, but incorporating many design
refinements to improve speed and aerodynamic efficiency. Two of
these machines were under construction in 1924, and on 12th September, with very little time left before the race, the prototype was taken
by road to the R.A.F. seaplane base at Felixstowe to be flown by test
pilot Captain Hubert S. Broad. Broad was then chief test pilot to de
Havillands, but he had done a lot of free-lance testing for Glosters, and
as he also had extensive floatwork experience he was an obvious
choice.

It was on Friday evening 19th September that the great moment
came. The race was less than five weeks away, but the Aerial Derby
had been won in 1921 with even less time to spare after a first flight, so
there was still hope. "Mr. Broad took the machine off on Friday
evening in a very short distance and there was a slight suggestion of
porpoising though the machine got cleanly off the water," said *The
Aeroplane*. "Mr. Broad made several circuits with the machine
evidently under perfect control. It was, however, somewhat tail-heavy,
but with the throttle nowhere near full open she was doing just under
200 m.p.h." Because of the tail-heaviness Broad did not open her out,
but it was plain that when properly trimmed she would satisfy the
Air Ministry's requirements for speed.

After a short flight Broad prepared to alight. He came in at about

85 m.p.h. and touched down perfectly, but just as everyone was congratulating themselves that the initial test had gone well the machine started to porpoise, and one of the forward float struts gave way. The machine immediately turned over and sank, the only part still visible being the tail unit, and it was feared that Broad was trapped. But within a few seconds he was seen clinging to the tail. He attributed his escape to the fact that he had been unhampered by either parachute or seat belt.

Shortly before this accident the Italians had withdrawn from the race, and now the British too were out; there was no time to get the second Gloster II into racing trim. The Americans had demonstrated their ability to race, and a second victory for the holders was taken for granted. But the Americans themselves decided differently. The National Aeronautic Association wrote to the Royal Aero Club to say that owing to the withdrawal of Italy and the accident suffered by the British they would not claim a walk-over but would cancel the race for that year. In view of the preparations they had made and their own loss of an aircraft, and the fact that they were giving their challengers another twelve months in which to catch up, this must rank as the most generous of all the many gestures that characterised the Schneider races. The Royal Aero Club at once cabled their "warmest appreciation of this sporting action", and they added the hope that Britain would be fully represented in the following year.

After the race was cancelled, a substitute seaplane meeting was arranged at Bay Shore Park for Saturday 26th October, at which the two CR-3s raced over the Schneider course and set up several new records. The R2C-2, however, was held back for entry in the 1925 Schneider, and its only flights in 1924 were its contractor trials.

1925

at Baltimore

Jimmy Doolittle—national hero

"NEVER in the history of British aviation have we tackled an International speed race in so thorough a manner. . . ." That was the verdict of *Flight* magazine on 17th September 1925, five weeks before the race for the Schneider Trophy was due to take place at Chesapeake Bay, the same venue as the one arranged for the previous year. And indeed it did seem at last as though Britain were putting her best work and effort into recapturing the trophy. Two new machines had been ordered by the Air Ministry in March 1925, ostensibly for technical development purposes but in practice for entry in the race, one from Supermarines and one from Glosters, the orders being made on the same basis as in 1924. Flying was to be at the Air Ministry's risk, with the insurance of personnel left to the competing firms. The Supermarine was to be a monoplane and the Gloster a biplane; both would be powered by Napier engines and would use Fairey-Reed metal airscrews. On 21st August *The Times* reported that trials to test the two new types were about to begin.

After the failure of the Gloster II in 1924 it was realised on all sides that Britain had a great deal to learn about high-speed aeroplanes. The experience gained by the development of aircraft of this type, it was decided, fully justified the allocation of a proportion of the money voted for experimental Air Force purposes. The most exciting development that resulted was the abandonment by Mitchell of the racing flying-boat and the recrudescence of the monoplane form promised in the design of the Supermarine S.4. In accepting that the small flying-boat had been rendered obsolete for racing purposes by the emergence of the Curtiss biplane on floats, Mitchell had looked for the further step forward that would render the Curtiss racers obsolete in their turn. Most attempts at producing racing aircraft in the early post-war years had inevitably followed the form taken by the successful high-speed military types of the war, and these were mainly biplanes. The increase of power available from aircraft engines had dictated the use of larger wing surfaces, and the weight advantages of the biplane were still marked. Moreover the streamlining of bracing wires and struts had developed to such an extent that the braced monoplane had little advantage over the biplane for the same total area. The development of the thick wing, however, and other improvements in structural design and materials, leading to the practical possibility of building a monoplane without external bracing, tended to swing the advantage back towards the monoplane. The feature that made the design of the S.4 so outstanding was that its wing, float chassis and tail unit were each complete cantilevers, no bracing wires being used at all.

Reginald Joseph Mitchell was born at Stoke on Trent in 1895, and after an engineering apprenticeship he applied for a job at Super-marines in 1916, and Hugh Scott-Paine took him on. He was appointed chief designer in 1919 at the age of 24, and chief engineer in the following year. Virtually self-taught, he combined plodding common-sense and unerring intuition with a quiet, subtle genius that was some-times mistaken for luck. All his previous designs had been flying-boats, and although he was a young man of great creative potential, full of new and practical ideas, his excursion into the twin-float mono-plane field was a courageous one. But he was not the first designer to turn back to the monoplane for racing purposes. The Americans had done so unsuccessfully in 1920, notably with the Dayton-Wright Racer, which took part in the Gordon Bennett race of that year but failed to finish; and perhaps more significantly, in December 1924 a Bernard-Ferbois mid-wing racing monoplane with a new 450 h.p. Hispano-Suiza engine had recaptured the world speed record for France, averaging 278·48 m.p.h. and beating the existing American biplane record held by Al Williams by about 12 m.p.h.[1] This was just about the gestation period of Mitchell's new design, and he may well have taken the Bernard as his starting-point; the design he eventually produced bore notable resemblances to it. For ten years, however, from 1914 to 1923, no important race had been won by a monoplane, and the success of the Curtiss racers suggested that biplane supremacy in speed events might continue; this was the situation into which Mitchell introduced his new design.

The S.4 was a mid-wing monoplane constructed mainly of wood. The cantilever wing had been developed in collaboration with the Royal Aircraft Establishment, and a trial wing had been tested to

[1] The Société d'Avions Bernard had been founded in 1919 by Adolphe Bernard himself, Louis Bécherau, and Mark Birkigt, founder of the firm of Hispano-Suiza.

destruction at Farnborough. The fuselage was of monocoque construction, but the front portion was a steel-tube structure, to which were attached the wing and the undercarriage struts. The higher wing loading of the monoplane type meant higher take-off and landing speeds, and landing flaps were fitted in an attempt to overcome this drawback. The floats, of the single-step type, were of wooden construction, and the only other protuberances were the external radiators, which were located under the wings. The flying trials were conducted at the R.A.F. base at Calshot, and on 25th August, five months after the decision was taken to go ahead with Mitchell's design, the S.4 made its first flight. The pilot was Henri Biard. Reg Mitchell, whose concern for the pilots who tested his machines bordered on the neurotic, had changed into a bathing costume and seated himself in a motor launch to watch the flight. "If anything happens," he told Biard, "I'll dive into the water and pull you out." But the flight went well.

Three days earlier, on 22nd August, Hubert Broad—on loan again from de Havillands—had taken the Gloster III into the air for the first time. Like its predecessor, the Gloster III was a single-strut biplane with normal wire bracing, with fabric-covered wings and a wooden monocoque fuselage. Wing-surface radiators were planned, but they were not ready in time for the race and external radiators were mounted instead, on the leading edges of the lower wing. Like the S.4 the Gloster was powered by a Napier Lion developing 700 h.p., which meant that it would be at least as powerful as any other entrant.

Neither pilot was completely satisfied with the early performance of his machine. Visibility in the S.4, according to Biard, was "perfectly dreadful". The wings were in the way, and once embarked on a take-off run, or once having alighted, the pilot couldn't see ahead at all. More than once Biard was lucky to escape collision on the water. And in the air the machine frightened him, although it behaved well enough during its initial trials, getting airborne smoothly and efficiently and seeming to fly safely and well. It was the unbraced single wing that worried Biard, perhaps because it was new to him, and once or twice, as he was turning during these tests, he thought he felt a tiny shiver in the wings, although it was so slight as to be almost imperceptible, and he put it down to an overworked imagination. There was no doubt that the plane was fast, and on a three-kilometre straight course at Calshot on 13th September, checked by official timekeepers, he set up a new world seaplane record of 226·75 m.p.h. This beat the existing record, which stood to the credit of Lt. George T. Cuddihy of

D 2

the U.S. Navy in a Curtiss racer, by 38·7 m.p.h., and Biard felt that he still had something in hand.[1] Yet he remained uneasy, for no apparent cause. Meanwhile Hubert Broad had quickly put his finger on the trouble with the Gloster III: directional instability was the fault, the symptoms being the sliding, skidding course that the machine seemed determined to fly. Time was too short for the structural redesign that was really necessary, but the inadequacy of the tail surface was rectified to some extent by increasing the chord of the ventral and dorsal fins. This brought a marked improvement in the air without eliminating the defect altogether. By mid-September, however, the performance of the two planes had reached the point of satisfying the Air Ministry, though both pilots harboured reservations about their chances at Baltimore.

A second Gloster III had been built, and although Britain had entered only two machines for the race it was decided to take the second Gloster as a reserve, with a reserve pilot named Bert Hinkler, whose services were lent by A. V. Roe. The Bamel was used at Felixstowe for practice, and this machine too was to be taken to Baltimore. But because of bad weather Hinkler flew the reserve aircraft only once at Felixstowe before the party packed up to sail for America, and even Broad was able to complete no more than an hour's flying on the actual Schneider machine.

Throughout the summer, air attachés in the relevant capitals were prying and probing to get what information they could about the performance of the competing machines and sending it back to their governments. British estimates were that the circuit speed of the Italian entry would probably be in excess of 200 m.p.h. and that the Curtiss racers might reach 235-240. The British party, which included the two designers, Mitchell and Folland, and two Napier engineers, plus a team of ten mechanics, all under the leadership of Captain C. B. Wilson of the Royal Aero Club, sailed from London in the *Minnewaska* on 26th September in optimistic mood, with the general approval and commendation of the British aviation world, summed up in the opinion already quoted from *Flight*.

The Italian team, as it happened, left Genoa in the *Conte Verde* on the same day. Contrary to published accounts, Italian participation this year was sponsored not by the government but by Aeronautica Macchi.[2] In the previous autumn Mussolini was reported to have

---

[1] Rittenhouse's speed of 227·5 at Long Island on 27th September 1924 was not flown under record conditions.

[2] Signor Muzio Macchi, answering a questionnaire prepared by the author.

ordered another competition for the design of suitable aircraft, but the task of organising the expedition fell exclusively to Macchis, and the whole expense of travelling and competing was borne by them. The only help they got from the government was the loan of the two Curtiss D-12 engines purchased by General Guidoni in the previous year. Unfortunately the engines had been so extensively tested by Fiats for the purposes of design study that they never produced their full rated power.

In an attempt to find something to compete with the Curtiss racers, Mario Castoldi, the chief Macchi designer, turned, as Mitchell had done, to the cantilever monoplane; but unlike Mitchell he did not abandon the flying-boat form. The wing was set low down on the hull, and the engine was mounted on struts at a considerable height above the hull and wing. The dimensions were greater than those of the British and American machines, the wing-span being 32'. The result was a flying-boat of highly distinctive appearance labelled Macchi 33; but although more seaworthy than the other entrants, it did not seem likely to match them for speed.

The design of the M.33 proved satisfactory in trials, but it was not very well liked by the test pilots because of the frequent vibrations of the cantilever wing. Two identical machines were entered for the race, to be piloted by Macchi test pilots Giovanni de Briganti, winner of the 1921 race in a Macchi 7, and Riccardo Morselli.

In America neither the Navy nor the Army felt they could afford the expenditure of funds necessary to build a new racer; but finally they decided that the stimulus to research and development that the Schneider and Pulitzer races provided would make it worth their while to go in together and share the cost. For a total expenditure of $500,000 they purchased four newly designed machines from the Curtiss company, and earmarked four new Curtiss V-1400 engines for them, of twelve that were being built. These engines were expected to deliver 600 h.p. at 2,350 revolutions per minute. The new racers embodied all the improvements made over the years to the type, while retaining the sleek original appearance and outline. One of the new airframes was tested to destruction, which left three flyable machines and a spare engine. Of these, two were entered for the Schneider on behalf of the Navy and one on behalf of the Army; this was the first time the Army had entered the contest. Al Williams was named as acceptance pilot for the Navy and Lieutenant James H. Doolittle for the Army. The first machine completed and fitted with the new engine was put through its trials during the second week of September—rather later than the first flights of the new British machines, though the basic Curtiss type had of course a history of success behind it—and this machine was subsequently used by both Navy and Army pilots as a practice machine. Two of the new machines were entered for the Pulitzer, which preceded the Schneider by eleven days; the third machine, the one that had been used for practice, was held in reserve.

On 18th September Jimmy Doolittle, a leading test and demonstration pilot stationed at McCook Field, the nerve-centre of military aeronautical development in America, covered two laps of the Pulitzer course at 254 m.p.h., putting the advantage firmly back with the Americans. Doolittle, small of stature and a former bantam-weight boxing champion, was of modest, quiet and unassuming personality, and during his early flight training his unusual ability was recognised. He was one of the first test pilots to combine theory with practice in research flying, and he was the first man to fly an aeroplane 'blind'. He had been chosen by the Air Corps to take a course in aeronautical engineering, and he had subsequently made a special study of the effects of high centrifugal and gravity forces on aircraft and pilot. Equipping himself with an accelerometer, he had practised the most violent aerobatics and deliberately subjected himself to the phenomenon of blacking-out, about which little was then known. But his experiments, although not without danger, were never foolhardy, and when caution was urged on him his answer always was that he calculated every risk he took.[1]

Doolittle knew that every pilot had his own theories about high-speed cornering and about which method involved the least loss of pace. If the plane was pulled round too hard, speed was killed. A pilot, he thought, should cut the pylon as close as possible without actually risking disqualification, but he should start to bank shortly before reaching the pylon so as to make his turn symmetrical; if a turn was entered and left smoothly it would approximate to an arc of a circle joining two straight lines. Sharper and faster turning, he thought, could be achieved by diving slightly while passing round the pylon, losing perhaps 50-100 feet; in his practice laps on the Pulitzer course he found that by using this method he lost very little on the turns. Doolittle also made a study of the wind conditions, flying as low as

[1] On 18th April 1942 Jimmy Doolittle led the first air raid on Tokyo, taking off from the deck of the *U.S.S. Hornet*. He subsequently commanded the Eighth U.S. Army Air Force in Britain.

possible into wind and considerably higher with the wind behind him; a 300-feet change of altitude, he found, could make a difference of 6-8 miles an hour.

On the same day as Doolittle's circuit speed of 254 m.p.h., Al Williams, helped by an initial dive from several hundred feet and backed by a following wind, covered a measured kilometre—so it was reported—at over 300 m.p.h. This, however, was a freak speed, and soon afterwards the Americans had to ban these diving speed runs because of the break-up of aircraft.

The new Curtiss machines were designated R3C-1 as landplanes and R3C-2 as seaplanes, and it was as landplanes that they made their first public appearance. The 1925 Pulitzer was held at Mitchel Field, Long Island on Tuesday 13th October, and as the challenging Schneider teams had arrived in America a week earlier, some of their members were able to attend the Pulitzer meeting and evaluate the performance of the new Curtiss racers at first hand.

At Mitchel Field the Navy machine was flown by Lieutenant Al Williams, the Army machine by Lieutenant Cyrus Bettis. The best time yet put up in the Pulitzer had been that of Al Williams in the Curtiss R2C-1 in 1923, when his average speed had been 243·67, and it was naturally expected that the improved machines, with more powerful engines, would leave this far behind. But the new V-1400 engines developed defects before the race, and although most of the troubles were alleviated, performance was affected. Al Williams, indeed, was hampered throughout by a faltering engine, and with more turns to negotiate than hitherto and with a stiff gale blowing, he could do no better than average 241 m.p.h., two miles an hour inferior to his speed of two years earlier. The race was won by Cyrus Bettis, but his speed, too—248·97—was regarded as disappointing, and with the Schneider Trophy to defend in little more than a week the Americans were deeply disturbed. The substitution of floats for undercarriage was expected to cost anything up to 30 m.p.h., and the British challenge, almost discounted three weeks earlier, began to look formidable again.

The British machines were already established—if that was the right word—at Bay Shore Park, the beach area facing Chesapeake Bay 14 miles south-east of Baltimore which was to serve as the base from which the race was to be run. As a base it was primitive in the extreme. There were no facilities such as hangars or sheds, and nothing had even been improvised when the British team arrived, so that the packing

cases lay out in the open. While the pilots kicked their heels in the
Southern Hotel in Baltimore—neither the Americans nor the Italians
had yet arrived—the Baltimore Flying Club built up the site from
scratch. The gradual slope of the beach, which meant that the water
remained shallow for some distance out, obliged them to undertake
dredging operations, and a slipway had to be laid to make it possible
for machines to be towed on cradles into and out of the water. Meanwhile a line of T-shaped canvas hangars or tents, with wooden floors,
work benches and electric light, was erected to accommodate the
competing machines, with direct access to the slipway. All this time
the British team waited, absorbing valuable time that would otherwise
have been available for practice.

All might still have been well if the weather had held. But it was
cold and wet, the rain seeped through the tents as though they were
sieves, and working on the machines became more and more unpleasant.
The only consolation was that everyone suffered the same privations,
although the Americans, when they arrived, had the full backing of their
Service organisations. The contrast with the comparatively luxurious
conditions provided at Cowes in 1923 could hardly go unremarked.

The British team had already suffered one serious misfortune on the
voyage out in the shape of an accident to Henri Biard; he had slipped
while playing deck tennis and broken a bone in his wrist. The injury
had mended quickly, but there was some doubt at first as to whether
he would be able to fly. There was a possibility that Bert Hinkler might
replace him, but it was soon realised that Biard's experience of the S.4
made him indispensable.

First to fly at Baltimore was Hubert Broad in the Gloster III, a short
test flight of fifteen minutes on 13th October. Biard took the S.4 for
two flights over the bay on the 16th, when he found that his wrist
seemed strong enough and his speed all he had hoped for and more.
But bad weather and illness—in the appalling conditions Biard contracted influenza for the first time in his life and was confined to his
bed—reduced the opportunities for practice, and finally a gale wrecked
the improvised hangar area, the tent housing the S.4 collapsed, and the
tent pole crashed down on to the tailplane, damaging it severely.
Mitchell was confident that it could be repaired in time for the race
but it was another serious setback.

The race was due to be run on Saturday 24th October, with the
preliminary trials the day before. The course was a triangular one of
50 kilometres which fitted neatly into the northern reach of Chesapeake

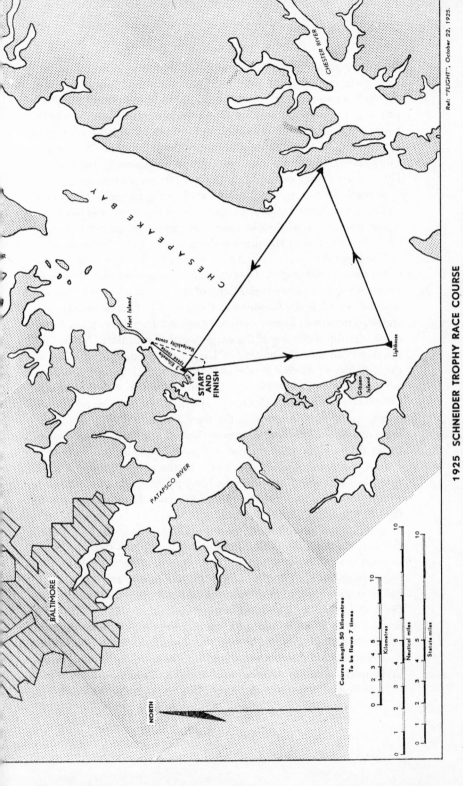

NORTH

CHESTER RIVER

CHESAPEAKE BAY

Hart Island.

3 Kilometres
Navigability Course
speed course
START AND FINISH
Lighthouse

Gibson Island

PATAPSCO RIVER

BALTIMORE

Course length 50 kilometres
To be flown 7 times

Kilometres
0 1 2 3 4 5 10

Nautical miles
0 1 2 3 4 5 10

Statute miles
0 1 2 3 4 5 10

1925 SCHNEIDER TROPHY RACE COURSE

Ref: "FLIGHT", October 22, 1925.

Bay; competitors would fly seven laps in all. Starting from a point in front of the judges' stand at the end of the pier at Bay Shore, they would fly south across the estuary of the Patapsco river and along Lake Shore Beach to the southernmost tip of Gibson Island, off which the light-house marking the first turning-point was situated. A left-hand turn of 105° would be followed by the crossing of the bay to Huntingdon Point on the far side, this leg forming the base of a rough isosceles. At Huntingdon Point a rather sharper turn of 120° would take competitors back north-west across the Bay to complete the triangle. The second and third turning-points, at Huntingdon Point in the east and Bay Shore in the north, were marked by pylons on barges. Judges were sited on the lighthouse and at Huntingdon Point as well as at Bay Shore.

The general impression in America was that the race would be one of the closest ever staged. The S.4 monoplane in particular, despite its misfortunes, was recognised as one of the fastest seaplanes ever put into the air, while the Gloster was thought to be capable of very high speeds. The Italian flying-boats, although not feared for speed, would come into the reckoning if the rough weather continued. Meanwhile the American team, consisting of Lieutenants Cuddihy and Ofstie of the U.S. Navy (selected for the 1924 team), and Lieutenant Doolittle, with Lieutenant Frank 'Hersey' Conant of the Navy as reserve and Lieutenant-Commander Homer C. Wick as captain, were settling down, although rivalry within the team was keen. What impressed observers most of all was the support Doolittle got from his understudy Cyrus Bettis—just as Bettis had got from Doolittle in the Pulitzer. "These two lone Air Service representatives," said the American magazine *Aviation*, "surrounded by Navy pilots, mechanics and crews, were more observed by their businesslike, modest bearing than any of the other flyers."

By nine o'clock on the morning of the preliminary trials, Friday 23rd October, Ralph Ofstie had left the slipway in a Curtiss racer, and soon afterwards he took off on the first test of the day. He was followed by Giovanni de Briganti in one of the low-slung monoplane flying-boats, and soon after at 9.30 came Hubert Broad in the Gloster. Then at 9.45 Biard climbed into the tightly-fitting cockpit of the S.4, half-way between nose and tail, and soon afterwards gave the signal to stand clear. After taxying out to the starting-line the all-white monoplane made a neat take-off after a very short run; but precisely what happened in the next minute or so remains obscure to this day.

Eye-witness accounts all agree that something went wrong.

9 (a) The Supermarine Sea Lion II demonstrates its manoeuvrability during the 1922 contest

9 (b) Some of the contestants at Naples. Left to right, Arturo Zanetti, Hubert Scott-Paine, Henri Biard, Alessandro Passaleva, Piero Corgnolino

10 (a) and (b)   Some of the French entries at Cowes, 1923.
Top, the C.A.M.S. 38. Bottom, the Latham, with the
C.A.M.S. 36 (tractor propeller) behind

11 (a)   Jake Gorton's Navy-Wright N.W-2 "Mystery" racer at Cowes, 1923

11 (b)   Henri Biard in Sea Lion III

12 (a)   The Blackburn Pellet—inverted—is withdrawn (Cowes, 1923)

12 (b)   Lt. Rutledge Irvine taking off in the second Curtiss CR-3

13 (a)   Lt. David Rittenhouse after his victory at Cowes

13 (b)   The 1923 pilots. Left to right: Lts. Rittenhouse and Irvine, R. W. Kenworthy, Lt. A. W. "Jake" Gorton, Lt. Frank W. "Spig" Wead, Henri Biard, Jean Duhamel, Lt. de Vaisseau Hurel

14 (a)　The 1925 British team on its way to America. Seated (front row) R. J. Mitchell, Capt. C. B. Wilson, H. P. Folland; (back row) H. J. L. "Bert" Hinkler, Henri Biard, Hubert Broad

14 (b)　Typical slipway scene at Baltimore. One of the Macchi M.33s is just visible top right

15 a, b and c. Progress of the Supermarine S.4 at Baltimore—
on the slipway, taking off, and being salvaged

16 (a) The Macchi M.33

16 (b) Hubert Broad in the Gloster III during the 1925 contest

"Captain Biard . . . flew over the pier and hangars making steep banks on the turn," said *Aviation*. Presumably he was testing the machine following the repairs to the tail; there is no record of any other air test. "He was seen to put the seaplane into a right-hand vertical bank and then immediately into a left-hand vertical bank. The observers from the ground suddenly realised that something was wrong for the machine appeared to stall and sideslip first one way and then the other from about 500 feet. After a half dozen of these right and left wing ups and downs, Captain Biard appeared to lose control completely and dropped about a hundred feet, pancaking into the bay. A great splash of water concealed the wreck and everyone on the shore was saddened over the probability that the pilot had been hurt."

Flight gave a similar account. "Biard made a circuit over the sheds and then flew out to the judge's cutter, coming back over the pier head. At a height of about 800 feet he was seen to make a steeply banked turn, which at first led the spectators to believe he was stunting, but it was soon realised that the machine was in difficulty and not under proper control. Some experts expressed the opinion that the wings had commenced to flutter, a phenomenon not unknown in cantilever mono-planes, but whatever the reason, Biard was obviously in trouble." *The Aeroplane* said: "Mr. Biard after getting off made several sharp turns and put the machine on to vertical banks. After the last it seemed to develop wing flutter and get out of control."[1]

In those last few seconds as the S.4 dived for the sea, Biard tried frantically to save the machine and himself. Somehow, according to *Flight*, he managed by skilful piloting to flatten out and reduce speed just before the plane hit the water, but the impact was still catastrophic. The floats gave way and the machine sank. To crash from such a height gave the pilot little chance, and the remark by the *Aviation* correspon-dent that "everyone was saddened over the probability that the pilot had been hurt" was little more than a euphemism: few doubted that Biard was dead.

Most demented of all the witnesses was the designer of the plane, R. J. Mitchell. He had again seated himself in the rescue launch; but as the boat raced to the scene of the crash it broke down.

First to reach the scene was Hubert Broad in the Gloster; he had just completed his navigability tests and he taxied straight over. The

[1] The symptoms of wing flutter were violent oscillation of the wing-tips accompanied by severe vibration of the whole machine. Serious structural damage could result.

surface of the water was littered with wreckage, but there was no sign
of the pilot. Then another piece of wreckage bobbed to the surface, and
Broad gave a gasp of surprise. He recognised a pair of pilot's goggles:
that was his first impression. But the goggles were still in place,
firmly fitted round the head of Henri Biard. This piece of wreckage,
although severely bruised and shaken, was vocal and animated;
miraculously Biard had survived.

Twice before, back in England, when flying the S.4, Biard had
experienced an eerie sensation of a 'ghost' plane following him, keeping pace with him as no other plane in England at that time could have
done, yet not seeming to be a shadow or reflection. He had had the
same sensation just before the crash. Now he found himself staring
through smeared, misted goggles at the anxious face of Hubert Broad.
Soon afterwards the launch arrived, and Mitchell and Biard grinned at
each other. "Is it warm?" asked Mitchell.

Later—according to a report in *Aviation*—the British issued an
official announcement on the cause of the accident: the S.4 had stalled
coming out of a steep turn at a height which did not leave the pilot
sufficient room to regain control. The wreck had been carefully
examined, it was added, and there was no evidence of structural failure,
nor was there any question of the wings having fluttered or of engine
trouble. This reassuring diagnosis, however, which appeared to put
the blame on the pilot, was not universally accepted, and it may well be
that it was deliberately fabricated to allay suspicions of faulty design.
The Italian contingent, though, were firmly of the opinion that the S.4
had stalled in a turn.

Was there wing flutter or not? Biard, in his own account, shows that
he clearly thought there was.[1] "She glided along the water," he wrote,
"rose in perfect style after a record short run, circled over the sheds up
into the icy blue dome of the sky till the buildings below looked like
dolls' houses, turned and sped away down-wind towards the spot where
the Judge's cutter lay all ready for the race itself.[2] Never had the
engine run so beautifully, or the machine answered so swiftly to the
controls. Round over the anchored cutter and back again towards the
pierhead at a speed somewhere round four miles a minute. Throttle
down the engine for the turn; over the pierhead and round again for
another straight run. And then the thing I had always known would
happen. . . .

[1] In *Wings*, published in 1934 by Hurst and Blackett.
[2] Surely this was a 'ghosted' account. It may possibly be suspect for that reason.

"As the wind caught the wings with colossal pressure on the turn, the flutter which I had noticed so faintly before that it only seemed fancy began with a vengeance. I worked feverishly at my controls—got the machine almost round—tried to relieve that awful pressure that was making the wings flutter almost like a moth's wings—felt the air tearing at them like a living, malicious thing superhumanly bent on smashing and twisting and wrenching this mechanical intruder and hurling it to destruction—spinning down like a leaf before a gale—and then with an effort which tore at every muscle in my body, I got her righted again and on an even keel, only to find that we had lost flying speed and it was too late. . . ."

Biard had freely confessed that the S.4 frightened him. He had risen from a sick-bed and may have been in no condition to fly so sensitive a machine. The official communiqué on the accident's cause was later confirmed by no less an authority than Major J. S. Buchanan, who represented the Technical Department of the Air Ministry at Baltimore, in a paper he read to the Royal Aeronautical Society on 21st January 1926; this paper contained the definite statement that the S.4 stalled and crashed into the sea. Yet the balance of opinion remains that in the design of the S.4 Mitchell overstepped the bounds o aerodynamic knowledge of the time and that the accident confirmed what had already been suspected in England—that the cantilever wing of the S.4 was subject to flutter. It is significant that, in the design of the S.4's successor, Mitchell abandoned the unbraced cantilever wing.

The loss of the S.4 left a gap in the British team, and it was determined to fill it by rushing the second Gloster III into service. Possibly through lack of forethought, but more probably because of the appalling conditions at Bay Shore, the ground team had concentrated on two aircraft only, and the reserve machine was not ready. Now it was hurriedly prepared for the navigability test. Meanwhile five of the competing pilots had completed the test and were anchored for the mooring-out test; they were de Briganti and Morselli, Doolittle and Ofstie, and Broad. Cuddihy had broken an undercarriage wire but was starting again at four o'clock. He impressed everyone when he finally got going again, but it was already obvious that the man they all had to beat was Doolittle, who during the morning had given, according to one account, "the most perfect exhibition of flying yet seen". Especially remarkable for an Army pilot were his alightings, which were far smoother than those of his Navy rivals and well up to the high standard set by the British team. The rear of his pontoons had no sooner touched the water than he instantly seemed to straighten out and come to a halt.

Whatever criticism of the unreadiness of the British team may be justified—and it would obviously have given Hinkler a much better chance if the reserve machine had been standing by fully tested and ready to go—the speed with which the second Gloster was got ready to compete was wholly creditable, and at five o'clock that evening the little Australian pilot, thrilled to be in the race after all, taxied out. His take-off was good and he was flying round strongly when a broken wing-bracing wire forced him to return, and by the time it was repaired the light was failing. Hinkler wanted to go out just the same, but Wilson, the team captain, decided it was too risky and ordered the attempt to be abandoned.

Under the rules of the contest, which required the preliminaries to be completed that day, Hinkler was now automatically out of the race. But a waiver was prepared and signed by all the other competitors which besought the contest committee to let Hinkler take his preliminary tests early next morning, in time for him to compete in the race at 2.30, and under this friendly pressure the referee gave way. Hinkler was duly launched from the slipway at daybreak next morning, Saturday 24th October, but half a mile off shore the water was so rough that he gave up and had to be towed in.

The conditions that had deterred Hinkler prevented any racing that day, and indeed the gale reached 65 miles an hour, becoming so fierce that most of the tents were blown down again, while 17 Glenn Martin S.C.1 floatplanes that had arrived to perform in a Naval Air Pageant that was to precede the Schneider race were torn from their moorings on the foreshore, seven of them being wrecked. The weather was not much better on the Sunday, forcing another postponement, but at daybreak on the Monday Hinkler was on the slipway again in the Gloster III ready for launching. This time the Italians demurred—they had agreed to waive technicalities three days earlier to give Hinkler a chance of competing, but with the long delay they felt it was possibly unfair to admit a fresh challenger, leading perhaps to complications on some future occasion if the precedent were established. The contest committee, however, having left their beds in Baltimore at three o'clock in the morning specially to give Hinkler a chance, allowed him to continue.

The gale of the previous two days had moderated but Chesapeake Bay was still swollen and ruffled by the waves that had smashed up the

Glenn Martins on the Saturday. Visibility, too, was minimal, but as soon as it was light enough to see the course and recognise the mark boats Hinkler was off down the slipway. Time was precious: he had to fly the course twice, land twice, taxi two stretches of half a mile each and then complete the six-hour mooring-out test, all before 2.30 that afternoon.

The small protected area near the shore was calm and the Gloster III took off comfortably and flew out to the starting-line. But out in the bay Hinkler could see that the boats that had gone out to observe his tests were rolling heavily. The water was still far too rough for sea-planes, but for Hinkler it was now or never. He came down from his first alighting so as to taxi over the starting-line, but as he tried to skim the wave-tops his floats were buffeted and shaken by the undulating surface. Suddenly one of the float struts cracked and gave way, and the machine tilted forward and settled in the water. The airscrew, still rotating, fouled the floats, and enough damage was done to put the plane out for a week. The disconsolate Hinkler, still sitting in the cockpit, was towed back to the slipway. Once again Britain was reduced to a single entry.

Conditions improved during the morning and by ten o'clock the contest committee were able to confirm that the race would take place. The pageant was curtailed by the absence of the Glenn Martins, but there was some formation flying and parachute jumping, followed by some thrilling stunt work by reserve pilot Frank Conant. Meanwhile the competitors were testing their motors and making final preparations for the race. All the engines were functioning well except the Curtiss D-12 of the second Macchi, and this machine had to be withdrawn.

By two o'clock the conditions had become as near perfect as they were ever likely to be. The early morning haze had lifted as the day warmed up, and the sun glistened on the highly-polished surfaces of the competing machines as they were towed down the slipway into the water. The bay was choppy but not rough, just right for floatplanes, and the wind was in the right quarter to suit the lay-out of the course. Each competitor had been allotted a five-minute period in which to take off, and in the absence of Biard, Doolittle would be first off in the period 2.35 to 2.40. At precisely 2.30 he taxied out from the beach area towards the starting-line in his black Army racer, and when he reached the rougher water of the bay he threw up a lot of spray, suggesting that the take-off might be exciting; but as he taxied across the starting-line at 2.38 he was going smoothly and his take-off was undramatic.

Broad was next, followed by Cuddihy and Ofstie, with de Briganti last, and each pilot got away comfortably within his five-minute span. The low-slung Macchi, wing-tip floats within inches of the water, gave the ranks of spectators along the bay shore a long take-off run for their money, but de Briganti was in complete control. By the time of de Briganti's take-off, however, the crowd were already hailing a new hero: Jimmy Doolittle, cutting the pylons to within a few feet in a series of near-vertical banks with his engine apparently full out, had completed his first lap, from a taxying start, at 223·15 m.p.h., a truly astonishing time. Broad had meanwhile set off after Doolittle, but the directional instability of the Gloster III was causing him to slide sideways on the turns, forcing him to take them wide, and he believed he was losing up to 20 m.p.h. over the whole course. He described the symptoms afterwards as "like the back wheels of a car on an icy road". When the time for his first lap came through it proved to be faster than any other Schneider plane had lapped in the past, but at 194·27 it was still much slower than Doolittle's.

A good public-address system informed the crowd of the race situation throughout. Speeds for completed laps, and mean speeds over the course so far, were posted on notice-boards within a minute, and the arrangements for the crowd, while greatly adding to the interest of the race, contrasted sharply with the lack of consideration received by the competitors. The biggest discomforts suffered by the crowd were the roar of the engines and the screech of the propellers; propeller-tip speeds in this race, with no reduction gear fitted, reached the speed of sound.

There were still another six laps in which anything could happen, and after their experience in the Pulitzer the Americans were suffering a severe attack of anxiety neurosis; but already the race looked like developing into an inter-Service battle between Doolittle on the one hand and Cuddihy and Ofstie on the other, and particularly between Doolittle and Cuddihy. The rivalry between these two men, both flyers of vast experience, both aged 29, had caught the imagination of the American public almost to the exclusion of the international angle, especially since the loss of the S.4.

When Cuddihy's time for the first lap was announced the Naval contingent, who had given the impression almost of over-confidence, fell omnousley silent: at 211·59 he was 12 miles an hour slower than Doolittle. There was time to catch up, but the indications were against it. Doolittle's handling of his machine was causing a sensation, even among the experts, who feared that the way he was cornering he would black out. There were three recommended methods of cornering: to bank sharply but slow down on the actual turn; to maintain full throttle but take the corners wide; or to climb at the turn while maintaining full power and make use of the height gained to dive into the straight. The Italians favoured the third method, Cuddihy and Ofstie the second; but Doolittle was ignoring all the precedents and cornering vertically at full throttle, sometimes gaining perhaps 50 feet or so though not intentionally. As he banked round the home pylon at low level he held his plane in so tight that the officials on the judges' stand felt the breeze from his propeller. His experience of high G-forces when testing machines to destruction before baling out, as he had been known to do at McCook Field, put him in a class by himself, and his precision flying at high speed was of a standard never seen before. Most pilots tended to black out at anything much above 4G, but Doolittle could stand 4G for fairly long periods and up to 8G for a short time.

Doolittle's superiority was underlined still further when Ofstie, in the machine in which Al Williams was said to have reached over 300 m.p.h. in practice, returned a first lap of 207·95. Both the Navy pilots were taking their turns very wide and neither was flying so direct a course as Doolittle.

To everyone's surprise the best cornering in the race next to Doolittle's was de Briganti's in the M.33. This graceful machine, expertly flown except for an unaccountable blunder in mistaking the course at one point, was hugging the pylons in the Doolittle manner, but at a speed of about 170 m.p.h. de Briganti was not subjected to the forces that were affecting Doolittle and the other Americans. Broad did better on his second lap and topped 200 m.p.h. on his third, and his cornering, despite his steering difficulties, was better than either Cuddihy's or Ofstie's, but he could not match them for speed. Cuddihy's second lap was only a fraction slower than Doolittle's first, but meanwhile Doolittle, unhampered by the taxying start, had pushed his lap speed up to nearly 234 m.p.h. If his engine held out he was a certain winner.

Engines: when the pressure was on in the Schneider, it was the engines that decided the issue. Whatever the shortcomings in design of the British seaplanes, the Napier Lion engine, although not approaching the American engines for reduction of frontal area, had given not a moment's anxiety since the team landed, and in Broad's Gloster III it was running perfectly now. The same could not be said of

the new Curtiss V-1400s, which were giving both Cuddihy and Ofstie a
worrying time, though Doolittle's had been trouble-free so far.

To the chagrin of the U.S. Navy, neither Cuddihy nor Ofstie was
destined to complete the course. Ofstie was forced down with engine
trouble half way round his sixth lap, alighting with a broken magneto
shaft in the centre of the bay, from where he was towed in; while
Cuddihy, holding on grimly despite a climbing temperature gauge,
was forced down near the end of his final lap when he ran out of oil and
his engine caught fire. He throttled back, put the blaze out with an
extinguisher, and alighted. He too was towed ashore.

Broad was still going well, and although he had been lapped by
Doolittle he was still outpacing de Briganti; if Doolittle faltered he
would win. But in fact Doolittle had already completed his last lap
when Cuddihy came down, so Broad was never quite so close to victory
as the final result suggested. As Doolittle rounded the last pylon he
zoomed up several thousand feet in a victory climb before coming in to
a perfect touch-down and being towed to the pier. His average speed
for the race of 232·57 m.p.h. had broken all seaplane records, and he
had also set up new records over 100 and 200 kilometres. Broad in the
Gloster flew a fine race to finish second at an average speed of 199·16,
and had it not been for his steering difficulties he must have run Doolittle very much closer; but his own opinion was that he would never
have caught him. The Gloster III simply wasn't fast enough.

The Americans regarded the race as the most interesting ever held
in the States, and Doolittle became a national hero. He had saved their
faces in thrilling fashion, and from the viewpoint of aviation progress
his times showed a remarkable advance on previous years. Next day he
set up a new world seaplane record by flying four times over a measured
3-kilometre straight in front of Bay Shore Park at an average speed of
245·71 m.p.h.; his speed would have been better but for turbulence and
a cross wind, but the figures showed how little he had been slowed
down in the race by the frequent cornering. Broad, too, had beaten all
previous records for the Schneider, and de Briganti had beaten all
records for flying-boats.

The latest Curtiss racer, designed by William Gilmore, and the new
V-1400 engine, designed by Arthur Nutt, had established a margin of
ascendancy for America over her rivals which, despite some teething
troubles, looked like deciding the final ownership of the trophy in the
following year. Yet there was consolation for the losers. The U.S.
Navy, holders of the trophy, had been humbled, and had the Army Air

Service not entered—for the first time—Britain, despite almost overwhelming misfortunes, would have won. Perhaps the genius of Mitchell
and Folland would provide an even more formidable challenge in 1926.
The Napier Lion had proved itself to be the best and most reliable
engine, with a power-weight ratio of virtually one for one (one horse-
power for every pound of weight), which was marginally better than
the V-1400; and Mitchell's own expressed view was that it was still
quite capable of winning the trophy.

For the Italians, too, the defeat had many lessons. They had been
wrong to rely on an obsolescent American engine, however reliable;
and in the event it had let them down in one case. Mario Castoldi had
designed the first cantilever monoplane to fly successfully in the
contest; but if they were to compete on level terms next year, and have
any chance of saving the trophy, they would have to abandon the
flying-boat form.

The British had gone to America with such high hopes and prospects,
but despite Broad's performance they accepted that they had been outclassed. This was bitter medicine, but the swallowing of it, and the
abandonment of illusions, was the finest tonic for the future. On their
return home they got down to analysing the reasons for their failure.

Despite the belief that had been current before the team left England
that preparations had been both punctual and thorough, it was apparent
in retrospect that insufficient time had been allowed. Minor troubles
had remained undiscovered until too late, while pilots had had no
chance to become accustomed to their machines or to become adept at
high-speed cornering: when Broad took off on his navigability tests he
had logged a total of only $1\frac{1}{2}$ hours on the type, while Biard had only a
few minutes more, and Hinkler had less than half an hour. The conditions at Bay Shore had been a contributory factor, and although there
was no suggestion of unfairness there was no doubt that these conditions had borne especially heavily on the British, who had placed too
much reliance on a preparatory period there. That was another lesson.

Four main factors were cited as leading to American superiority.
First and of paramount importance was the general cleanness of design
and elimination of parasitic resistance; even the S.4 had suffered from
excessive engine drag. Second, the introduction of flush or integral
wing radiators was said by the Curtiss company to be responsible for
an improvement of 20 m.p.h. at speeds approaching 250; they were an
essential part of any future design. Third, the latest Reed propellers
used by the Americans, of the forged type (produced only just in time

for the race), had been more efficient than the sheet type used by the British. And finally, the American pilots had been better organised and better trained. There was nothing but praise for the performance of the British pilots under difficulties, but the example of the Americans in entering a team of Service pilots would have to be copied, it was thought, and a period of at least six months' training allotted, if the best was to be got out of any new design.

These factors inevitably led to a consideration of the changing pattern of the Schneider race and its economic implications. While experts still believed that it was essential for the progress of aviation to maintain such contests, many doubted whether the Schneider races offered an ideal testing ground. From the sporting and spectacular viewpoints they were an outstanding success, more so now than ever before, and they had stimulated some astonishing technical and scientific progress; but they had moved beyond the scope of the private owner or private firm and had come to depend increasingly on government sponsorship. What would be the attitude of governments in the future, and of the British and Italian governments in particular? Both were urged to put the design and construction of next year's machines in hand immediately in a determined effort to prevent the Americans from capturing the trophy for good; but their chances of success seemed negligible, and the danger was that under these circumstances both governments would decide that further effort was pointless, besides being potentially damaging to national prestige.

1926

at Hampton Roads

"The race must be won at all costs."

Benito Mussolini

WHEN the lessons of 1925 had been absorbed it was clear that neither Britain nor Italy had much chance of overtaking the Americans within a period of twelve months. Yet to their credit neither nation thought in terms of abandoning the trophy altogether. All the competitors at Baltimore were agreed that October was too late in the year for racing, and since new machines could not be got ready in time for the summer of 1926, a postponement until 1927 was thought both by Britain and Italy to be inevitable, although no final decision could be taken until the F.A.I. met in Paris in January.

The entry by the Americans of a full Service team in 1923 and again in 1924 and 1925 had changed the whole nature of the Schneider race, and the increasing technical complexity of racing aircraft made preparations for an annual contest uneconomic if not actually impracticable. But the importance of the further development of high-speed machines was recognised, and another well-learnt lesson was that only government sponsorship could produce the conditions necessary for a successful challenge. The attitude in Britain, as expressed unofficially by Sir Sefton Brancker, the monocled Director of Civil Aviation, was that if the next race were put off until 1927 the Air Ministry would see it through.

A factor that militated against challenging nations and greatly reduced the time available for preparation was that the regulations for the next contest were not drawn up until the F.A.I. met at the beginning of each year; and until it was known whether or not there would be any change in the race conditions, new designs for expensive specialised aircraft were a gamble that neither governments nor private enterprise could afford to take. Criticism in Britain and Italy of the way the closing months of 1925 were frittered away was therefore misdirected. There remained a strong body of opinion that pure speed races were of no lasting value to the aviation industry and tended to produce freak machines, and when the F.A.I. eventually met on 11th January 1926 a proposal was put forward by Italy, supported by France, that competing machines should be obliged to carry a useful load of 550 lb in addition to pilot and fuel, and that the length of the circuit be increased from 50 to 500 kilometres. The Americans naturally interpreted this as a sly attempt to eliminate the Curtiss racers: "Aren't they tricky fellers?" was their reaction. But the Italians insisted that the existing regulations tended to produce machines that were useless for any purpose other than racing, leading constructors into heavy expenditure with no chance of finding a market for either aircraft or engines, and making it difficult to get government backing. The idea was opposed by Great Britain as well as the United States and was rejected, but it illustrated the planning difficulties.

Meanwhile in Britain Air Vice-Marshal W. G. H. Salmond, Air Member for Supply and Research at the Air Ministry (A.M.S.R.), had carried out a review of the 1925 race and reached two main conclusions: (1) that Britain was close enough to America in design and performance to approach a race in 1927 with confidence, and (2) that however good Britain's machines might be, her effort would be wasted unless the pilots and ground organisation operated at maximum efficiency. He therefore suggested that the Royal Air Force take over responsibility for the next Schneider team: this was the only way to do full justice to whatever efforts the Air Ministry might make, directly or indirectly, to win the trophy. But on 29th December Sir Hugh Trenchard, the Chief of the Air Staff, re-stated a basic principle on which he believed the R.A.F. should stand: Service machines and Service pilots should not be entered for private races. This looked a difficult barrier to circumvent; but it presented no problem to the Air Chief Marshal. Every principle could be broken if the occasion warranted it. Any such abandonment of principles, however, could only be justified by success. And Trenchard was prescient enough to foresee that even success would bring problems. Britain would be expected to act as host for any subsequent race, and there was the expense of sending a team to America to be borne first. Could the Treasury, in what was a stringent financial period, be persuaded to foot the bill? Trenchard's immediate solution was to go ahead with the production of high-speed machines under the existing development budget, irrespective of any final decision on entering the race, and meanwhile to get the views of the Secretary of State for Air, Sir Samuel Hoare.

Hoare believed that the race was a special case. The Treasury would need careful handling, but the advantages, he thought, were obvious. In addition to the technical and training angles, there was the propaganda side. "With anything so new as flying," he wrote, "special efforts must be made to enlist the support of public opinion. I can scarcely imagine a better way . . . than by winning a cup which rightly or wrongly is regarded as the blue ribbon of air racing." The Air Council remained opposed to any action which might lead to habitual participation in such events, but Trenchard's decision to go ahead and order the machines stood.

The British, however, had completely misread the atmosphere in America, where there was a stubborn determination to run the race in 1926 and have done with it. The outlook of the Americans had changed radically since their generous gesture of postponement in 1924. The speed records set up by their racing aircraft since 1921 had brought banner headlines but little business, at home or overseas; the demand for planes and engines of the racing type was too small for big sales and big profits. Meanwhile the impression was gaining ground that the limit of performance of racing aircraft was not far off, or anyway that a watershed was about to be reached. The possibility was even canvassed that human tolerance in piloting at high speeds was approaching the ultimate. These were problems that offered exciting scope for research; but it was a field for which the government were not prepared to provide further funds, and as appropriations were reduced so development work tapered off. The Americans were anxious to concentrate on translating their years of racing experience into the production of modern fighting planes; and even more important, their eyes were turning increasingly towards the field of air commerce and air transport. The stunt and the record men, amongst whom the Schneider pilots were misguidedly lumped, had had their day. The last race for the Pulitzer had been run in 1925, and for the Americans this was a convenient moment to wrap up the Schneider Trophy as well.

On 12th September 1925 President Coolidge announced the appointment of a President's Aircraft Board, which became the vortex of American discontent with her aircraft industry. The board recommended three separate five-year production programmes, to give continuity and stability to the industry, and the first one to be announced, in accordance with the new priorities, was the Air Commerce Act of May 1926. This was followed by the announcement of a five-year Naval programme in June and a similar Army programme in

July. In these programmes the contest for the Schneider Trophy had no place.

There was no Billy Mitchell now to fight the military case; absorbed in his campaign for a separate Air Force, and out-manoeuvred politically by the shrewd Rear Admiral Moffett, he had become a man consumed by an obsession. In February 1925 he had been removed from his post, and later that year, after severely criticising his superiors and accusing them of incompetence and criminal negligence, he was court-martialled and suspended. On 27th January 1926 he resigned.

Nevertheless the Americans had no intention of relaxing their grip on the trophy. The contest would be staged in 1926 as planned, challenge or no challenge. There were no funds available to build new planes, but the Curtiss racers that had proved victorious in 1925 would be made available again, cleaned up still further and fitted with new and more powerful engines. There was little doubt that they would be good enough to win.

On 16th December 1925 the Americans informed all likely competitors that the race would he held at the Naval Air Station at Hampton Roads, Virginia in the week beginning 24th October 1926. Lobbying by Britain and Italy began at once and continued right up to the time of the F.A.I. meeting of 11th January, and all possible influence was brought to bear to secure a postponement, but the American representative who attended the meeting—Commander J. C. Hunsaker—was unmoved.[1] His contest committee, in fact, had voted unanimously against such a postponement. But the British obstinately retained their faith in their powers of persuasion, and they still hoped to win the Americans round. Failing that, they expected to be able to put them in the unenviable position of having no challenger for the decisive contest; they did not believe the Americans would go through the farce of staging the final race with no opposition.

On 23rd January 1926 the Royal Aero Club informed the American National Aeronautic Association that Britain would be unable to compete in 1926, and they added a formal request for a postponement until 1927. The association, ostensibly the governing body in America, professed sympathy towards the British request, but pleaded that they were entirely in the hands of the naval and military authorities, who remained adamant. Accusations of unsportsmanlike conduct—which

---

[1] Dr. Hunsaker had had charge of the design of the Navy-Curtiss flying-boats for the Atlantic flight after theArm istice.

found little sympathy even in Britain—were treated with disdain. The contest was an annual one, and the attitude was that but for the gesture of 1924 the trophy would belong to America already. If Britain expected the holders to wait until some challenger produced an aeroplane good enough to win, they must be unusually naive. These were understandable attitudes; and in addition the Americans fell back on the rather sanctimonious excuse that they would be "failing in their duty to the donor of the trophy" if they postponed the race a second time.

The reaction in Britain remained one of disbelief; and unshaken faith in the personal approach led Sir Sefton Brancker to sail for America in late February to make a final appeal. He saw Orville Wright, chairman of the contest committee, and Godfrey A. Cabot, President of the N.A.A.; but the news of his pilgrimage was that he "wasn't getting much change". There was still time for Britain to enter—the closing date was 31st March—but so far as the Air Ministry was concerned the decision against it had been made. To attempt to rush new challengers into production at this stage would be to invite disaster.

Rumours that entries might be forthcoming from private individuals then became current, and it was confirmed that both Sammy Saunders and Colonel W. A. Bristow, a prominent consulting aeronautical engineer, were planning to build racing machines as a private venture and enter them for the race. Drawings of the Saunders machine, a low-wing monoplane, were ready, and the small frontal area and clean lines looked extremely promising; while Bristow had completed a design for a monoplane powered by an air-cooled engine. Trenchard's initial reaction was one of relief; here was the ideal opportunity for the R.A.F. to pull out altogether. But his views were not shared by Salmond, whose attitude was that any challenge in 1926 would be a waste of money, whether public or private, and that private entries would only stiffen American determination to hold the race. The more the Air Ministry thought about it the more irritated they became, and they were soon exerting pressure on Saunders and Bristow to withdraw. Their entries could have, it was argued, no chance of winning, and they would only provide the Americans with another excuse for making world-wide propaganda about their supremacy. There was some force in this, but it was an odd position to take up for a government department which had continually urged private enterprise to meet the challenge.

At a meeting at the Royal Aero Club on 19th March, attended by representatives of the Air Ministry, the Society of British Aircraft Constructors, and the Club, the refractory firms were bought off with promises of future orders and it was "unanimously" decided not to offer a challenge that year. This decision, it was emphasised, did not mean that the development of high-speed machines in Britain was to be abandoned; on the contrary, the Air Ministry confirmed that a considered policy of high-speed development had been decided upon, and that orders for new racing machines had been placed with three firms— Supermarines, Glosters and Shorts—together with an order for 12 new engines. It was expected that the new machines would become available for trials during the late summer. If the Americans persisted in their plan to hold the race in 1926, the Air Ministry promised to encourage the setting-up of a new speed record immediately the result was known, to nullify any propaganda advantage the Americans might gain; but this particular tit-bit was not released for public consumption. The official communiqué was less defiant: "These machines will be thoroughly tested out and as a result further machines will be built which will be available for the race in 1927 if it is still open." But what was the chance of that condition being fulfilled?

Since the Americans remained unwavering in their opposition to a postponement, and since the Italians were far behind the British (the French had already intimated that they would not be challenging), it seemed that Britain was finally conceding the trophy. But colouring all their dealings was the hope that the Americans, faced with the fiasco of a walk-over, would eventually be forced to give in. "It is almost impossible to imagine an international trophy of this nature being competed for by one nation alone in the absence of other entries," wrote Geoffrey Salmond.[1] Thus it came as a rude shock when Sir Sefton Brancker, on his return empty-handed from the United States early in April, brought the news that a challenge had been received by the N.A.A. from the Royal Aero Club of Italy.

The entire British strategy for getting the race held over was thus overthrown at one blow. Now there was a challenge there would have to be a race. If there was a race the Americans would win. The trophy —and the kudos—would be theirs for all time.

The Italians were attempting something that the British, far in advance of them at Baltimore, had dismissed as impossible. It seemed an unrealistic, reckless, selfish action, and the British were furious.

[1] Subsequent events lent this opinion an unexpected irony.

What they did not know was that the initiative had come from the
Italian government: Mussolini, the Italian leader, had ordered that the
race was to be won at all costs.

* * *

After the 1925 race, very few people in Italy believed that their
country would ever enter the Schneider contest again; to that extent
the information passed on by the Royal Aero Club to Trenchard in
London was soundly based. At Baltimore the Italians had been "hopelessly outclassed"; that had been the verdict of the United States Air
Corps News Letter, and this and other comments had deeply wounded
Italian national pride. Rather than expose themselves again to such
humiliation, most Italians were ready to fade out of the contest quietly.
It was in the hope of restoring a waning self-confidence and prestige
that Mussolini ordered, towards the end of 1925, that the prospects for
making a worthwhile challenge in 1926 should be investigated.

At this stage the chances of success seemed virtually nil. Not a
single suitable engine or aeroplane was under construction or even
under consideration in the whole of the Italian aircraft industry. Even in
1925 the Italians had had to rely on the Americans for an engine, and if
they were to enter the competition in 1926 they would almost certainly
have to rely on the Americans again. In December 1925 an American
company—probably the Curtiss company, though the name of the firm
was not divulged—was asked by the Italian government to build a
number of engines for installation in their Schneider racers for the next
contest. On 6th January 1926 the American firm replied that they could
not build engines of the type requested for a foreign power as these
engines had been developed in cooperation with the American government.

The Italians were thus thrown back on their own resources, and at
the end of January Mussolini, announcing another competition between
Italian factories to produce a possible challenger or challengers, called
the brains of the Italian aircraft industry together and made it absolutely
plain what he expected of them, promising whatever finance was
needed for the development of an aeroplane and an engine. The lesson
of 1925 was that it was impossible for any one firm to bear the financial
burden, and the government promised to absorb all the risks of the
flight tests and cover all the contest expenses. The combined experience
of Macchis and Fiats made these firms the inevitable choice, and a
contract was let for the supply of five machines, two for training and

E

three for the race. The minimum contractual speed was 380 k.p.h.—
just under 240 m.p.h.

By 4th February Fiat engineers under Tranquillo Zerbi, taking the
Curtiss D-12 on which they had done so much bench testing as their
starting-point, had begun work on the design of a water-cooled 12-
cylinder engine of similar pattern, and construction was started on the
15th; the engine was given a compression ratio of 6:1 and was
expected to develop 800 h.p. Every engine owes something to previous
designs, and the Italians were not alone in learning from the Curtiss
D-12; but they followed the basic design closely, time and their lack of
experience of racing aero-engines forcing them to take this course. The
crankshaft was built by Vickers in England. Meanwhile Mario Castoldi,
who had been ill in bed when Mussolini's orders reached him, got up at
once and started work on the design of a new airframe.

Mario Castoldi was born near Milan in 1888, and although described
by contemporaries as an average student he did well as a youth at the
Milan Polytechnic and during the war he entered military aviation as
an engineer. He soon gravitated to the experimental side, and in 1922
he joined Aeronautica Macchi at Varese. He was not, by all accounts, a
great theoretical aerodynamicist, but his ideas were intuitive and
original, and he had a flair, in a period of rapid and diverse aeronautical progress, for sifting what was likely to be durable from the
designs of others. This propensity for absorbing good ideas was
paralleled by a pathological jealousy of all original ideas of his own,
and he even avoided taking his own design teams fully into his confidence. To confuse competitors he produced inaccurate sets of drawings and left them where they might be stolen or copied, and on one
occasion he had a fit of near hysteria when he suspected that production
of parts of a Macchi machine had been based on the wrong drawings.
In the climate of the time, however, when everyone was copying
everyone else, his deviousness was not altogether unjustified.

In designing a machine to follow the M.33 and eclipse the performance of the Curtiss racers Castoldi found himself facing entirely
new problems; but confidence in his ability was so great that the task
was unanimously assigned to him. And within a few days of being
given the commission, Castoldi presented to Rome a design which,
while undoubtedly original in concept, expressed in dramatic form all
he had learnt at Baltimore—in the art of streamlining from the
Curtiss racers, in the monoplane form from the S.4, and in float design
from the Gloster. In practical terms this meant, first, the abandonment

of the central hull employed in all previous Italian Schneider entries and the substitution of twin floats; second, further development of the monoplane wing used by both Castoldi and Mitchell in the previous year (following the disaster to the S.4 and the wing vibrations of the M.33 Castoldi chose a braced rather than a cantilever wing); and third, the employment of skin-type radiators and Curtiss-Reed metal propellers. The Italian Air Ministry attached its best draughtsman, Signor Filipa, to Macchis to work with Castoldi, and the first drawings reached the experimental shop on 10th February. By 25th March the final design had been begun in detail, and by 15th April the building of the fuselage had started. In all other respects the project was going forward and designs were being reproduced as soon as drawn.

The first of the training aircraft was delivered at the beginning of July, and Romeo Sartori, Macchis' chief test pilot, completed the maiden flight successfully on the 6th. The two training machines had a slightly larger wing-span and an engine of 600 h.p., against the 800 h.p. expected from the contest machines. Some of the early flights—and a broken undercarriage—disclosed the limitations of Sartori as a float-plane pilot, and for high-speed work a more experienced pilot was requested. The man selected was Major Mario de Bernardi.

In mid-June Britain's air attaché in Washington reported that the Italian entries were firm and that there was no question now of a postponement; but Trenchard, on information supplied to him by the Royal Aero Club, remained sceptical. Rumours persisted throughout July that the Italians would not come up to scratch, but the Macchi company, neglecting their other contracts, worked day and night. At the beginning of August, after a demonstration flight in front of General Verduzio, who had replaced General Guidoni as Director of Aircraft Construction (Guidoni had been sent to Britain as air attaché), the provisional decision to enter a team for the contest was confirmed. The first contest machine was ready for testing by mid-August, $2\frac{1}{2}$ months before the race, and after a short period of engine and float trials the Macchi 39, as it was designated, had its first flight at Schiranna Air Station on Lake Varese on 30th August. The pilot was again Sartori.

In the ensuing weeks three more machines were delivered, and the team of pilots chosen for the race began to assemble at Schiranna. Led by Commandant the Marchese Vittorio Centurione, a 26-year-old nobleman, the team was to consist of Major Mario de Bernardi, Captain Arturo Ferrarin and Lieutenant Adriano Bacula. De Bernardi was 33, Ferrarin 31 and Bacula 32. De Bernardi, who had learnt to fly in 1913, had been a wartime fighter pilot. Ferrarin, chief test pilot to Fiats, was the hero of a record-breaking Rome-Tokyo flight in 1920 and a pilot of world renown; his selection followed political pressure by Fiats. Only Centurione and de Bernardi had arrived at Schiranna so far.

On 17th September de Bernardi made the first speed run over a measured 3-kilometre course and recorded 414 k.p.h.—nearly 260 m.p.h. This set up a new record for seaplanes, but the flight was unofficial and the speed was kept secret. Carburation troubles caused the loss of a good deal of potential flying time in this period. Then on 21st September Centurione, flying one of the new machines—the training version—for the first time, stalled sharply on his first turn after take-off and with insufficient height to recover crashed into the lake. The days when a pilot might hope to survive such a catastrophe were over, the machine was lost and the Marchese was killed.

The incident inevitably threw a pall of gloom over the Italian preparations, and there was no more flying for six days. The carburation troubles and the loss of one aircraft had between them delayed the race preparations by about a fortnight, at a time when every day was vital, and it began to look impossible to get the team to Norfolk in racing trim by 24th October. A request was therefore sent to the N.A.A. for a short postponement. The Americans were as determined as ever to fly the race that year, but they acceded to the Italian request, and the race was put back to 11th November, despite a strong protest from the Royal Aero Club of Great Britain, who rightly queried the legality of a postponement for any reason other than from day to day for unsuitable weather. But putting strict legality on one side the American decision was again a generous one, and in challenging it Britain was pursuing a lost cause.

Eventually de Bernardi resumed practice flights on 27th September, and Ferrarin and Bacula arrived at Varese at the end of the month. Take-offs and alightings on water were a new experience for Ferrarin, but within a week he was fully competent and was flying the M.39. With his arrival a keen personal rivalry developed between him and de Bernardi which culminated in a thrilling aerobatic display in the training machines. Curiously, while de Bernardi asked for a reduction of the rudder surface, Ferrarin asked for its increase: Castoldi's reaction was to increase the bottom fin area but to leave the rudder surface unchanged.

Bacula, too, had started practice flights, as had the reserve pilot,

Captain G. Guasconi, but there was very little time for further trials in Italy, and on 12th October the team, accompanied by their aircraft, sailed from Genoa on the *Conte Rosso*. De Bernardi was appointed team captain, and the party was placed under the overall direction of Major Aldo Guglielmetti.

* * *

The fiction that the Schneider race was still a 'club' event was overtly preserved to the extent that entries were made on behalf of the respective aero clubs: just as the three Macchi challengers had been entered by the Royal Aero Club of Italy, so the American defenders were entered by the National Aeronautic Association of America. Before this was done, however, the Secretary of the Navy had authorised the Bureau of Aeronautics to make three racing planes available to defend the trophy.

The Americans were well aware that, despite the Italian intention to compete, they could still be left at the last moment without a challenger, and they were determined that if this happened the race should not be the fiasco that everyone predicted. The answer, they believed, lay as in 1925 in a race within a race. The Army Air Service was not involved this time, but another form of inter-team contest was inherent in the variety of power units the Americans had chosen.

The three machines selected to represent the United States were the identical Curtiss R3C-2 racers which had successfully defended the trophy the previous year, modified in two cases to accommodate new engines. The third machine, the actual winner in 1925, retained the 600 h.p. Curtiss V-1400 engine of that year. The new engines were a geared 1A Packard developing 700 h.p., and a Curtiss V-1550 direct-drive engine also developing 700 h.p. Apart from the minor modifications necessary to accommodate the new engines there was no change in the airframe structures, though smaller pontoons were fitted, more streamlined in shape and with a rounded nose instead of the sharp point characteristic of their predecessors. The machine with the new Packard engine was designated R3C-3 and the one with the new Curtiss engine R3C-4.

The Curtiss racer remained a very small machine, with a wing-span of only 22 feet; the lower wing, with a span of 20 feet, was slightly shorter than the upper. The overall length from hub to tail, not including the projecting pontoons, was 20 feet. Curtiss-Reed duralumin propellers of the forged type were retained, and at 2,500 r.p.m. they pulled the machine through the air at approximately 10 feet per revolution, giving an efficiency rating of 89%. Many racing aeroplanes of the period were so delicate to fly that control could easily be lost through over-correction, but the Curtiss racers embodied a system of geared control which gave hands-off stability in straight and level flight. Another advantage for the pilot was that although the cockpit was a tight fit he was able to wear a parachute, and the cockpit had hinged sides for rapid escape.

Despite some last-minute misgivings the R3C-2 racers had been successful in 1925, proving distinctly faster than their rivals, and their re-appearance in 1926 under increased power was a logical step. Developed from a long line of Curtiss racing aircraft, all built to a basic design which had been refined and improved annually, they were the visible result of extensive pioneer engineering, and of concentrated research work in aeronautics and aerodynamics, allied to five years' racing experience at international level. Flown by three of the U.S. Navy's most skilled racing pilots, they looked certain to win.

The entry into the racing field of another engine manufacturer added considerably to American interest in the race, and to their prospects of victory. The Packard company already had wide experience in the manufacture of aircraft engines for long-distance patrol seaplanes, and it was natural that the Navy should turn to them for a racing engine to compete with the Curtiss engine and at the same time help to secure the trophy. Victory for one or other of the new engines would inevitably influence the authorities in the placing of orders, so competition was keen. The Packard company had forced the compression ratio of their engine up to 7·6:1 to get 700 h.p., and the Curtiss company, knowing this, had increased their own compression ratio to 7·5:1 to get the same power. Compared with the D-12 engine of 1923, the V-1550 developed 240 more horse-power for a 50 lb increase in weight.

The American team, which was announced early in September, was headed by George Cuddihy, who had first been chosen in 1924 and who had been forced to drop out on his final lap when in second place in 1925. The other pilots were Lieutenants Frank 'Hersey' Conant, a reserve in 1925, and William C. Tomlinson, both of the U.S. Navy; and Lieutenant Harmon J. Norton of the U.S. Marine Corps. The team captain was again Lieutenant-Commander Homer C. Wick.

Within a few days of the start of training, one of the American team was killed. On 13th September Harmon J. Norton, in attempting after a high-speed practice run in the winning 1923 machine to slow down so

as to formate on two Army aircraft at 2,000 feet, stalled and went into
a vertical dive, crashing into six feet of water on the Potomac River
near the naval base at Anacostia. Just before he struck the water he
tried to roll his machine out of trouble but was unsuccessful. Cyrus
Bettis, winner of the 1925 Pulitzer and the man who had backed up
Doolittle so ably at Baltimore, had been killed three weeks earlier, and
the depression that descended on the American team was difficult to
shake off. To some extent it paralleled the Italian loss of Centurione,
which came a week later, though in the case of Norton an obsolescent
machine was involved. The replacement drafted in was Lt. C. Frank
Schilt, like Norton one of the outstanding flyers in the Marine Corps
and an experienced pursuit pilot.

The intended American line-up for the race was now as follows:
Cuddihy was to fly the R3C-3 (Packard engine), believed to be the
fastest American plane, and certainly the most difficult to fly; Hersey
Conant was to fly the R3C-4 (Curtiss engine); and Frank Schilt
would fly Doolittle's 1925 R3C-2, leaving William Tomlinson as
reserve. At this stage the postponement of the race was probably not
unwelcome to the Americans. The Italians arrived in New York from
Genoa on 23rd October and soon afterwards transhipped to Hampton
Roads. To greet them Hersey Conant, checking his time with a stop-
watch, set up a new unofficial record at Anacostia on 27th October in
the R3C-4 with a speed of 251·5 m.p.h. over a 4½ mile straight course,
which he covered twice in each direction; this was nearly six miles an
hour better than the official record still held by Jimmy Doolittle. It
was inferior, though, to the time recorded by de Bernárdi in the
Macchi 39 over Lake Varese five weeks earlier.

These, of course, were early days, and the American team had not
yet moved down to Hampton Roads. But there was another tragic setback when they did so. On 30th October Hersey Conant, flying a
training plane from Anacostia to Norfolk Virginia to superintend the
unpacking of his racer, crashed when low-flying across Winter Harbour, 30 miles north of Norfolk, apparently having hit a fish-stake pro-
truding from the water. That was half the original team wiped out.
30-year-old Lieutenant Carleton C. Champion, an experienced racing
pilot and already named as a stand-by reserve, filled the vacancy.

There was more trouble for the Americans when Champion took up
Conant's racer, the R3C-4. In the course of the flight the wing radiators
were badly buckled and distorted through detonation of the motor
caused by excessive steam formation, and Champion, badly shaken,

alighted with the engine all but ruined after an uncomfortable flight. The team had been using a mixture of 40% benzole and 60% petrol instead of the 75/25 proportion recommended by the makers.[1]

Meanwhile the Italian party had established itself at the Naval Air Station at Hampton Roads, facing the bay in which the race would take place, where they were allotted a hangar and full facilities, in contrast to the primitive conditions at Baltimore in 1925. The Fiat engines were prepared and mounted in their respective aircraft, and in the last days of October and the first days of November they were exhaustively ground-tested. The braced low-wing monoplanes drew admiring crowds, but there was scepticism among the experts, spiced by many subtle hints about plagiarism of design. This did not depress the Italians: to beat Prohibition they had smuggled a plentiful supply of Chianti in the floats of their machines, so that the victory they looked for could be celebrated in appropriate fashion.

On 3rd November de Bernardi flew one of the M.39s—it was the machine assigned to Bacula—for the first time in America. It proved an inauspicious start. After only five minutes in the air de Bernardi was preparing to alight when the engine began back-firing and the petrol caught fire. He put the plane down immediately, smothered the flames with his leather flying jacket, and then used a fire extinguisher borrowed from an American seaplane that hurried to his aid. An incident that might have had disastrous consequences was thus kept under control, but it did not inspire confidence in Italy's chances. Neither did a series of engine tests next day; Bacula's machine needed two new pistons, for which the reserve engine was raided, and Ferrarin's failed to give full power due to the old trouble of faulty carburation. Castoldi, who had a morbid fear of sabotage, suspected the fuel supply, and he insisted on drawing his fuel from the same source as that used by the American team, rejecting a whole train-load specially ordered by Fiats. The sparking plugs, too, seemed to be performing indifferently, and the type was changed to that used by the American team.

With the race only a week off, both teams still had many mechanical problems to solve. Cuddihy was getting disappointing results with the R3C-3 (Packard), which had developed lubrication troubles since its reassembly at Hampton Roads, and the R3C-4 and the Macchis were all undergoing engine repairs or tests. The R3C-4 was not ready until 8th November, three days before the race; there were no spares

---

[1] With the primitive fuels in use, almost pure benzole had to be burned in these high-compression engines to avoid detonation.

available to replace the damaged wing radiators, so they had to be repaired as efficiently as possible. The result was a satisfactory cooling system at the expense of additional drag, and therefore some loss of speed. The test flight was entrusted to Cuddihy, and after the test a new unofficial speed record of 256 m.p.h. was claimed. With the Packard engine still performing moderately it looked as though the R3C-4 would carry America's main hopes, and many Americans felt that Cuddihy, as the most experienced racing pilot in the team, should be transferred to this plane.

The trouble was that the Packard-engined Curtiss was extremely difficult to fly. Increased engine revolutions to get more power had already resulted in propeller-tip speeds in excess of the speed of sound, and since engines develop most power at high speed and propellers are more efficient at a lower speed, a reduction gear had been introduced in the Packard between the engine and the propeller. In this case the reduction gear caused the propeller to rotate in an anti-clockwise direction.

Propeller torque had become a serious hazard on take-off, and this was accentuated in the R3C-3, in which the right float became completely submerged at full throttle. Although the tail fin had been offset in an attempt to correct the torque, the tendency to bury the right wing continued almost up to take-off speed, and the rudder correction necessary to counteract the torque was in the opposite sense to that to which pilots were accustomed. Getting airborne in the racing machines of the period was difficult enough anyway, in the absence of variable pitch propellers, and the whole problem was intensified in the R3C-3. Cuddihy had mastered the subtleties adeptly enough, but he was an exceptional pilot, and much as he wanted to fly the fastest plane he was reluctant to hand over the Packard to someone else at this late stage.

The news that Cuddihy had reached 256 m.p.h. on a routine test flight dismayed the Italians, especially as it was believed that Cuddihy had been taking it fairly easily and had had something in hand. Next day, however, word went round the base that the Americans were doubtful about their timing and that the actual speed had been slower, and the Italian mood fluctuated with each fresh rumour. Even the countenances of the American team were carefully studied for signs of confidence or uneasiness, and a lugubrious Homer C. Wick and a care-worn George Cuddihy gave the Italians further encouragement. Champion's uncomfortable flight in the R3C-4 had been another talking point and it was rumoured that he might find himself left out

E 2

altogether. On the same day, 9th November, the Italians' own engine tests progressed well and morale soared.

The amount of actual test flying, however, was extremely limited, and all the competitors were careful to avoid any sort of circuit from which their speed might be estimated. Thus the Italians were kept in doubt about the American potential and vice-versa. The indications were, though, that there was practically nothing to choose between the two teams, anyway so far as the aircraft were concerned. The Packard-motored Curtiss was reputed to have reached 258 m.p.h. in one of its early test flights, the Curtiss-motored machine was expected to do at least 256, and the Italians had claimed a speed of about 258 over Lake Varese. If an official handicapper had been employed he could not have produced a closer race.

What about the pilots? How would they compare? The Americans, with their much wider racing experience, expected to have the advantage here, as they had done in previous years. But the loss of half the original team in the course of training was bound to be felt, however good the replacements. And on 9th November the slim, dashing Arturo Ferrarin gave a convincing example of the skill and courage of Italian pilots; after taking off smoothly for a trial flight over the circuit he was caught out in a sudden and unexpected squall. The wind rose to gale force, and it rained so torrentially that the circuit was blotted out and Ferrarin with it. Despite this Ferrarin kept control and orientation, and just as the watchers were giving him up for lost he came in and alighted in perfect order and was towed to the slipway. The way the Macchi behaved, and the poise of the pilot, drew unstinted admiration. "After such a trial," said one newspaper, "the Italian aircraft can do without the navigability test, and all doubts about the ability of Italian pilots have been dispersed." The Americans had had a glimpse of what they were up against.

The sudden change in the weather that had given Ferrarin the chance to display his skill reduced opportunities for flying next day and caused a postponement of the navigability trials from 10th to 11th November, and even then it wasn't possible to start until late afternoon; so it was decided to continue them next day and to run the race itself on Saturday the 13th. Fortunately the elements relented and there was no repetition of the storms of 1925.

The high state of training and readiness achieved by the Americans in each of the previous three years had not been approached this time and there were still worries about both their major contenders, while

the Italians had had even less flying time at Hampton Roads than the
Americans. Since their arrival de Bernardi and Ferrarin had made five
flights between them and Bacula only one. The race was an absolute
lottery, even more so than on many occasions in the past. Whereas the
Americans had the stimulus of the outright capture of the trophy to
sustain them, the Italians drew equal inspiration from their desire to
frustrate them, and from a cable received that day from Mussolini
calling on them to conduct themselves so as to win respect for their
country. This was doubly heartening as reports were current in America
that there had been an attempt—one of several—on Mussolini's life.

At 4.15 p.m. on 11th November de Bernardi, the Italian captain,
took off from in front of the Naval Air Station in the first of the Macchi-
Fiat racers, climbed gracefully away and set out across Little Bay for
his navigability trials. There was no time limit for completing the
trial, and de Bernardi took the opportunity to give his plane a brief but
thorough try-out. As with the other competitors, this would be his last
time airborne before the actual race. The quick, smooth take-off
characteristics of the Macchi were especially noticeable, comparing
well with the pitching tendency of the Curtiss racers, which the smaller
floats tended to accentuate.

The light was already beginning to fail when de Bernardi came in to
land after completing his trials, and this may have accounted for the
accident which followed. The motor launch which went out to tow him
in ran into his starboard float and punctured it so badly that the
machine had to be hastily brought in. This was an error of race
organisation, for which the Italians were not responsible, and the
contest committee ruled that they could repair or replace the pontoon
and undergo the mooring-out test next morning. Nevertheless it was
an unfortunate setback, which contributed to a serious Italian error of
judgment before the day was out.

At 4.45 p.m. Frank Schilt took off in the winning 1925 machine,
and three minutes later he was followed by Adriano Bacula. The
American biplane with its blue naval markings made a colourful contrast with the scarlet Macchi monoplane, and as the two planes competed together in the failing light they presented a striking spectacle.
By 5 o'clock both had completed the trials successfully and anchored for
the mooring-out test. Meanwhile George Cuddihy, deciding it was too
late to complete his trials that evening, took the opportunity for a
final test flight in the R3C-3 (Packard) before competing next
morning.

The engine of the third Macchi had also been warmed up, and the pilot, Arturo Ferrarin, was anxious to complete his trials so as to moor out that evening, when the water was likely to be calm, rather than chance the conditions next day. This had become doubly important since the enforced delay in de Bernardi's mooring-out test: if both machines were caught in bad weather next day it could be disastrous for Italy's chances. Ferrarin, unwisely as it turned out, regarded the rapidly falling light as the more acceptable risk, and at 5.15 he took off in good style and sped out across Little Bay. He completed his first alighting successfully, but after heading out into the bay for a second time he disappeared behind some ships in the harbour and failed to reappear. It was now almost dark.

Ferrarin in fact had suffered an engine failure and had come down safely in the bay; but he was drifting about with a dead engine, and he was in imminent danger of being run down in the darkness by some passing vessel. Tug boats, passenger boats and ferries criss-crossed the bay every few minutes. A motor launch went out and failed to find him, but he was spotted from the air by a Service flying-boat that joined in the search. The pilot alighted and taxied close enough to Ferrarin to converse with him, but neither man could understand the other so the flying-boat pilot, aware of the danger to both of them, taxied in a circle round Ferrarin in complete darkness for the next two hours, manipulating his fuel mixture whenever the lights of a vessel approached so that his exhaust ports spat a warning fire. Eventually the motor launch found them and took Ferrarin in tow.

It was nine o'clock that evening before the Italian mechanics were able to get to work on their diagnosis, and they soon found what had caused the trouble—a broken connecting rod. The crankcase was fractured at four or five points and several other connecting rods had failed. Next day was the last on which the navigability trials could be run, and it looked impossible to repair the engine in time. The mechanics declared that it would be equally impossible to get the reserve engine—already raided for Bacula's machine—repaired and mounted in 24 hours, and the exclusion of Ferrarin seemed certain. His absence would have been such a severe blow, however, that Silvio Scaroni, the Italian air attaché, together with Muzio Macchi, son of the founder of the firm, and Signor Ferretti, in charge of the Fiat contingent, called the team together and asked for an all-out effort, reminding them no doubt of Mussolini's order, and of the cable received from him the previous day. Exhausted as they already were after the strain of the previous fortnight, they worked all night and throughout the following morning to produce one serviceable engine from the bones of two, and at two o'clock on Friday afternoon the engine was mounted and tested on the ground and at four o'clock Ferrarin took off and completed the trials, his engine functioning perfectly.

The temperature was rising even more steeply in the American camp. Homer C. Wick, the team captain, had fallen ill, and Rear Admiral Moffett, Chief of the Naval Bureau of Aeronautics, had assumed the leadership. Confronting him, with little time for consideration, was the decision as to which machine Cuddihy was to fly, and, if it was to be the R3C-4, who was to be assigned the task of coping with the Packard. Moffett, in fact, had very probably made up his mind already; but no inkling of his intention was allowed to leak out. The official position that Thursday evening, as disclosed by Press enquiries, was that a final decision would be taken at 9 o'clock next morning. Meanwhile final ground tests of the American machines had revealed that the fuel pump on the R3C-4, which raised gasoline from the floats to the main tank, was sticking, and a new pump was installed.

There was another shock first thing Friday morning when it was announced that Carleton C. Champion was unwell; but no hint was given as to whether he would be fit to fly or who might take his place. This, even more than in the case of the team captain, had all the hallmarks of a 'tactical' illness, possibly suggested by Moffett; but still the public was kept in suspense about the final composition of the team.

Early that morning both the modified machines, the Packard and the Curtiss, were out on their 'dollies' on the platform in front of the air station, with their engines ticking over and warming up; and very shortly two men in flying gear were seen to be approaching. One of them was recognised immediately as George Cuddihy. The other proved to be reserve pilot William 'Red' Tomlinson. All queries were finally resolved when Cuddihy climbed into the cockpit of the R3C-4 (Curtiss) and Tomlinson made for the R3C-3 (Packard). Cuddihy's qualms about giving the Packard to any pilot less experienced than himself had evidently been resolved, or more probably overruled.

The weather was almost perfect, with a balmy easterly breeze and a brilliant sun. Cuddihy was lowered down the slipway first, and after a perfect take-off he climbed steeply away. In three years' experience of Curtiss racers he had developed a masterly technique, and his alightings, taxyings and general handling were a nice blend of the workmanlike and the spectacular. After completing his trials he was towed to his mooring position about 300 feet from the shore. Next came Tomlinson in the R3C-3. He had never flown the Packard-engined plane before. After leaving the slipway he turned dead into wind and began his take-off run, but the characteristic pitching motion of the Curtiss racers and their tendency to jump out of the water before reaching flying speed soon had him in trouble. He bounced badly and looked certain to somersault, but somehow he recovered and climbed unsteadily away. Once properly airborne, however, he showed a surer touch, and he spent the next half-hour feeling his way and getting accustomed to the machine. Then, after 38 minutes' familiarisation, he decided he was ready to attempt his first alighting.

Turning over land, he was making his approach to Little Bay from the edge of the flying field which ran right down to the water's edge when he was baulked by a Service machine which had just taken off. The pilot's field of vision in the Curtiss racers was poor, and Tomlinson soon lost sight of the offending plane. The safest thing was to go round again. His second approach was unhampered and he seemed to come in well, but he misjudged his height at the last moment and held off too soon. He was only a few feet above the water, but the plane dropped heavily and then bounced, damaging the starboard float. The wing-tip on that side dropped, and Tomlinson applied port aileron to correct it. The plane immediately did a side somersault to port and plunged upside down into the water. Tomlinson, squeezed into the tiny cockpit and hampered by his flying gear, was trapped as the aircraft lay submerged with only the underside of its pontoons showing. But he was alive and unhurt, and after being under water for several seconds he struggled clear and pulled himself up on to one of the up-turned floats, waving reassuringly to the slipways. He was brought in suffering from little worse than a ducking, but the wrecked R3C-3 was out of the race.

By putting Cuddihy in the R3C-4 the Americans had acknowledged that this was their No. 1 choice, but the loss of the R3C-3 was nevertheless a crippling blow to the team. It was no satisfaction to Cuddihy that he had warned against the change of pilots.

After Ferrarin had completed his test that afternoon, Tomlinson appeared again in flying clothes and took off in a standard Curtiss Hawk, which the Americans were entering to complete their team. To show that he had not lost confidence or spirit, Tomlinson "put up about the finest show of trick and fancy flying that the spectators had seen for a long time", according to one account, and he completed the

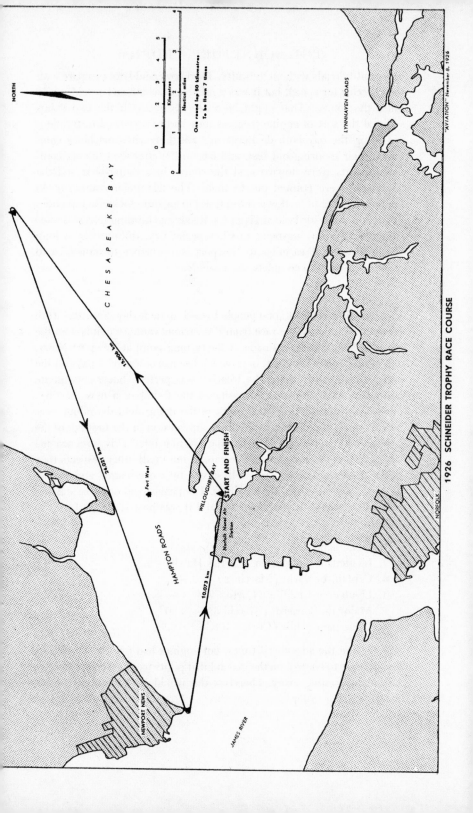

NORTH

0 1 2 3 4 5
Kilometres

0 1 2 3
Nautical miles

One round lap 50 kilometres
To be flown 7 times

CHESAPEAKE BAY

13,906 km

24,051 km

HAMPTON ROADS

Fort Wool

Willoughby Bay

START AND FINISH

Norfolk Naval Air Station

10,073 km

NEWPORT NEWS

JAMES RIVER

NORFOLK

LYNNHAVEN ROADS

"AVIATION" November 8, 1926

1926 SCHNEIDER TROPHY RACE COURSE

navigability trials without difficulty. The Hawk could not compare with
the Macchis for speed, but it was a reliable machine and would surely
finish the course. That might be a decisive factor if the two teams
suffered the sort of engine troubles they had experienced in training.

During the day both de Bernardi's and Ferrarin's machines completed their mooring-out test, and late in the afternoon the six competing pilots were flown round the course in a flying-boat and the
landmarks were pointed out to them. The triangular course, of 50
kilometres, was to be flown seven times in an anti-clockwise direction,
beginning at the air base at Hampton Roads and heading north-east for
9½ miles to a turning-point in Chesapeake Bay, followed by a long
south-west leg of 15 miles to Newport News before turning back to
Hampton Roads to complete the triangle.

*   *   *

A crowd of about 30,000 people turned up next day, Saturday 13th
November, to view the race from the various vantage points—on the
flying-field at Hampton Roads, at the turning-point at Newport News,
and at Old Point Comfort, over which the machines must pass on the
long south-westerly leg. The weather was perfect, but a last-minute
change of wind direction necessitated the fixing of a new starting-
point. Instead of taking off in front of the flying-field the pilots were
briefed to continue straight from the slipways on to the first leg of the
course, taking off after crossing the starting-line. This screened the
take-off from the majority of spectators, but in all other respects they
had a good view and were well served by score-boards and public-
address systems recording lap times. The provisional order of starting
had been decided by drawing lots, and it was posted on the board as
follows:

1. Lieutenant Bacula (Macchi 39)—2.30
2. Lieutenant Tomlinson (Curtiss Hawk)—2.35
3. Captain Ferrarin (Macchi 39)—2.40
4. Lieutenant Cuddihy (Curtiss R3C-4)—2.45
5. Major de Bernardi (Macchi 39)—2.50
6. Lieutenant Schilt (Curtiss R3C-2)—2.55

These were the advertised times, but engines had grown so complex
and difficult to control on the ground that pilots were given 15 minutes
latitude in getting away. Therefore this would not necessarily be the
actual starting order.

That morning the Italian team, with their air attaché, worked out a tactical plan. The presence of the Curtiss Hawk in the race appeared at first to pose no threat; but it was realised that here was a plane that was certain to finish, whatever happened to the speedier entrants, so it was worth holding one machine back and nursing its engine specifically to make sure of beating it. This self-sacrificing task was given to Adriano Bacula. A speed a little in excess of 200 m.p.h. was considered to be quite enough to leave the Hawk far behind, and this was what Bacula was to aim at. Meanwhile, still uncertain what speed to expect from the Americans, de Bernardi and Ferrarin would be ready to force their engines to the limit, though de Bernardi's propeller, set at slightly coarser pitch, gave him a small advantage. Two members of the team who were not actually flying were to station themselves at a point in the bay where they could judge the situation and where their signals would be seen by the pilots, and their most important task would be to let the Italian pilots know if the Curtiss racers—and especially Cuddihy—were forced to retire. If that happened, de Bernardi and Ferrarin would throttle back and make sure of finishing. This simple, straightforward plan was of course unknown to the Americans, who were unable to make any worthwhile tactical plan themselves as their only real chance of winning—unless all the Macchis broke down—lay with George Cuddihy. Cuddihy himself was optimistic. During a test that morning his engine had turned up several hundred revolutions more than normal, and the 9'1" propeller previously fitted had been replaced by a propeller 9'4" in diameter. This had left the engine developing maximum power at 2,600 revs.

A further piece of opportunism was worked out by the Italians—or more specifically by Ferrarin—just before the race. He was timed to take off five minutes ahead of Cuddihy, with de Bernardi five minutes behind. Ferrarin decided to take advantage of the 15-minute rule and delay his take-off until after Cuddihy, and to fly immediately behind him, regulating his speed according to the American's, making sure of overtaking him but not necessarily opening right out. That would leave de Bernardi clear to race at maximum speed all the way. It was another example of the selflessness of the Italian teamwork, in which all personal rivalries were submerged.

Bacula began warming up his engine on the slipway at 2.28, and he appeared to have reached a good speed as he taxied across the starting-line. His take-off run lasted less than half a minute, he was airborne by 2.35, and the smoothness of his take-off and the small amount of spray thrown up were impressive. Three minutes later Tomlinson crossed the line in the Curtiss Hawk, and soon afterwards Bacula's machine came into view again as it approached Hampton Flats on the far side of the Roads, making for the second pylon at Newport News.

There was a short delay now as Ferrarin, right on cue, affected to be having minor trouble warming up his engine; and Cuddihy, anxious not to spend too long with his engine running, decided, as Ferrarin had expected, not to wait for him. Immediately Cuddihy began his take-off run Ferrarin's engine trouble miraculously cleared and he chased after him, getting airborne less than a minute behind him. De Bernardi followed in his own time at 3 o'clock and Schilt a minute later.

While this pantomime was being played out, Bacula was completing his first lap, and his time was announced and posted on the board. His average speed was 209·58, which caused a gasp of surprise and disappointment, even from the more partisan of spectators, most of whom were desperately keen to see the home side win but wanted to see a close race. That Bacula might have been deliberately conserving his engine did not occur to anyone at this stage; and as it happened his main petrol tap had worked loose and he was flying with only one hand on the controls, losing time on the turns in consequence.

At 2.53 Tomlinson completed his first lap at a speed of only 137·31, but he got a sympathetic cheer from the crowd. And a minute later the spectators really had something to excite them. Cuddihy, going much faster than anything seen so far, and taking the pylons much closer than the Italians, completed his first lap, and the voice of the announcer, thundering across the enclosure, revealed his speed. He had gone round at 232·427 m.p.h., nine miles an hour better than Doolittle's first lap in the previous year, and 23 m.p.h. faster than Bacula in the Macchi. Even if Bacula's machine was the slowest of the Italian entries, it didn't look possible for any of them to catch Cuddihy.

American euphoria, however, was short-lived; close on Cuddihy's tail came Ferrarin. After flying low over the heads of the spectators he made a 90-degree turn over the home pylon and hared off for a second time into the bay. The impression that he had already caught up slightly on Cuddihy was confirmed when his lap speed was announced as 234·61 m.p.h., just over two miles an hour better than Cuddihy's.

For a moment the other contestants were forgotten in the absorption of the personal struggle between Cuddihy and Ferrarin. Cuddihy chalked up 236·18 for his second lap, better than Ferrarin's first, but along came Ferrarin even closer on his tail with 238·75. It looked like a two-man race—until de Bernardi completed his first lap and his time too was chalked up. 239·44 m.p.h. put him well beyond Cuddihy, possibly out of reach, especially if he improved his time in subsequent laps as the others had done. Schilt was making about 230 m.p.h. on the R3C-2, which was a good lap time for the plane, but he could not match the Italians. Nevertheless it remained a thrilling contest, with crowd excitement mounting with each lap. The delight of the Italian contingent was unmistakable; all doubts of their superior speed were gone, and with the team occupying first, second and fourth positions they were now entirely in the hands of their engines.

The tension on the ground, however, was dwarfed during the third lap by the tension that developed in the air. First Ferrarin found that his engine was overheating; he kept after Cuddihy according to plan, but the needle of his oil gauge had fallen steeply and he feared that his oil pressure was failing. Then Cuddihy, who had hitherto felt that his plane was functioning better than ever before, noticed that his fuel gauge showed only 25 gallons, and he began to operate the hand-pump to lift the gasoline from the floats. There was no reaction from the gauge. Was the hand-pump sticking again, or was it the gauge itself? He went on pumping fiercely.

For Cuddihy the fuel problem was a threat for the future, a possible failure on a later lap, but for Ferrarin the danger was immediate. His speed on his third lap reached 243 m.p.h., but as he rounded the home pylon it was obvious that his engine was failing. The dark smoke that had been streaming from the exhausts of all three Macchis was now greatly accentuated in Ferrarin's case, and soon after starting his fourth lap he left the course and circled beyond the hangars before coming in to alight with his engine almost dead. In his machine, at least, the gauge had told the truth: the persistent heavy drop in oil pressure had reflected the loss of almost all the available oil, caused by a broken pipe-line.

The threat that the Italians would take first and second places was removed, and victory now lay between de Bernardi and Cuddihy. The Italian had a clear advantage over the first three laps with an average of 244·95 against Cuddihy's 237·76, but Cuddihy was improving his times on each lap and a small mistake by de Bernardi could cost him the race. Cuddihy, still pumping furiously but flying a better course than the Italian and taking the pylons more aggressively, got a tremendous cheer from the crowd when his fifth lap of 242·16 was announced, his best so far. But although de Bernardi's speed dropped off after a very fast third lap of 248·52, he did not seem to be losing much by taking the corners wide, and he was still ahead.

He was certainly in no danger from Schilt. One of the wires bracing the wing of the R3C-2 to the floats had carried away at the lower end, and it was dangling loose, causing so much wing and aileron flutter that the stick was vibrating violently. Only by a tremendous effort was Schilt maintaining his speed.

By the beginning of his sixth lap, de Bernardi too was showing signs of distress. From a low-flying circuit less than 100 feet above the water he had climbed to 600 feet. His engine, like Ferrarin's, was over-heating, and he had climbed in an effort to find cooler air. Cuddihy, almost exhausted by his efforts at pumping, was nearing the end of his final lap. If de Bernardi faltered now it was America's race. But with two thirds of his final lap completed and in sight of the finish, George Cuddihy had the mortification, despite all his efforts, of having his main tank run dry. The engine stopped and he alighted at once down wind. For the second year in succession he had been forced down on his final lap. Two miles distant lay the home pylon, the distinction of second place, and an outside chance of the trophy.

When they towed Cuddihy in they found that his pontoon tanks were half-full. His pumping had been of no avail. Some idea of the physical and mental effort he had expended was revealed to those who saw him climb out of the cockpit. His right hand was so blistered and swollen that he could not use it, and the arm hung limp at his side.

Meanwhile the cheers of the crowd were all for de Bernardi. His climb to 600 feet had steadied his temperature gauge, and he came down low again for his final lap and shot across the finishing-line at well over 250 m.p.h. His average speed for the race—246·50—had broken all seaplane records. With the enforced retirement of Cuddihy it was Frank Schilt who chased him home, his average of 231·36 for the course being only one mile an hour slower than Doolittle's at Baltimore. Bacula was third with 218 m.p.h. and Tomlinson fourth with 137.

In nine months the Italians, after taking up a challenge that the British had rejected as unrealistic, had produced a machine that had ended the years of American supremacy and rescued the Schneider Trophy from what had seemed certain extinction. The fight put up by the Americans had been a determined one, and even in defeat the Curtiss biplane had proved magnificent, the speed margin being almost entirely a matter of superior power; but the scarlet Italian monoplanes had proved victorious, and their superiority was confirmed four days later when de Bernardi set up a new world speed record over a straight course of 258·87 m.p.h.

It had fallen to the Italians to demonstrate the solution to the structural problems of the racing monoplane, and they deserved all the congratulations that were heaped upon them. The satisfaction of the team was subtly expressed in a telegram from de Bernardi to Mussolini. "Your orders to win at all costs," he cabled, "have been carried out."

The cost had indeed been high. Both Macchis and Fiats had been completely disorganised by the effort, and work on other contracts had been disrupted. Even with the generous government subsidy both firms had lost heavily. The government too had suffered from the delay in delivery of contracts for standard service types. But the game had been worth the candle, and there were no recriminations.

The cost in terms of human life had borne more heavily on the Americans, but the Italians did not forget their own scars. When they got back to Italy General Italo Balbo, the Italian Air Minister, accompanied by de Bernardi and Ferrarin, dropped a wreath from a Macchi flying-boat at the spot on Lake Varese where Centurione died.

PART IV
LAST LOVE

1927

at Venice

"I think I'm going to win."

Flt. Lt. S. N. Webster, R.A.F.

Britain's preparations for a provisional entry in a hypothetical contest at an unnamed venue on an unknown date went forward slowly but surely throughout 1926, so that when news came through of Italy's victory at Hampton Roads, valuable progress had already been made. Meanwhile efforts to turn the contest into a biennial one looked like succeeding, and the next race seemed unlikely to take place before 1928. The form that Britain's entry would take, however—whether the Air Ministry would lend the machines back to the manufacturers, as in 1925, or whether they would organise the team themselves—was still undecided; the industry itself wanted a Service team to assume full responsibility, but the Air Ministry remained reluctant. Trenchard was still dead against forming a racing unit in the R.A.F.; but he agreed that certain pilots could be selected to try out any high-speed machines that Geoffrey Salmond might produce.

Specifications for three new types of high-speed seaplane had been drawn up by the Air Ministry in March 1926. The main requirements were speed at low altitudes, controllability at high speeds, stability, manoeuvrability, and seaworthiness, and there were also special provisions as to performance; speed at 1,000 feet had to be not less than 265 m.p.h., and alighting speed had to be not more than 90 m.p.h., though these criteria could be varied at Air Ministry discretion. An extensive programme of wind tunnel tests with quarter-scale models of the three types of machine—the Supermarine S.5, the Gloster IV and the Short 'Crusader'—designed primarily to test performance, was begun in the same month, and this extended to ancillary items such as floats, wing radiators and airscrews.

Quite fortuitously the Air Ministry found themselves with three markedly different machines, whose characteristics and performance, when contrasted and evaluated, could not fail to help resolve some perennial arguments. The S.5 was a monoplane, the Gloster IV a biplane: what the biplane offered in reduced weight was generally considered to be offset by its increased drag, but a direct comparison between the latest models of each type would now be afforded. Similarly, the air-cooled engine still had its devotees, its principal advantage being lightness of construction, compensating for greater frontal area by a lower weight-power ratio: all racing aeroplanes of the recent past had used water-cooled engines, and the aim of the designers of the Short Crusader was to demonstrate the possibilities of incorporating an air-cooled engine in a high-speed racing machine.

Variations to the two Gloster IIIs that had competed at Baltimore, such as the fitting of integral radiators and modifications to the wings and tailplane, followed by exhaustive air testing by Hubert Broad, yielded much empirical information to help H. P. Folland in designing the Gloster IV, but this advantage was denied to the other designers, who had to rely on the wind tunnel tests. For R. J. Mitchell, after the failure of the S.4, these tests were especially significant.

In designing the S.5 Mitchell eventually settled for five major improvements on the S.4. First came the lowering of the wing; the mid-wing form saved a small amount in frontal area and gave a slight speed advantage, but the pilot's view had to be opened up. Second, the unbraced wing and chassis of the S.4, whatever the truth about wing flutter, had been high in structure weight, and the wire-bracing system introduced in the S.5 between floats, wing and fuselage brought an appreciable saving of overall resistance, according to the wind tunnel tests, and a calculated speed increase of 5 m.p.h. Third, a smaller fuselage and floats, and the re-shaping of the Lion engine by Napiers to give better streamlining, gave a reduction in body resistance which was expected to add 15 m.p.h. Fourth, the substitution of integral for external radiators brought an estimated speed increase of 24 m.p.h. And finally came increased horse-power and—after some of the engines had already been made—the gearing of the propeller drive, by means of which a further 30 m.p.h. was hoped for. Together these improvements meant an expected speed increase of not less than 70 m.p.h., bringing the top speed up to the region of 300 m.p.h. With such a substantial speed advance it was thought that Britain could look forward to the next race with confidence.

In the opinion of many the Napier Lion, the engine used in both the S.5 and the Gloster IV, had already been pushed up to near-maximum power for its weight consistent with reliability, and a redesign of the Rolls-Royce Condor was considered. But the Lion was eventually preferred, and a further substantial improvement in power was achieved. By increasing the compression ratio to 10:1 and raising engine revolutions to 3,300 per minute, 898 h.p. was developed by this engine on the test bed. A total dry weight of 928 lb gave a power-weight ratio of just under 1:1. Of even greater value, however, was the lessening of head resistance brought about by a substantial reduction in frontal area and more efficient cowling. When the plans for this engine were first drawn up, the results of research into the advantages of reduction gear were still awaited, and the first engines produced were of the direct-drive type. Later, when definite evidence became available of the improvement to be expected in airscrew efficiency, a reduction gear was included, and both geared and direct-drive engines were available for the race.

In addition to their fundamental differences, each of the three British types had its own distinctive features. The fuselage of the S.5 was probably smaller in cross-sectional area than any previously built. There was no room for a fuel tank, and the fuel was stored in the starboard float. This brought bonus advantages in that it improved stability and helped to balance engine torque on take-off and to some extent in the air. In the Gloster IV, careful redesigning of the fuselage and floats and the blending-in of components where they joined brought a reduction in head resistance of 40% as compared with the Gloster III. This, in conjunction with power and other improvements, gave a total speed increase of 70 m.p.h., similar to that of the S.5. The Bristol 'Mercury' radial engine of the Short Crusader, an improved version of the long-established Jupiter, with nine cylinders disposed radially round its crankshaft, brought a 12% reduction in weight, but the aerodynamic resistance of the body was high. Nevertheless wind tunnel tests suggested that cowling of the cylinder heads would give a top speed of 260 m.p.h.[1]

While these designs were in preparation, the formation of a high-speed flight was planned within the R.A.F. to accept and test the planes when they were completed, and on 1st October 1926 Squadron Leader Leslie J. Slatter was posted to Felixstowe to command the new flight. Three other pilots were posted in to join him, and three high-speed aircraft were allocated for practice—the two Gloster IIIs left over from the 1925 race and the Bamel. This new establishment was a

[1] Colonel W. A. Bristow was in charge of the Mercury engine project and the aircraft was designed by W. G. Carter, formerly a draughtsman and designer with Sopwith.

natural development of the ordering of the machines for experimental
Service use and did not imply acceptance by the R.A.F. of any responsibility for the race. The cost of the machines was charged to the
normal research and development vote; Treasury sanction would be
needed if R.A.F. responsibility was to be extended further, and no such
sanction had been applied for. The overt Air Ministry position
remained that, although certain machines might be lent back to
manufacturers if the aircraft industry decided to enter a team, the
Schneider was a race between private clubs. Much was happening,
however, behind the scenes.

The logic of the argument that the work of the high-speed flight was
ideal training for the Schneider race was tacitly accepted at the Air
Ministry; as Geoffrey Salmond put it, two birds would be killed with
one stone. But Trenchard's mind was troubled by conflicting influences.
On one side was his intense dislike of the idea of a Service unit competing in private races, with all the undesirable publicity—as he saw it
—that would inevitably follow. Against this was his conviction that
Britain's failure to win in 1923 and 1925 and to enter at all in 1924 and
1926 had been due to lack of organisation, something that, in an
enterprise of this nature, only Service discipline could provide. He was
still trying to resolve this inner conflict when he learned from the
Royal Aero Club on 19th November that in future the trophy was to be
defended every two years instead of annually and that the next contest
would not be held until 1928.

This on the face of it was good news, but Trenchard was still
nursing his grudge against the Royal Aero Club over their inaccurate
forecasts of 1926 and his reaction was one of distrust: they had been
wrong then, they might be wrong again now. Perhaps he reasoned
that the Italians would not be so stupid as to give Britain two years in
which to catch them up. And on this matter his instinct proved correct.
A longer period between races suited challengers better than holders,
and unknown to the Royal Aero Club the Italians were about to re-
open the question of holding the next race in 1927, when their chances
of repeating their victory would be highest. The Americans would have
no time to build new machines, Britain's new seaplanes would scarcely
have undergone a thorough test, and France would have no time to
build at all.

Italy's request, put forward in mid-December, was referred to an
extraordinary conference of the F.A.I. in Paris on 25th January 1927,
and the necessary support from other countries—hardly any of whom

had the slightest intention of competing—was obtained. The Royal Aero Club, who had long been campaigning for a two-year gap between races, surprisingly raised no objection. They were getting their orders from the Society of British Aircraft Constructors, whose attitude was that the new British machines had been designed to beat the Italians by a margin in 1927 and that the margin might not carry into 1928. About the Americans and the French they naturally took the same view as the Italians. But they did not consult the Air Ministry, as a result of which Trenchard first learned of the decision from a newspaper report. "Every bit of information that has come to me about the Schneider Cup from the Royal Aero Club during the last two years has been incorrect," he complained. In his anger he denounced the decision as a blunder; but on reflection he seems to have agreed with it. Anyway, within a month he had made up his mind. Lending the machines back to the manufacturers, and the pilots with them, did not appeal. The only way to approach the task was to accept full operational responsibility, running the entry like any other Service unit and bearing the cost. That would require Treasury sanction, which might be difficult to get.

A letter arguing the case for Service participation went to the Treasury on 29th March 1927. British aircraft, it said, had competed in 1923 and 1925, but due to imperfect organisation had been unsuccessful. Nevertheless the design of new high-speed aircraft had been stimulated and valuable experience in problems such as head resistance had been gained. The high performance of some of the aircraft types now in regular use in the United States Air Services was largely attributable to the lessons learnt in racing contests; if entries were properly organised, further technical lessons were undoubtedly derivable. The Air Council therefore wanted to enter a team for the 1927 race, taking full responsibility for both finance and organisation. Unless the current entry was made on this basis the Air Ministry believed that Britain would fail again. Such failure would be damaging to prestige. The American entries in 1923 and 1925, and the Italian entry in 1926, had been entirely organised and manned by Service personnel, and the Air Council thought that this course should be followed for the British entry in 1927. They were, they stressed, far from contemplating that such representation should be an annual event. The additional expense involved was estimated as not exceeding £2,500.

Winston Churchill, Chancellor of the Exchequer from 1924 to 1929, took a predictable attitude. The Treasury "found it hard to believe" that the prestige of either Britain or the Royal Air Force would be affected by the failure of British aircraft to win the race; they therefore took it that the Air Council intended to refer to the prestige of the British aircraft industry. They were not satisfied that the reluctance of the British aircraft manufacturer to incur the cost of the advertisement furnished sufficient ground for the shouldering of the burden by the taxpayer. But Churchill did not close the door: he asked for further information on the nature of the expected experience which could not be obtained by ordinary non-competitive flying.

Faced with this request the Air Council on 27th April devised an appropriate rejoinder. The building and flying of high-speed aircraft was productive of valuable results both in research and technical development: they listed head resistance, engines and the problems of power-weight ratios, structural questions, and ancillary items such as propellers, radiators, carburettors, plugs, lubrication, control mechanisms, and float design. The stimulus to research and progress was difficult to produce in a vacuum: where the Air Council could not dangle the carrot of possible production orders, the necessary inducement to manufacturers was lacking. The test of airmanship for pilots was impossible to reproduce except under international racing conditions. Since 1922 all successful teams had been organised and manned by Service personnel and a team not organised on these lines had little chance of success. These arguments satisfied the Treasury, and on 13th May they authorised the Air Council to accept full responsibility for finance and organisation. They stressed, though, that this sanction must not be regarded as in any way carried forward to any subsequent year. Special sanction would always have to be applied for again.

At the very moment when the British government were being urged to assume responsibility for entering a team, the United States government were preparing to pull out; but this fact, not surprisingly, found no place in the cajolings of the Air Council. In the final weeks of 1926 the Americans had under discussion a plan for participation in the next race under which personnel, machines and equipment would be sent to Italy in an aircraft carrier, to give adequate facilities and to reduce financial obligations; but it was never more than tentative. Having changed the whole nature of the contest by introducing highly organised Service teams, they now innocently put forward the proposition that the Schneider Trophy should be to aviation what the America's Cup was to yachting—an international sporting competition with no bearing on the development of military aircraft. Meanwhile the Navy Department was piously claiming to have "fostered racing as far as it could". But the truth was that the Americans, having got what they wanted out of the competition, and aware of the prodigious effort that would be required to win it again, sought to downgrade it. They were frank enough, though, to admit that the law of diminishing returns was operating; valuable information had been obtained, but the information likely to be got through a continuance of racing activity "would not be commensurate with the expenditure". The emphasis remained on air transport, and the Americans were more concerned with a new venture called the National Air Tour, which was designed to try out transport planes and encourage interest in air transport.

On 9th February 1927 Curtiss Dwight Wilbur, Secretary of the Navy Department, announced that the U.S. Navy would not be entering for lack of funds; Congress, he said, had made no specific appropriation for such an entry, and the use of current funds would mean curtailing other important Service activities. To send a full Service team to Italy, involving the construction of say five machines and eight engines, would cost $500,000; but by putting the cost so high he was deliberately discouraging participation, and it is significant that no compromise solution was suggested. In the next breath he was expressing the hope that a private American entry would be forthcoming. The Navy, seeing little chance of winning, was getting out. Hopes that the Army Aviation Department might take up the challenge were soon dashed for similar reasons, but a blank entry for three machines was nevertheless made by the National Aeronautic Association.

As soon as it was known that the race was to be run in 1927, air attachés in Rome, Washington, London and Paris were again busy reporting back to their masters on the activities and progress—so far as they could ascertain them—of rival powers. Each country's need was for an intelligence study of the aircraft with which it might have to compete. The information that reached London at the end of January was that no French manufacturer had a racing machine under construction or even under consideration: French manufacturers were still handicapped by the paucity of government orders for fighter aircraft, and for the industry generally there was not enough work to go round. The possibility of a French entry was discounted in London, and it was thought extremely unlikely that any private American entry would materialise. That left the Italians as the only opposition to be feared.

This somewhat complacent appreciation was rudely shattered on 24th March when it was announced that a group of New York sportsmen were giving $75,000-100,000 towards building a plane to regain the world's speed record, still held by Florentin Bonnet for France at 278·48 m.p.h., and to win back the Schneider Trophy. This was America's last chance to complete the necessary three wins in five years (1923, 1925, 1927) to qualify for permanent possession; and when the details were known the news gathered substance. The plane was being designed and built by the Kirkham Products Company at Long Island, New York (Kirkham was a former employee of the Curtiss Company, as were several of his team), and it would be powered by a new Packard four-bank 24-cylinder engine reputed to develop 1,200 h.p. at 2,700 revs, giving a top speed of over 300 m.p.h. The pilot would be Al Williams—Lieutenant Alford J. Williams, winner of the Pulitzer in 1923 and America's greatest racing pilot—and he had obtained leave from the Navy specially to compete. Like Doolittle he had a sporting background, having once been a baseball pitcher with the New York Giants, and like Doolittle he had a keen analytical mind, which brought him key appointments in research test flying and as an instructor in combat tactics. He also possessed a law degree. The designers of the Kirkham-Packard had considered turning to the monoplane form, but Williams, a biplane man, and a great advocate of the well-proven Curtiss design, would have none of it, and a biplane it was to be. The American practice of building biplanes, it was thought, might yet prove to be justified, and Williams was not the only one who believed that given equal power the Curtiss biplane would have beaten the Macchi monoplane in 1926. The margin had been narrow enough to lend credibility to this view.

When further details of the Kirkham-Packard were available they confirmed that it would probably prove to be the highest powered single-engine plane in the world. Two 12-cyclinder Type V-1500 engines, one inverted and one upright, were joined to a common crankshaft; the arrangement of the cylinders in four banks of six to form an 'X' shape produced a somewhat blunted nose, but the general streamline form was good. The construction was otherwise orthodox. Fuel was carried in both pontoons.

* * *

When the R.A.F.'s high-speed flight was first formed, the pilots were mostly transferred from the Marine Aircraft Experimental

Establishment already in being at Felixstowe, since it was felt that marine experience was essential. Among these pilots the only one who was retained right through the training period was Flight Lieutenant O. E. Worsley. Volunteers for high-speed flying had meanwhile been called for by the Air Ministry, and out of some 20 or more who put their names forward, two—Flight Lieutenant S. N. Webster and Flying Officer H. M. Schofield—were selected and transferred early in February. Their selection reflected a change of attitude by the Air Ministry, in that neither man had previous floatplane experience. But Webster had flown more than a hundred different landplane types and had been transferred from the experimental establishment at Martlesham Heath, where he was a test pilot, while Schofield was a versatile pilot who had served with Slatter, the commander of the flight, before. Both men had to face a certain natural resentment at the intrusion of landlubbers, but they adapted themselves readily enough.

The flight, however, soon ran into difficulties. Bad weather restricted flying and often stopped it altogether, and there was no sign yet of the promised new machines. Slatter's problems in welding the flight into a team were thus exacerbated, and his leadership was criticised by Trenchard. He himself, although a good administrator, was not in the same class as a high-speed pilot as most of his men, and inevitably he had to lead from behind. No one yet knew whether the R.A.F. would be directly involved in the race itself or not, and a sense of urgency and purpose was lacking. When flying did become possible, jealousies and friction were not uncommon.

The situation improved in the spring, and in May the first of the new machines, the Crusader, was delivered. Its acceptance trials, however, were flown by Bert Hinkler, and the pilots of the high-speed flight, aware by this time that they were to fly in the race and impatient to get to grips with their machines, were frustrated by a further spell of bad weather. During this period one pilot was posted away from the flight, and after consulting the list of volunteers for a replacement Slatter asked for either Flying Officer R. L. R. Atcherley or Flight Lieutenant S. M. Kinkead, both of whom he knew. Sam Kinkead, who at 30 was one of the most highly decorated men in the Air Force, was like Slatter a South African, and the choice fell on him; but Atcherley's turn was to come.

Next to be delivered was the first Gloster IV; and early in June Worsley left for Calshot to fly the prototype S.5. By mid-July the whole flight, except for the Crusader, had moved to Calshot, and

F

although there was still very little flying in the actual race machines
the atmosphere at once was entirely different. Slatter's policy was to
give each pilot a fair trial on each type. Webster had his first flight in
the S.5 on 14th July and Schofield on 1st August. Two days later
Schofield began tests on the second Gloster IV, which reached 277
m.p.h. on its first run. The S.5 had begun at 280 and was working up
towards 300.

The main problem with the Gloster IV was visibility: the pilot's
view forward was bad. But this was a question of basic design and
nothing could be done about it before the race. It was impossible to see
anything over the top plane at all, or below it except at the tips, and
the water thrown up over the cockpit in the early stages of take-off was
blinding. The view when flattening out before alighting was equally
bad. The danger of collision was always present, but there was nothing
for the pilots to do but minimise it as best they could.

The S.5, after an early alteration to the tailplane to correct nose-
heaviness, showed no vices at all once it was airborne. "Very very
nice, no snags," was Webster's log-book comment after his first flight,
and he noted an estimated speed of 284 m.p.h. The aircraft was
wonderfully positive on the controls, a factor of enormous importance
for high-speed work at low level. But the take-off involved a specialised
technique. When the throttle was opened the port float would almost
bury itself in the water due to torque and the machine would start to
swing to the left; at the same time the bow wave from the floats was
sucked up by the propeller, sending a wall of spray over the cockpit.
The trick was to keep the head down for a few moments and apply
opposite rudder; the moment the floats came up on the step the spray
disappeared and vision was much improved. The main danger during
the take-off was porpoising, for which the only sure remedy was to
close the throttle and try again; otherwise the amplitude of the pitching
was apt to increase, until the machine became airborne without flying
speed.

The alighting technique was straightforward enough, though it
required patience and a light touch. Owing to the high loading and the
absence of wing flaps the approach speed was fast and the gliding angle
flat. Up to two miles of alighting space was needed, depending on wind
and water. The necessity for a tail-down alighting, touching water on
the heels of the floats, entailed a long and careful hold-off to ensure that
all flying speed was lost first. To touch down on the step of the floats
was to bounce into the air again, with the consequent risk of stalling.

The other trick with the S.5 was getting used to the tiny cockpit: for a
tall man it was far too cramped. The right arm and the right knee got
in each other's way on take-off, and the rudder bar was uncomfortably
near. Schofield later described how he had to squeeze himself into the
cockpit, letting himself down sideways, so that his shoulders were
below the top of the fairing, then turning to face the front of the machine.
"In my case", he wrote, "it needed no ordinary effort to get my
shoulders home."[1]

The race aircraft were not yet ready for exhaustive testing, and
meanwhile the pilots spent much time in practising cornering on hack
machines. If, as was thought likely, the contending machines vere
evenly matched, time lost or gained on cornering might be decisie. A
scientific study of the problems involved in cornering at high speed
was made, and the conclusion was reached that theoretically at least it
did not pay to gain or lose height on the turn, although practical
considerations might make a small gain in height necessary. A tight
turn was better than a loose open one. With the type of circuit employed for the Schneider race, the best possible mean speed for the
course was considered to be about 3% less than the top speed of the
aeroplane. This sounded a formidable target but the pilots took it
seriously and practised assiduously. Time for such practice, however,
was restricted by a further break in the weather, and by the emergence
of an unforeseen transport problem; it was found that the packing cases
that would contain the aircraft couldn't be sent overland because they
were too large to pass through the Simplon tunnel into Italy. They
would have to go by sea, and that meant an earlier start.

The first consignment—the original S.5 (number N.219), the
Gloster IVA (number N.222, direct-drive engine) and the Crusader—
left Britain for Venice on the *S.S. Heworth* on 17th August, and the
remaining machines—two S.5s (N.220 and 221) and the Gloster IVB
(N.223, geared engine)—left ten days later in the *Egyptian Prince* for
Malta, where they were to be transferred to the aircraft carrier *Eagle*.
A 'Flycatcher' was also sent as a hack machine. The race was scheduled
for Sunday afternoon, 25th September, which if all went well left about
three weeks at Venice for further practice.

* * *

Although the British were again seriously short of preparation on
their race machines—Webster, for instance had flown the S.5 only

[1] *The High Speed and Other Flights*, by H. M. Schofield (John Hamilton, 1932).

twice at Calshot—they were further forward than either the Italians or the Americans. The disruption suffered by the Italian aircraft industry in 1926 could hardly be tolerated again, and a breathing space was needed. Yet the natural reaction had been to hold the next race as soon as possible while the lead was still held, avoiding any basic redesign. Nevertheless the Italians were aware of the thoroughness of British preparations, and Castoldi, in redesigning the M.39, had aimed at a speed in excess of 300 m.p.h.

The Macchi 52—following the victory of the M.39 the next multiple of 13 was chosen for luck—was substantially similar to the M.39, but it was smaller in length, wing-span, wing area and tailplane, though as it was also lighter the wing loading was not much greater. The floats too were smaller, and their volume was less. The most distinctive new feature was the sweep-back of the wings, which was far more marked than in the M.39. The fuselage had a flatter back, the hump back of the M.39 being levelled off though not disappearing entirely, and this gave better streamlining as well as improving the pilot's forward view. The fuselage was made to measure to fit the new A.S.3 engine, which was similar to the A.S.2 of the previous year but was boosted to 1,000 h.p. by raising the compression ratio and the revolutions per minute. The engine was also smaller in frontal section, and by the use of alloys its weight was reduced to 950 lb. Material for five of the new engines had been ordered by 11th March; this time, with Britain emerging as the most likely competitor, the crankshaft order went to Krupps.

The Italian team, supervised by Colonel Tacchini, assembled at Varese for training on 16th May, flying at first the four M.39s left over from the previous year. Three M.52s were being built. From the start it seems that the atmosphere was different. The knowledge that the Americans were not entering a Service team, and doubts about Britain, made it difficult to recapture the spirit of challenge and urgency that had pervaded preparations in 1926. Confidence gave way, perhaps, to complacency. New pilots with their names to make might have injected fresh impetus, but de Bernardi and Ferrarin were chosen again. The stalling characteristics of the Macchi racers, however, were delicate, and one new pilot, Lieutenant Borra, was lost during the training period. It was the engines, though, which gave the most trouble.

In England, Napiers had achieved a substantial increase in horse-power for a modest increase in weight; Fiats planned to go one better with an increase in horse-power and a decrease in weight. Whether the

new Napier Lion, developed from Rowledge's original design by G. S.
Wilkinson, would stand up to 50 minutes' running at full power, which
it would have to do to last out the race, remained to be seen; even more
uncertainty surrounded the stamina of the engine built by Fiats. Of
twelve engines being prepared for possible installation in the new
Macchi racers, six are said to have broken down during bench tests and
been damaged beyond repair. Another problem was that the 1,000 h.p.
that Fiats were contracted to produce was not being achieved.

In America, Al Williams was experiencing the same sort of frustrations as had afflicted so many private entries in the past. The fitting of
pontoons to his Kirkham-Packard, for instance, caused considerable
delays; the first pair proved unsatisfactory and a new set had to be
built. Unofficial reports credited Williams with a speed of 275 m.p.h.
over a carefully checked course on an early test flight, but there were
still many faults to be eradicated and it was apparent that more time
would be needed to get the plane ready. It was no good going to the
expense of shipping the plane to Venice unless it reached a satisfactory
standard beforehand, and towards the end of July Williams put the
situation to the National Aeronautic Association and they contacted
the Royal Aero Club of Italy on his behalf. "Earnestly urge 30-day
postponement to Schneider Cup race," they cabled. In view of the
postponement agreed to by the Americans after a similar request in
1926, little doubt was felt in America that the request would be granted.

At the beginning of August General Balbo presided at a meeting of
the organising committee responsible for the race. Whatever difficulties the test flights at Varese may have been undergoing they were
evidently not regarded as likely to be disastrous to Italy's chances, as
the attitude of the committee was that, much as they would dislike
refusing the Americans after their generosity in the past, they would
prefer not to postpone the race. It was possible, though, that reponsi-
bility for the rejection might be avoided by sending the request on to
the British. The buck was duly passed, and the Royal Aero Club,
possibly as reluctant as the Italians to face American competition,
replied on 3rd August (after full consultation this time with the Air
Ministry) that the rules did not allow of any postponement except from
day to day on account of bad weather. This was the regulation that the
Americans had refused to invoke in 1926 despite pressure from the
Royal Aero Club; it would have enabled them, of course, to walk away
with the trophy. It must be said in fairness to the British, however,
that a month's delay would have caused a complete upheaval of all

their arrangements and added considerably, perhaps disastrously, to the cost of participation and to the time lost by the manufacturers, all of whom were providing full servicing teams; such delay was genuinely insupportable.

A brief cable rejecting the request was sent to the N.A.A. by the Royal Aero Club of Italy, but the matter was thought to have such political overtones that the Italian government weighed in with a somewhat hypocritical cable on the same day. "The American proposal to postpone the date fixed for the Schneider Cup Race for one month", they cabled, "would have been favourably received by Italian aviation, to which American aviation extended such exquisite courtesy last year in deferring the date of the race so as not to exclude the Italian team. The fact that England is competing in 1927 makes a difference of circumstances, however, and in consequence the Ministry was obliged, before accepting the American proposal, to ascertain the views of the British Air Ministry. That Ministry has today communicated that the postponement is contrary to Article 8 of the regulations, according to which the date must be definitely fixed before March 1st. England opposed acceptance of the proposal and added that if it were to be accepted, it would possibly entail withdrawal of British participation." After stressing the organisational, technical and meteorological difficulties that would arise from postponement, the cable continued: "All the circumstances so far set forth are therefore markedly unfavourable and constitute an insurmountable obstacle to the spontaneous and lively desire of Italian aviation to meet the wishes of their brave and gallant comrades. . . ." But no amount of sugar-coating could sweeten the pill, and the Americans, after all they had done to preserve the contest as something live and meaningful, were bitterly resentful. To them, of course, it appeared that the British were responsible, and the British ambassador was left in no doubt of American disgust. On 16th August in a cable to the Foreign Office he referred to the ill-feeling caused by the British decision "although they [the Italians] favoured acceptance", and he urged the Air Ministry to agree to a postponement. The Foreign Office reply straightened the matter out. "The view of the Italian air authorities as represented to the Air Council", they cabled, "was in entire agreement with that of the Royal Aero Club."

American newspapers remained caustic, but the Americans finally accepted that in the circumstances their request had been unreasonable, and President Coolidge responded to an N.A.A. approach by authorising the use of the cruiser *Trenton* to take Williams and his plane to Venice. Even this gesture, however, was unavailing. By the end of August Williams had managed no more than four flights in his Kirkham-Packard due to bad weather, and he had still been unable to do better than 275 m.p.h. This, he considered, was not good enough, and on 9th September the final decision was taken to withdraw.

* * *

The advance members of the British team, Squadron Leader Slatter and Flight Lieutenant Worsley, arrived in Venice on 30th August, and next day the *Heworth* docked at San Andrea with the first consignment of machines. San Andrea is on a small island at the northern end of the lagoon, opposite the main channel for shipping approaching Venice, and a flying-boat base was situated there. The Italians had cut a waterway about 300 yards long into the island, on each side of which were hangars and slipways; the British established themselves on one side and the Italians prepared to use the other. The work of unloading, assembly and launching was greatly speeded up by the facilities available, but this advantage was offset by squally weather and a choppy sea which prevented any flying for a full week after the planes were assembled. Meanwhile Kinkead, Webster and Schofield had arrived by train. The pilots were accommodated at the Excelsior Palace Hotel on the Lido beach, and the ground crews in the Italian sergeants' mess at San Andrea. Slatter had almost certainly decided by now to put Webster and Worsley in two of the S.5s and Kinkead in the Gloster IVB.[1] Schofield was booked for the Crusader, but this machine was unlikely to take part in the race, leaving Schofield available for either the third S.5 or the Gloster IVA if required.[2]

At 11 o'clock on Saturday morning 10th September Slatter took off in the S.5 on the first test flight at Venice; after a series of turns over San Andrea he covered the full Schneider course, which was out over the open sea facing the beach. Fifteen minutes later Kinkead took off in the Gloster IVA and made a fast run along the beach. Next day, 11th September, after Webster had flown the S.5, Schofield prepared to take off for his first flight at Venice in the Crusader.

Schofield had had several uncomfortable rides in the Crusader, and

[1] In Venice the team was under the overall command of Air Vice-Marshal F. R. Scarlett, Officer Commanding Coastal Area.

[2] Although the available documents appear to confirm that all three S.5s were despatched to Venice, there is some doubt as to whether N.221 was actually sent. It never flew there.

he had never completely got rid of a feeling of claustrophobia when the cockpit hood was clamped into place. It was a confinement that was rare for the racing machines of the time, and Schofield had likened it to being nailed in a coffin. Now, after the manufacturer's ground team, the Service mechanics and fitters, and finally the Air Ministry inspector, had all done their checks, Schofield climbed aboard and the lid was clamped down.

Undiscovered by all these independent checks, a fault was present in the re-assembly of the airframe which was virtually certain to cause disaster unless Schofield himself discovered it before he attempted to take off. Reversed controls—controls which act in the reverse sense to normal—were the dread of every test pilot of this era; so deadly were the results that today it is illegal to design controls susceptible to such a mistake. The control wires to the aileron circuit on the Crusader had been threaded through the wrong holes. Given sufficient height, a pilot might recover in time from the shock of the unexpected and get his plane down safely; but if a wing dropped on take-off, the instinctive correction applied by the pilot would put the wing-tip on that side straight in.

In the excitement of the moment, Schofield's cockpit check seems to have been perfunctory. With so many experts about he can hardly have anticipated such a blunder. In the event of a crash, blame would certainly fall on the civilian and Service teams, and on the inspector; but the final check was the pilot's, by observation of the reaction of the controls to movements of the control stick. And it was on the pilot that the principal blame—and the physical burden —would fall.

Schofield began by revving and closing the throttle intermittently to test the plane's taxying characteristics; then he headed out into the lagoon. But as he did so, some premonition made him discard his plain glass goggles, which the pilots preferred because they were more comfortable, for a Triplex pair. It was some time before the Crusader showed signs of willingness to leave the water; and once airborne Schofield held her down, to make sure of having ample speed and control. Suddenly there was a terrific bump as a gust hit the starboard wing, and the wing on that side dropped abruptly. Schofield immediately corrected, but the result was a rapid accentuation of the tilt. The starboard wing went over beyond the vertical, the wing-tip struck, and in the next instant the machine disappeared in a fountain of spray, with Schofield still locked in the cockpit.

When the Crusader hit the water it broke in two, and Schofield was

washed out of the cockpit with such violence that his clothing and
flying boots were torn off and he was deposited in the sea in his shirt.
Miraculously he had broken no bones, though he later turned black and
blue from head to foot. The tail floated and he clung to it, and he was
soon picked up. Part of the frame of his goggles was embedded in his
face, and the safety glass was smashed to atoms; had he not changed his
goggles before take-off his eyes would certainly have suffered injury.
As it was he was limping about on sticks within a few days.

That, not surprisingly, was the end of flying for the day. But the
arrival within a few hours of the aircraft carrier *Eagle*, accompanied by
four destroyers and with the remaining machines on board, gave the
British no time to brood. More troublesome was the weather, which
again prevented flying for several days.

The loss of the Crusader had occurred in the full glare of publicity;
complete secrecy surrounded the preparations of the Italians. The team
had arrived and the pilots were staying at the Hotel Danielli, so clearly
they were not practising elsewhere; but their machines did not arrive
at San Andrea until 19th September, six days before the race, and then
they had to be re-assembled. The Italian hangars were only just across
the water from the British, and occasional glimpses of the scarlet
Macchis were gained, but little of value was seen until Tuesday
evening, 20th September, when the first Macchi was flown by de
Bernardi. Bad visibility had made high-speed work inadvisable all day
and the Macchi was never fully opened up throughout its test. So the
British were not much the wiser. Most interesting to them was the
method of cornering practised by de Bernardi during a trial run over
the course; he repeatedly employed a climbing turn, diving into the
straight afterwards to regain speed. This was the method decided
upon by the Italians for the race; it was one of the methods that had
been assessed and rejected by the British.

In a determined effort to provide the contracted 1,000 h.p., Fiats had
introduced new pistons of magnesium alloy at a very late stage. There
was no time for exhaustive trials; the crucible would be the race itself.

It was not until 21st September, four days before the race, that the
Gloster IVB and the second S.5 could be flown, but on that day the
weather was kinder and both machines were tested, the Gloster by
Kinkead and the S.5 by Webster. A new geared engine had arrived in
the meantime with a strengthened crankshaft, and Slatter had had this
fitted into the second S.5 (N.220), to be flown by Webster, installing
a direct-drive engine in Worsley's S.5 (N.219) as a safety measure in

F 2

case the geared engine caused overheating, which it was prone to do.

Webster's test of the geared S.5 was satisfactory, but when Kinkead was about to alight in the Gloster IVB his spinner came adrift and struck the propeller, causing damage to the propeller shaft. Even worse was the news that fumes in the cockpit, a fault that it was thought had been corrected at Calshot in both the S.5 and the Gloster by ventilation from air ducts in the wings, had affected Kinkead so badly that he was confined to his room all next day. The excuse given out was that he was suffering from malaria. The chances of the Gloster taking part in the race seemed slender, but a determined effort by the ground crew brought the machine back to full serviceability in time for the navigability trials on the Friday. Meanwhile all the Macchi 52s had been air tested, although they had done nothing more than short practice spins at something less than full speed. The pilots seemed afraid to let them go.

The navigability trials were duly held on the Friday, in a marked channel in the shelter of the lagoon about a quarter of a mile wide; so much for 'seaworthiness'. The crowds on the Lido saw little of this, the best view being vouchsafed to the sailors aboard the *Eagle*. Shortly before nine o'clock the three British planes were towed into position on their floats; they were Webster in the geared S.5, Worsley in the direct-drive S.5, and Kinkead in the geared Gloster. After they had taken up position it was learned that the Italians would be at least an hour late, due to last-minute tuning-up of their engines. There was a long wait, but shortly before 10.30 the British received permission to proceed without the Italians. Kinkead was just taxying towards the first mark at 10.32 when the tugs towing the sloping ramps or barges on which the M.52s were being protected suddenly steamed into the middle of the fairway. It looked as though Kinkead would be baulked, and indeed he seemed to misjudge his take-off and leave the water very late, but he climbed safely over the top of the approaching tugs and completed his tests without further difficulty.

The Italians had now pulled over to the side of the channel, and Webster had a clear run; but he too misjudged his speed and distance. In his case he took off too soon, before he had reached the end of his taxying run, apparently hitting the crest of a wave and bumping off inadvertently. Worsley followed. Altogether the British machines behaved better in the air than on the water, but the proximity of the Italian convoy may have accounted for this. Anyway, no reproving flags were raised and all three pilots were directed to carry on to the mooring-out test when they alighted, so it was assumed that the trials were safely behind them.

The first of the Macchis, flown by de Bernardi, reached the starting-line at 11.42 and opened out immediately, in contrast to the somewhat reluctant take-offs of the British. The plane got off in a remarkable short run and went through the tests in impressive fashion, under perfect control throughout; and the other two Macchis put up almost equal performances. There was no denying the professionalism of the Italian pilots, the only possible criticism being that they tended to show off during and after the tests with gratuitous displays of aerobatics. The tentative and inaccurate taxying and manoeuvring of the British team was difficult to account for except on the grounds of interference.

The first opportunity for direct comparison between the two sets of machines came at the mooring-out position; six red mooring buoys had been placed alongside the canal bank about 25 yards apart, and the line-up of the machines was an imposing one. Despite the flattening of the back of the M.52s, the S.5s with their beautiful straight lines contrasted well with the curved, cigar-like shapes of the Italian machines, and the colourings—the scarlet of the Macchis, the silver and blue of the S.5s and the blue and gold of the Glosters, all glinting in the afternoon sun—presented a memorable picture. In the middle of the afternoon, however, the weather broke, heavy rain and hailstones as big as pebbles beat down on the machines, and it was a tribute to the various constructors that no damage was done. There was, however, one major surprise: at four o'clock the judges announced that Webster had been disqualified. As he had been given no warning sign at the time and had been waved on to his mooring-out test, which his machine had almost completed, the news caused a sensation. The geared S.5 was expected to be the fastest of the challenging machines and its exclusion from the race would be a disaster for Britain. But Webster took the setback philosophically and arranged to re-fly the tests at nine o'clock next morning, and when the time came he passed them without further incident. Teased beforehand with the prospect of an Italian victory, the reticent Webster was moved to a brief comment. "I think", he said, "that *I'm* going to win it."

Apart from Webster's tests, Saturday was a day of final tuning-up and tactical discussion for both teams. The outings of the Macchis had been so rare and fleeting that it had been impossible for the British to assess their probable speed; hence the British pilots, forced to take a pessimistic view, planned to fly at full throttle throughout. Whether the two geared engines would stand up to such a gruelling test was uncertain, but there was confidence in the direct-drive engine in Worsley's S.5, so to this extent his was the 'safe' machine. Across the narrow channel the Italians could be seen at work on their engines, and it transpired that another engine had cracked up during the trials. The Italians decided to repeat the tactics of 1926 by making sure that one machine at least completed the course, and an A.S.2 engine from the previous year was fitted into the third Macchi, to be piloted by Federico Guazzetti. The Italian team hardly seemed weakened by this substitution; like the British they were including a 'safe' machine.

The enthusiasm of the Italian people for the Schneider contest was immense, and Venice was en fête with flags, banners, tapestries and posters, while the trophy itself was on public view in St. Mark's Square. The Italian State Railways were running half-fare excursions from all over the country, the canals were crowded with gondolas and small boats of every description, and thousands of tourists were overrunning the narrow streets. On Sunday morning, the day fixed for the race, huge crowds were fighting for places in the ferries plying across to the Lido, where the beach had been cleared for spectators; and conditions in the Excelsior Palace Hotel became chaotic as hundreds of visitors jostled for vantage points to the discomfort of residents. But the day had begun badly for weather, a strong wind and a heavy swell making sea conditions in the gulf unsuitable and even dangerous, and at lunchtime the Italians reluctantly decided on a 24-hour postponement. The hordes of day-trippers flocked disconsolately back across the lagoon to Venice, their excursion spoiled.

Despite the many thousands who were disappointed, the delay only served to intensify the excitement and tension of the occasion. Monday morning seemed little more settled at first, with sky overcast, and there was still quite a swell in the gulf, but the wind had dropped and the lagoon was calm. While race officials hesitated, all the pilots agreed that, if the weather stayed as it was, and if the glare of the sun remained obscured, it would be an ideal day for fast times. Eventually it was announced that barring a sudden deterioration the race was on.

The Italians had forecast that the weather wouldn't clear for two or three days, and on Sunday evening the British pilots had relaxed. If they didn't exactly go on a binge they certainly had more to drink than they would have done had they expected to fly next day. Fortunately there were no hangovers.

The course covered the usual 50 kilometres, in an anti-clockwise

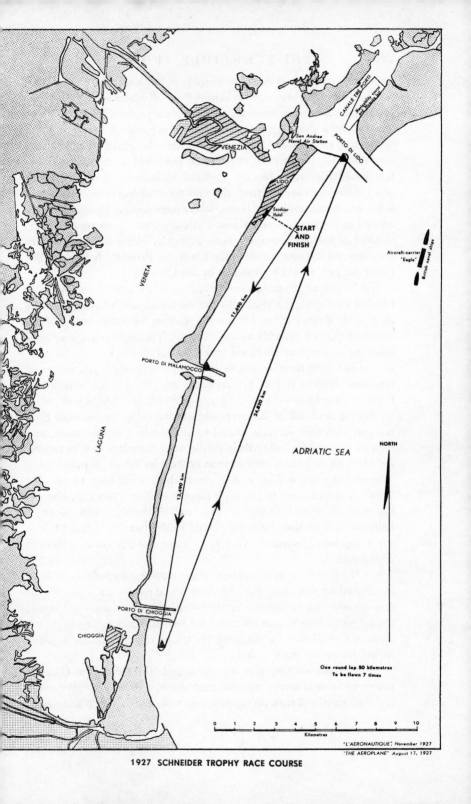

1927 SCHNEIDER TROPHY RACE COURSE

direction, starting and finishing in front of the Excelsior Palace. The first turning-point was a gentle one at Porto di Malamocco, where the pylon was mounted on the mole protecting the port entrance. This was followed by a short leg to a second turning-point off Chioggia. The course then ran back and forth along the whole length of the Lido beach —north to the larger mole at Porto de Lido, and south back past the Excelsior Palace again towards Porto di Malamocco. It was the finest of all Schneider courses, from the viewpoint of spectators and pilots alike, and the throng on the beach, where huge scoring boards had been erected at intervals, was estimated at 200,000. Private parties were situated at various vantage points, especially along the mole at the northern end and on the roof of the Excelsior. From the balcony of the tower the race would be watched by the Crown Prince.

The British team was ordered to line up off the mole at the Porto di Lido by two o'clock, and at 1.40 the machines were towed gently on their floats down the canal from San Andrea, followed shortly afterwards by the red Macchis on their barges. The sight of the machines lining up in preparation raised an emotional cheer. For the Italians, here at last were their heroes, de Bernardi and Ferrarin, the victors of Hampton Roads; and if de Bernardi was actually the champion, Ferrarin as a local man was the popular idol, mobbed wherever he went. Stories of official Italian pessimism following the setbacks they had had with their engines tended to be dismissed as affectation, and their avoidance of speed trials in public was interpreted as wise tactics, for which there were successful precedents. The British, for their part, were nearing the end of a long road which went back to the Air Ministry specification of eighteen months earlier, when this moment had seemed so comfortably remote, and to the disappointments of Baltimore before that. Now they could hardly bear to watch. "It is a very long time", wrote C. G. Grey, "since one felt quite as thrilled over a race."

For the first time in the history of the contest, competitors were to be allowed a flying start. Each machine would receive a warning signal five minutes before its due starting-time, and then a second signal giving permission to take off. After the second signal an interval of ten minutes was allowed for warming up, taking off and accelerating, and diving across the starting-line.

At 2.29 the starting-gun was fired and Kinkead in the Gloster, drawn to be first away, took off from the assembly area, executed a climbing turn, and then dived across the mole with a penetrating roar,

perfectly lined up for the starting-point. Soon he had flashed past the
Excelsior Palace and made off towards Chioggia. But heading back to
the Porto di Lido on the long northern leg he found it difficult to keep
properly lined up on the distant pylon because of the poor vision in the
Gloster, and even with the long, straight beach as a guiding line he
deviated considerably. Before rounding the northern pylon he came
down low over the water, where his field of vision was better, and
except for rising slightly to clear the mole he stayed there. He turned
smoothly in a half-circle and came out on a perfect line down the course.
But when he completed the lap the time posted, although beating all
previous Schneider records, was disappointingly low at 266·5 m.p.h.

Before Kinkead reached the Porto di Lido turn, de Bernardi had
taken off in the first Macchi and headed strongly for the starting-line at
a height of 200 feet. The characteristic note emitted by the Fiat engine
was noticeably rougher and more crackly than the Napier, and the
course of the Macchi was marked by a trail of oily smoke, but its speed
on the straight looked superior. De Bernardi's method of cornering
was the same as that demonstrated at practice and involved a spectacular
climb into the turn to a height of 600 feet and a dive into the next leg to
gain speed; this process was followed on the basis that height would
probably be gained during the turns anyway so a virtue might as well
be made of it. It drew the applause of the crowd, but its efficacy had yet
to be proved. There was a shock for the Italians when the time for de
Bernardi's opening lap was posted: the official timekeepers made him
half a second slower than Kinkead.

The fact was that the race officials, situated on the beach in front of
the Excelsior, had an imperfect view of the course as a whole and the
lap times they were announcing were not always accurate. Two other
independent but unofficial timekeepers were recording the lap times—
one for the Royal Aero Club in the official timing hut and the other
for the Air Ministry on the Excelsior roof. And as a result of this
independent timekeeping the British knew that de Bernardi's actual time
was 15 seconds better than the time announced and that his average speed
was 275 m.p.h., nine miles an hour better than Kinkead's. In the opinion
of the British contingent, only Webster in the geared S.5 had much
chance of beating him.

Webster was next away. It was his first fully loaded take-off in the
S.5, but he managed it nicely. He did not fly quite so low as Kinkead,
and he did not seem to take his corners so sharply, but he looked to be
going quite as fast as de Bernardi; according to the timings recorded by

the Air Ministry and the Royal Aero Club his first lap was almost exactly the same, promising an unbearably close race. The circuit, however, was filling up, Guazzetti, Worsley and Ferrarin all taking off at intervals, and the race was becoming confusing for anyone trying to keep all the contestants in view. As the last machine headed for the line it started to rain.

It was during this period of confusion, before the spectators had improvised a method of following the race intelligently with the eye, and before the steady accumulation of recorded lap times revealed a recognisable pattern, that the real drama of the race unfolded. The first the spectators knew of it was when Ferrarin, on the point of crossing the starting-line, was seen to be flying left wing low and with his engine giving out a note even rougher than de Bernardi's and missing intermittently. Suddenly there was a cloud of smoke and a burst of flame and the Italian was seen to climb shakily and turn off the course behind the Excelsior Palace before heading back for San Andrea. And although few were aware of it, an even greater disaster had already befallen the Italian team. De Bernardi, who had been going so well, had developed engine trouble soon after starting his second lap and had turned west at the far end of the course near Chioggia. In the distant haze few saw him go, but he too was on his way back to San Andrea.

The two Macchi 52s with the boosted engines were out of the race, and when the crowd realised it they fell into stunned silence. Guazzetti with last year's engine was still going well, but he was outpaced by all three British machines and he had no chance unless they cracked up.

Kinkead at this point was going faster than Worsley, and according to the British timings his second lap was faster than Webster's first. Would the biplane outfly the monoplane after all? At the end of Kinkead's third lap there was a sensation: the loudspeakers and score-boards credited him with a lap time of six minutes 26 seconds, a new world record of 289 m.p.h. for the lap. With two hairpin bends to negotiate it was clear that his speed on the straight must have been 300 m.p.h. The cheers were all for Kinkead; but to the independent timekeepers it was immediately apparent that a mistake of 20 seconds had been made in the official lap time, reducing the average speed to 275 m.p.h.

From this point on Kinkead's times fell away slightly, and indeed he was having trouble again with the spinner on his airscrew boss, which had cracked just where the blade went through it. A small strip of the

17 (a)   Lt. George T. Cuddihy and his Curtiss R3C-2, 1925

7 (b)   Lt. James H. Doolittle (left)
with Lt. Cyrus Bettis, 1925

17 (c)   Doolittle passes over the
scoreboard at Bay Shore, 1925

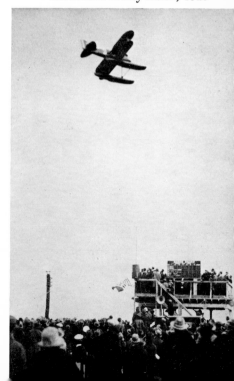

18 (a)   One of the scarlet Macchi M.39s rounding a pylon during the 1926 race, and (inset) de Bernardi's M.39 before the race

18 (b)   Major Mario de Bernardi being chaired after his victory. On extreme left is designer Mario Castoldi

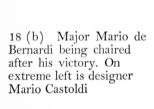

19 (a)   The Short Crusader at Venice, 1927

19 (b)   Captain A. Ferrarin and his Macchi M.52, 1927

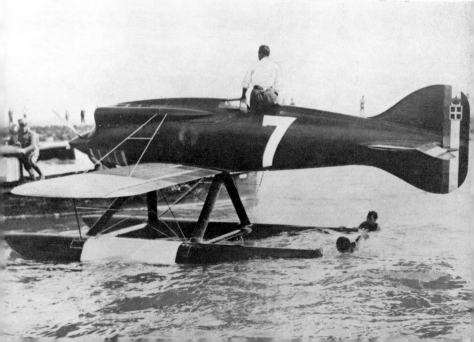

20 Kinkead, at low level in the Gloster IV, overtaking Worsley in the S.5 (Venice, 1927)

21 (a)   Part of the huge crowd on the Lido beach watching Webster
in the winning S.5

1 (b)   The British team at Venice, 1927. Left to right: Flt. Lt. H. M. Schofield, Flt.
.t. O. E. Worsley, Flt. Lt. S. N. Webster, Flt. Lt. S. M. Kinkead, Sqdn. Ldr. L. S. Slatter

22　Three of the Italian designs for 1929. The Fiat C.29 (top);
the Savoia-Marchetti S.65 (middle); and (bottom) the Macchi
M.67

23 (a)   Lt. Alford J. Williams, U.S.N.

23 (b)   Ramsay MacDonald, the British Prime Minister, with Flt. Lt. G. H. Stainforth

23 (c)   The Italian team with the Prince of Wales, 1929. Left to right: Lt. R. Cadringher, Lt. G. Monti, Captain A. Canaveri, Lt.-Col. Mario Bernasconi, Warrant Officer T. Dal Molin and Sergeant-Major F. Agello

24 The mooring-out, 1929. Left to right: Monti's M.67, Waghorn's S.6, Dal Molin's M.52R, D'Arcy Greig's S.5, and Cadringher's M.67. Behind them is the launch used by the R.A.F. as a floating headquarters

cracked metal had wrapped itself round an airscrew blade, setting up a vibration that threatened the engine with disintegration. After completing his fifth lap Kinkead followed Ferrarin and de Bernardi into retirement, and in doing so he probably saved his life. When the propeller gear was stripped down it was found that it would have come adrift in another few seconds of flight.

Fortunately for the nerves of the British party, Webster and Worsley were lapping with wonderful consistency, Webster's times particularly hovering round the 280 mark and varying hardly at all. Yet even Webster was having his worries; his engine cowling had loosened, and he had been forced to reduce his engine revs slightly, though curiously his speed was unaffected. Worsley's best lap was his third—275·8, only four miles an hour slower than Webster's, with Guazzetti another eleven miles an hour behind. The two British pilots, inspired perhaps by Kinkead's example, seemed to corner better with every lap, and the Napier engines were giving not a moment's concern.

Once Webster, taking the mole corner in his accustomed style just behind Guazzetti, left the Macchi far behind as the Italian banked violently and shot skywards, demonstrating beyond all doubt the wastefulness of the method; but Guazzetti's persistence with the old A.S.2 engine was keeping the Italian defence of the trophy alive, and it was not until towards the end of his sixth lap that he faltered. On that lap he took the northern turning-point very wide before charging straight for the roof of the Excelsior Palace. Blinded by petrol squirted into his face from a punctured fuel line, he just managed to leapfrog the hotel at the last moment and put the Macchi 52 down safely in the lagoon.

When Webster turned into the straight towards the finishing-line he looked at his watch. He had been racing for 46 minutes, and he had calculated that the seven laps would take him just under 51 minutes. Had he in fact flown only six laps? It looked very much like it. He had always ridiculed the idea that it might be possible to miscount, and the seven holes he had punched in the improvised lap counter on the dashboard stared back at him in confirmation; but he decided to take no chances, and he began an extra lap. Worsley, who had started after him, was of course still racing, so he could get no guide from him. The huge crowd that had watched the start of the race was already thinning out, partly in disappointment at the Italian débâcle, partly because of the rain; but had Webster been able to hear the frenzied cheering as he approached the line, or had his eye wandered off the course to the thousands of arms raised towards him in salute, he would have been left in no doubt.

When it was seen that he was flying another full lap the exultant British party gasped with apprehension. The machines had been fuelled on the basis of seven laps plus an adequate margin for take-off and return, but an extra lap was outside their calculations. If Webster ran out of fuel there could be disaster for Britain yet. But on alighting after his eighth lap he still had 7 gallons left.

Webster's average speed for the race was confirmed as 281·65 m.p.h., beating the world speed record for any type of plane by 3 miles an hour. Worsley averaged 273·01. These two men, by flying a perfect course despite haze and light rain, and by accurate cornering, had both attained a figure of only 3½ per cent below the optimum for their machines. They were entitled to feel that they had done everything within their power to win the race, and they were naturally elated. "Now let's celebrate," said Webster.

For the Italians their failure, sickening as it was for them, was not unexpected; the doubts they had expressed before the race had been genuine enough. What actually happened to the Fiat engines is a story which, like the S.4 and wing flutter, has never been fully told; but it seems that they pushed up the compression of the A.S.2 engine, increased its revolutions and reduced its weight without having sufficient time to test it thoroughly and ensure that it didn't break down under the consequent stresses. This was the substance of the view put forward by *The Aeroplane*. The alloy in the replacement pistons, too, is said to have been defective, Guazzetti's engine failing before the race, when he changed to the A.S.2, and de Bernardi's and Ferrarin's during the race itself. Mario Castoldi was characteristically acidulous about these failures. "That wasn't horse-power," he is reported to have said. "It was donkey-power." He vowed to go elsewhere for his engines next time.

Had de Bernardi been able to continue he would probably have finished second, judging from his first lap, beating Worsley; and had it not been for fears of a breakdown his first lap might have been faster than it was, beating Webster too. The improved aerodynamic design of the Macchi 52 was confirmed by Guazzetti's speed over six laps, which was 11 miles an hour faster than the Macchi 39 at Hampton Roads with the same engine.

The failure to produce a reliable engine for the 1927 race remains unexplained. Something went radically wrong in the preparation period, and last-minute doctoring failed to put it right. How near the Italians were to a second victory was underlined six weeks later when de Bernardi set up a new world speed record for any type of plane of 296.94 m.p.h. The Americans, too, had narrowly missed the boat, Al Williams being reported to have flown an unofficial 322·6 m.p.h., though this had not been under controlled conditions and a wheel undercarriage had been substituted for floats. The British would clearly face a formidable challenge next time.

The huge Italian crowd took the result in good spirit, and the defeat seemed not to reduce the popularity of de Bernardi and Ferrarin one jot. It was this sort of adulation of successful pilots that Trenchard had feared, and he made a point, at the Schneider Trophy banquet at the Savoy in October, of playing down individual glory. The R.A.F., he said, had many other pilots who could as worthily have upheld the honour of the country, a sentiment that was echoed by the modest Webster.

By this time, however, the main controversy centred around what sort of organisation would be needed for the defence of the trophy, and what form Britain's next entry might take. The Air Ministry had assumed responsibility for the 1927 race on a 'once only' basis, and on that basis they had had the support of the Treasury. Whether or not these two government departments fully understood the implications of victory, those implications were about to catch up with them.

1929

at Calshot

"Let's find a sheltered spot and have a talk."

Sir Henry Royce

By setting up a new world speed record of 296·94 m.p.h. on 4th November 1927, Mario de Bernardi had done for Italy what the British Air Ministry had hoped to do after the 1926 race—stolen some of the thunder of the Schneider victory. Yet there was no comparison between the two feats. One consisted of a few short sprints over a straight 3-kilometre course, lasting only a few minutes, the other was a gruelling comparative test of engine and airframe stamina and piloting skill over 350 kilometres, lasting the best part of an hour. Nevertheless there was disappointment in Britain that it had not been possible to set up a record in excess of 300 m.p.h. directly after the 1927 race, and although the high-speed flight was disbanded on its return it was reformed early in 1928, Sam Kinkead being retained for an attempt on the record.

On the afternoon of 12th March 1928, after a delay of several days through bad weather, Kinkead took off from Calshot in a specially-tuned S.5 (N.221, the spare machine in 1927) to go for the record. That he would beat it seemed certain, but conditions were again imperfect, and by the time he began his first timed run it was late and a mist was forming over the water. A glassy sea made judgment of height difficult, and worst of all there was no horizon. Kinkead, perhaps, should have waited for the morrow. Anyway he went into his approach dive towards the measured straight and never pulled out.

The Air Ministry called for volunteers to replace him, and the man eventually selected was Flight Lieutenant D. D'Arcy A. Greig, a leading exponent of formation aerobatics, who took over on 1st May. Meanwhile on 30th March de Bernardi, flying a modified Macchi 52 designated M.52R, had boosted his existing record to 318.57—further evidence of Italy's lack of preparedness at Venice and of her determined progress since then. It was more than six months—4th November 1928—before D'Arcy Greig was able to attack the record, and he then raised it so fractionally that it was insufficient to constitute a new record. For the moment Italy had had the last word.

Earlier that year, on 1st May 1928, Jacques Schneider, after apparently recovering from an appendicitis operation which had prevented him from attending the 1927 race, died suddenly at Beaulieu-sur-Mer, where he had been recuperating. The contest to which he gave his name had developed so disproportionately since he inaugurated it that his death passed almost unnoticed; but he died, as it happened, at a moment when the next contest, after much political manoeuvring behind the scenes, seemed likely to prove the most truly international of all. Britain, Italy and America all planned to enter, France was a serious contender for the first time for many years, and there were even reports that Germany might be represented, for the first time since 1914.

* * *

After Churchill's stern warning of May 1927 that Treasury support for that year was not to be taken as a precedent, Britain's Air Ministry did not look for government backing for the next race; it was assumed by Trenchard and the Air Council that the Treasury attitude would be uncompromising. But curiously enough, in a situation in which the R.A.F. might have been expected to act the part of the importunate child and the government the repressive parent, the roles were entirely reversed. It was the government who pressed hard for a second victory and the Air Ministry who resisted.

The Air Council had hardly had time to formulate their objections to further R.A.F. participation when, on 7th October 1927, they were asked by Sir Samuel Hoare to consider their plans for the next race. "My mind is quite made up", wrote Sir Samuel, "that if the next contest is to be held in England the Air Ministry must be responsible for seeing that there is a really efficient British entry." The Air Council, however, were not to be browbeaten: quite apart from the probability of Treasury opposition, Trenchard believed that it was definitely to the detriment of the R.A.F. and its officers that they should be exploited in this sort of competition. It was recognised that the victory at Venice had created a new atmosphere in which the Treasury's attitude might soften; but Trenchard was prepared for the moment to shelter behind the inferred threat of Treasury inflexibility. He therefore wrote to the Royal Aero Club asking them to appoint a committee to discuss the next contest, and at the meeting that resulted the Air Ministry position was made plain: the next contest should be the sole responsibility and expense of the Club, the Air Ministry merely assisting by the loan of such high-speed aircraft as were available.

Confronted with this blunt statement of disengagement the Club were equally direct. Without the same support as in 1927, they said, their prospects of retaining the trophy were remote. They also raised the question of race organisation: the government would surely wish to offer facilities and hospitality to foreign entrants similar to those given by the Italian government at Venice. But above all they professed themselves dismayed at the prospect of running the race without the direct assistance of Service pilots and ground personnel. They were emphatic that this assistance had been one of the determining factors at Venice, and they did not think the trophy could be defended without it. They went on to argue that the contest had assumed the character of a competition between governments and that any relaxation of effort would gravely imperil Britain's prestige in the air.

Trenchard, dismissing these arguments as mere bluff, finally replied to Hoare on 14th November. First he stressed the financial angle: indeed he exaggerated it. The Treasury, he said, had only given their consent in 1927 on the understanding that this did not form a precedent, and the next race, with ten times as many guests to be put up, lunched, dined and entertained, would cost infinitely more than when the Italians were hosts. Next he entered the political field, declaring that contests of this kind could only lead to complications and even diplomatic incidents, and citing the principles of the United States, where the President (so Trenchard maintained) was determined that his government should no longer support competitors. And finally he came to his real objection, for which he produced no evidence whatever —the bad effect on the young officers who took part.

Trenchard's irritation at the adulation of his pilots, although consistent with his known distaste for the 'ace' mentality, seemed almost to amount to jealousy. It led him so far astray as to commit him to an argument that contradicted the case he had put forward the previous year. He evidently realised this, as after concluding that from the Service point of view he saw no advantage in the race he added the patent afterthought: "although it might have been a benefit in the past".

Hoare tried to persuade the Royal Aero Club to organise Britain's entry, but the Club's reaction was to draft a plea for full government support. It was unfair, they argued, to saddle individual companies

with the financial responsibility for research and development when it
was the government who would ultimately benefit. There was no need,
they thought, to question that there was an adequate return if the
trophy was won: the gain in prestige and orders was sufficiently
apparent. But this inference was challenged in the aeronautical Press by
C. G. Grey, who pointed out that America had held the trophy for
three years without any flood of American aircraft being deposited in
Europe, while there was no indication that Italy had sold a single
aeroplane abroad as a result of her win in 1926. Winning the trophy in
1927 had unquestionably done Britain good, but the next task was to
get down to the production of commercial aircraft on a commercial
basis.

In mid-December came an event which gave everyone a breathing
space: General Balbo, on a visit to Britain, took the opportunity to
discuss the future of the Schneider contest with Hoare, his object being
to change the race into a biennial one while putting the responsibility
for such a change on to Britain. Under pressure, however, he agreed
that Italy would prefer a contest every two years, and at the annual
meeting of the F.A.I. in Paris in January 1928 a formal decision was
taken to hold the contest biennially, three wins in five successive
contests to constitute an outright victory.

Meanwhile Hoare had been down to Chartwell to discuss the whole
situation with Churchill, and he found the Chancellor much more
sympathetic to the idea of full Treasury support than Trenchard and
the Air Council had found it expedient to assume. Churchill and other
members of the Cabinet whom Hoare consulted all pressed the view
that the Air Ministry should spare no effort to secure another victory,
and it gradually became clear that full government backing was assured.
On 25th February 1928 Hoare told Trenchard that the concurrence of
the Chancellor could now be assumed and that the Air Ministry could
go full steam ahead with the development of machines and engines for
the next contest; and a week later Trenchard, having finally put his
objections aside, was busy laying down the procedures to be adopted,
through the ordering of the machines right down to the formation of a
high-speed flight, its composition and the choice of a commander.

* * *

Italy's defeat at Venice came as a traumatic misfortune after their
triumph of a year earlier, and it was inevitably followed by a demand
for change and reorganisation. The massive effort that followed was

largely due to the dynamism of General Balbo, who saw, even more than Mussolini, the possibilities for technical advancement that the contest offered. One of the strengths of the Italians was that they were quick to learn: they had adopted American methods—the concentration of effort into one aircraft and one engine manufacturer, with full Service backing—to win at Hampton Roads, and now they proceeded to adopt British methods as the best way of beating the British. This meant competition and diversification—the widening of the net to take in all the leading airframe and engine manufacturers—and a longer period of training. The answer to the first requirement came in the production of four different types of high-speed machine designed specially for the 'Coppa Schneider'; the answer to the second lay in the creation of a high-speed school. But such reorganisation would take time, hence Balbo's visit to London.

The high-speed school was established at Desenzano on Lake Garda in April 1928, thus removing high-speed training from the Macchi preserve at Lake Varese; the choice of Desenzano was dictated by considerations of weather, transport, air space, and accommodation, combined with the need for remoteness and secrecy. The lake was large enough to offer facilities equivalent to the open sea without the draw-backs of corrosion and lack of shelter; it was the unlimited natural run-ways available to seaplanes which gave them the advantage over the racing landplanes of the time. In addition to the training of pilots the school was to concern itself with associated problems of aerodynamics and engineering, together with research into all aspects of high-speed flight, and skilled teams of scientists, laboratory assistants, mechanics and fitters were assembled. The eight pilots chosen to attend the first course all had high-speed experience, and from this initial course the team for the 1929 race was to be chosen. Their names were Captains Motta and Canaveri, Lieutenants Monti and Cadringher, Warrant Officer Dal Molin, and Sergeant-Majors Agello, Huber and Gallone. Of these, all but two were later selected for the race.

Most of the flying on this initial course was done in the three M.52s left over from 1927 and the M.52R, which had a smaller wing-span and tailplane and a reduced support section for the floats. By this time the British had decided to hold the 1929 race in the Solent, and the proposed circuit was reproduced on Lake Garda for practice purposes.

The four new Italian designs could hardly have differed more widely. First was the Macchi 67, designed by Castoldi and the direct descendent of the M.39; it reverted from the sweep-back of the M.52 to a straight, symmetrical wing. The multiple of 13 was avoided this time, but the figures were chosen to add up to that number. Construction was again largely of wood, though the rear part of the fuselage up to the pilot's seat was metal. The main constructional problem lay in dispersing the heat from the engine, an Isotta-Fraschini direct-drive of 18 cylinders in three banks of six (the same lay-out as the Napier Lion but with two extra cylinders in each bank) developing 1,800 h.p.; the exterior was practically all radiator surface. Three Macchi 67s were being built.

Of the other new machines, the Fiat C.29 was the smallest, with a wing-span of only 22 feet and a length of 18: it was built on orthodox lines round the latest Fiat engine, the 1,000 h.p. A.S.5, then the lightest engine of its power in the world. The airframe structure was all metal, and although the wing area was only 77 square feet the wing loading was kept low. Most distinctive was the Savoia-Marchetti 65: two 1,000 h.p. Isotta-Fraschinis were mounted in tandem, one tractor one pusher, and the pilot was sandwiched between contra-rotating propellers in the engine nacelle. The tail unit was mounted on twin outriggers or booms. Most ingenious was the Piaggio-Pegna Pc.7, the fruit of many years of study by designer Giovanni Pegna: the principle was the elimination of floats and the adoption of a waterproof fuselage, but it was not a flying-boat. Separate engine systems drove a marine propeller at the rear to get the craft hydroplaning and a normal tractor airscrew once the nose was clear of the water.

From these four ambitious designs it seemed likely that the Italians would produce several worthy challengers.

* * *

Whatever doubts there may have been in aeronautical circles of the military and commercial value of high-speed research, it is significant that the Schneider victories of Italy in 1926 and Britain in 1927 helped to precipitate a crisis of confidence in the French government's handling of aviation. It might not be necessary to compete with America, but a long lead by European neighbours posed a recognisable threat. Under Raymond Poincaré's coalition government the French economy had recovered strongly, and the old excuse of financial stringency had lost conviction. There was a growing feeling that France was being left behind, and an awareness that the aviation industry needed the stimulus that international competition could provide.

In the spring of 1928 the Minister of Marine (the man responsible for aeronautical development) ordered two new racing seaplanes from the Société d'Avions Bernard and two from the firm of Nieuport-Delage; and subsequently three engine constructors—Hispano-Suiza, Lorraine and Gnome-Rhône—were called upon to produce prototype racing engines of from 1,000 to 2,000 h.p. for possible installation in the new machines. These machines were intended to set up new world speed records and to compete in the next contest for the Schneider Trophy; but there was very considerable ground to be made up. Public opinion remained dissatisfied, and on 14th September 1928 a French Air Ministry was created, the first Air Minister being M. Laurent Eynac, a wartime pilot and a man who had already served in various government posts connected with aeronautics.

The Bernard company designed two new wire-braced mid-wing monoplanes, the HV. (Haute Vitesse) 40, which was to be powered by a Gnome-Rhône 'Mistral' radial engine of nine cylinders, expected to deliver about 1,200 h.p., and the HV.42, which was to be powered by a new Hispano-Suiza W-type motor of 1,200-1,500 h.p. The two machines, designed by engineer Roger Robert, who had recently joined the company, were otherwise similar. They were made entirely of wood except for their metal ailerons and dural floats supported by tubular steel struts, to which Lamblin radiators were fitted. The Nieuport-Delage company (Delage was the name of the chief designer) based their design on the same formula that had produced the successful Macchi and Supermarine racers, and the power unit chosen was the new Hispano-Suiza.

Soon after his appointment Laurent Eynac announced that his government had decided in principle to enter a team for the 1929 Schneider; but he added the proviso that the aircraft were expected to require lengthy trials and that actual participation in the race would depend on what progress was made and whether they had a real chance of victory. Meanwhile in Germany a design was produced by Dorniers very similar in form to the Savoia-Marchetti 65, but it got no further than the model stage.

* * *

In America the view remained that the performance of racing aeroplanes had risen more rapidly than had the ability to put what was learnt into practical use; therefore the government still intended to stand aloof from the Schneider race. A deputation to President

Coolidge of 12th January 1928, headed by Lester Gardner, editor of *Aviation*, urged the sending of a representative United States team to Britain, but it failed to change the government's mind. Nevertheless the irrepressible Al Williams was again determined to enter, and he succeeded in enlisting powerful private backing, together with strong avuncular support from Rear Admiral Moffett and the Navy Bureau of Aeronautics. His plane, a mid-wing monoplane this time, developed from the Kirkham biplane of 1927 and still owing much to the Curtiss lineage, was actually designed in the Navy Department and built at the Naval Aircraft Factory at Philadelphia. A non-profit-making firm called the Mercury Flying Corporation, formed by a group of patriotic sportsmen with whom various commercial firms cooperated, provided the necessary funds. Models of the 'Mercury' racer, as it was styled, were tested in the wind tunnels of the Washington Navy Yard and proved to be technically and aerodynamically sound, and John S. Keen, of the Naval Aircraft Factory, supervised construction. The same engine as the one used in 1927—the 24-cylinder geared Packard —was installed, but modifications to it gave a small power increase and a reduced frontal area. Fuselage, wing and fixed tail surfaces were wooden; control surfaces and floats were of metal. Early in August 1929 the Mercury was transported to the naval station at Annapolis for flight tests because of the lack of space on the Delaware river. The Navy Department promised to transport the plane across the Atlantic if during trials a speed in excess of the existing world record of 318 m.p.h. was achieved.

For Britain it was inevitable that they should rely on further development of the existing Supermarine and Gloster designs. But to keep their lead both aircraft needed more power, and the Napier Lion, boosted from its original 450 h.p. of ten years earlier to 898 h.p. at Venice, was surely nearing its limit. The question for the designers was whether they should go for a new engine, with all the uncertainties and risks that that involved, or stick to the power unit which had served them so well in the past, relying on a small improvement in horse-power and the maximum practicable reduction in head resistance and weight to hold Britain's lead. According to Major G. P. Bulman, a leading test pilot who had been made responsible for engine development at the Air Ministry, Mitchell was suffering from so many qualms and misgivings about this decision that he went to Bulman for advice. The only possible alternative to the Lion would be a new engine from Rolls-Royce, a firm of whom Mitchell had had some experience. "What do you think of these chaps at Derby?" asked Mitchell. Bulman, who knew them well, said he had a hunch that they could do it if given the chance. "Right," said Mitchell, "that's decided it."

Overshadowed by Napiers immediately after the war, Rolls-Royce concentrated in the immediate post-war years mostly on new marks of existing engines. Then, under the pressure of Richard Fairey's desire after the 1923 Schneider race to build the Curtiss D-12 engine in England under licence for the Fairey 'Fox'—a desire that was largely frustrated by the Air Ministry, who felt that British firms should be encouraged to produce suitable types—Rolls-Royce were stimulated into producing the Kestrel, as it later came to be known. One of the D-12 engines was stripped and examined, but Royce eventually decided to design afresh. The Kestrel differed radically from its forebears in that each of the two banks of six cylinders was formed from a single aluminium-alloy block, resulting in a very light and rigid engine. It was supercharged, and although it first appeared as a direct-drive unit it was soon available in geared form. In its various marks it powered many British and foreign aircraft of the period, and from it was developed the 36·7-litre Buzzard, larger and more powerful than the Kestrel but similar in design, and giving 825 h.p. at 2,000 revolutions per minute at sea level.

By the time the policy decision that Britain's 1929 entry was to be government backed had been translated into an executive one it was too late for Rolls-Royce to attempt a completely fresh design, but the Buzzard served as a useful starting-point: many of the moving parts of the new engine, especially in the early stages, were the same. Rolls-Royce's ability to construct a racing engine under Air Ministry contract in 1929 can thus be directly traced to the pressures arising from the success of the Curtiss D-12 at Cowes six years earlier, and to the Air Ministry's timely interference when this engine looked likely to flood the British market.

The Rolls-Royce management were by no means unanimous in wanting to accept the contract; indeed the Managing Director, Basil Johnson, firmly believed that the company should stick to the motor-car. But three men who were in favour, E. W. Hives, A. J. Rowledge and A. C. Lovesey, went down to see Royce at his home and head-quarters at West Wittering in October 1928 and found him enthusiastic. It was a bright autumn morning and Royce suggested a stroll along the beach; as they walked he pointed out the local places of interest. But Royce, who walked with a stick, was a semi-invalid, as Montague

Napier had been, and he soon tired. "Let's find a sheltered spot," he said, "and have a talk."

Seated on the sand dunes against a groyne, Royce sketched the rough outline of a racing engine in the sand with his stick. Each man was asked his opinion in turn, the sand was raked over and adjustments made. The key to the engine was simplicity. "I invent nothing," was Royce's philosophy, "inventors go broke." Like the Kestrel and the Buzzard the new engine would have only 12 cylinders, against the 18 of the Isotta-Fraschini and the 24 of the Packard. The bore and stroke would be 6″ by 6·6″ and the compression ration 6:1. The secret of increased power would lie in supercharging.

On Rowledge's recommendation Royce had brought in an expert on supercharging from the R.A.E. in 1921 named James Ellor, a man who had advanced further in what was then an embryonic science than anyone else. The power of an engine depends on the mass of air it can consume in a given time, and a supercharger provides a means of getting additional air through an engine of given size and capacity. Ellor had introduced supercharging in aero engines in its fullest sense for the first time in the Kestrel and the Buzzard; part of his design was a forward-facing air intake which converted forward air energy into pressure energy, unique at that time. Another great advantage of supercharging—provided it could be made reliable and provided the higher stresses could be contained—was the reduction of frontal area and engine length. The 'R' (racing) engine supercharger was designed to have the largest diameter consistent with the airframe design.[1] Other changes from the Buzzard were an improved induction system and a higher engine speed. But it was by supercharging that the quart was to be got out of the pint pot.

Royce eventually guaranteed to produce an engine of around 1,500 h.p., privately informing James Bird of Vickers-Supermarine (the firms had amalgamated in 1928) that he hoped to give him 1,800. The engine was modified to ensure better streamlining, and around this outline Mitchell began work on the design of what was to become the S.6. The new engine would inevitably be much bigger and heavier than the Lion, so the S.6 had to be considerably bigger than the S.5. The general concept, however, was the same, and although the weight fully loaded rose from the 3,250 lb of the S.5 to 5,771, the percentage weight of the wings and other components was reduced by careful

[1] It was necessary to use a double-sided compressor in order to handle an adequate airflow.

design. The wings and tail surfaces were all-metal, and semi-monoco-
que construction was used as in the S.5. With the increased engine size
and consumption, both floats were now utilised as fuel tanks.

Meanwhile Folland was going ahead with the design of the Gloster
V, developed from the Gloster IV and using a supercharged Napier
Lion as an insurance against failure of the new Rolls-Royce engine.
Wind tunnel tests proved highly encouraging, but the addition of the
supercharger contributed to an inconvenient increase in weight, and
when a repositioned wing was tried to allow for the shift in the centre
of gravity it was found impossible to locate it and still give an adequate
view forward. This, and not any disillusion with the biplane form,
finally forced Folland to turn to the monoplane, and the result was the
Gloster VI. The boosted Napier Lion developed 1,320 h.p., considerably less than the Rolls-Royce engine, but the Gloster machine was
smaller and lighter and was expected to rival the S.6 for speed.
Indeed one of the selected Schneider pilots, Flight Lieutenant G. H.
Stainforth, given the choice, preferred the Gloster to the Supermarine.

The R.A.F.'s high-speed flight, kept in being operationally first by
Kinkead and then by Greig, had been reformed with the race in mind in
February 1929 with the posting in of Squadron Leader A. H. Orlebar
to command. 33 years old, Harry Orlebar had joined the R.F.C. in 1916
after seeing service with the Army at Gallipoli, where he was
wounded; he had been a Martlesham Heath test pilot alongside
Webster, so he was fully equipped professionally, and he was staff
college trained. Slim and almost gaunt in appearance, with high cheek-
bones and aquiline nose, he was tactful, energetic and self-effacing, and
besides being a superb organiser he had the requisite social flair. He
found himself commanding a remarkable team.

D'Arcy Greig, asked some time earlier for his opinion, had named
three of the pilots of his Hendon Display aerobatic team of the previous
year, and this had accounted for Stainforth and two others, Flight
Lieutenant H. R. D. Waghorn and Flying Officer R. L. R. 'Batchy'
Atcherley. Waghorn, winner of the Sword of Honour in his year at
Cranwell (when Atcherley had been adjudged best pilot), had been one
of the men on the short list in 1927. George Stainforth, a former Sand-
hurst cadet, and a crack shot who had been R.A.F. Champion in 1928,
was quiet, serious and imperturbable, and Dick Waghorn, ruthlessly
conscientious, was possibly even more reserved, but they were
leavened by the gaiety and dash of Atcherley and Greig, the two
practical jokers of the team. (Greig had also suggested John Boothman,

with whom he had flown at an earlier display, but he was overseas.)

After practice at Felixstowe on hacks and the Gloster IVs the flight moved to Calshot in April, where they began to fly the S.5s. But August came and there was still no sign of the new machines. The race was due to be run on 6th and 7th September. Meanwhile training was largely devoted to finding the most efficient method of cornering, the prospect of increased speeds necessitating a further study. At first it was thought that a level turn would still be best, but there was a feeling that it might be wise to let the machine climb slightly. Owing to aileron drag there was a strong tendency to climb at the start of the turn, and in order to counteract this it was necessary to use a lot of rudder. The theory was that a slight climb might cause less loss of speed than the extra surface drag involved in the use of rudder. Two scientists were attached to Calshot from the R.A.E. to keep a record of accelerations, speeds and climbs based on instrument readings, and they finally evolved the perfect turn, in which the tendency of the machine to climb was not resisted too strongly.

The final shape of the S.6 could not be decided until the engine to be provided by Rolls-Royce had been fully developed, and this accounted principally for the late delivery. By May, designing, detailing and production of the first engines had been achieved and the 'R' engine was born. But engine shape, power, installation features, cowlings and consumption were still being developed and adjusted, and every change meant some alteration to airframe or components. On 14th May, running at 2,750 revs per minute, the engine gave 1,545 horse-power, but after fifteen minutes parts began to fail.

Throughout that summer the test beds at Derby reverberated with the sound of the new engine, and of the auxiliary engines which were an integral part of the test rig. There were three of these, all 600 h.p. Kestrels. Two were driving fans, one to cool the new 'R' engine crankcase and the other to disperse the noxious fumes that filled the test house; both these engines were running at full bore during testing. The third auxiliary engine drove a special fan which provided an air-flow into the forward-facing air intake of up to 380 m.p.h., simulating the conditions that would be encountered in flight. This was necessary because it had been found in earlier tests, with the Kestrel and other engines, that serious de-tuning of the carburettors due to air velocity effects on the pressure balances could otherwise take place in flight.

When the wind was in the prevailing direction the noise of these four engines going at full blast could be heard all over Derby. The sound acted as a barometer of progress; when the new engine ran sweetly there was optimism, when it remained silent for long periods there was despair. The target that men like Rowledge, the designer, Hives, in charge of the experimental department, Dorey, who supervised the testing, and Lovesey, technical assistant to Hives, had set themselves was an hour's run of a proof engine at maximum speed and boost. The test runs were usually started at eight o'clock in the morning, and Rowledge, at his home outside Derby, could hear the roar of the engine over his breakfast; if it was still running as he set out for the factory he began to hope. He learned to time his arrival for one hour after the test started, but day after day silence descended as he drove in, sometimes only just before he arrived. Thirteen times the engine—not always the same one—broke down before the hour was up; but on 27th July, less than six weeks before the race, it was still running as Rowledge drove triumphantly through the gates.

Within another few days the stage was reached when a halt had to be called to development and a decision taken to sink or swim with the power already obtained. A satisfactory life of 100 minutes at 1,850 h.p. had by then been achieved, and the proved engine was transported to Supermarines. Meanwhile the fuel problems that had been causing valve distortion, overheating and the sooting up of plugs had been solved by F. R. Banks, representative in England of the Ethyl Export Corporation; Banks had also assisted Napiers two years earlier. Benzole, high in anti-knock qualities and not subject to detonation, had been in use at Derby so far, but 'Rod' Banks, with no time for lengthy experiment, mixed a 'cocktail' of 78% benzole and 22% aviation spirit, plus 3 c.c. per gallon of tetra-ethyl lead for the suppression of detonation and attendant pre-ignition troubles, and this proved about right.

The first S.6, N.247, was launched at Woolston on 5th August (Bank Holiday Monday) and towed to Calshot. The morale of the team soared, only to sag visibly in the next few days as Orlebar, carrying out the first tests, found that he couldn't get the machine off the water. There was still no sign of the Glosters.

* * *

The setbacks and delays suffered by Britain were meanwhile being paralleled in France and America. The two seaplanes being built by the Bernard company, HV.40 and HV.42, had both reached a stage by May 1929 at which airframe problems were more or less resolved, and both types made their initial flights in the following month; but the

engines were still a long way from racing trim. The Gnome-Rhône
Mistral was still undergoing bench tests and it was becoming clear that
it was unlikely to be ready in time. The Lorraine was still being developed, and even the new Hispano-Suiza was behind schedule. To fill
the gap an existing Hispano-Suiza V-type direct-drive engine was
boosted to a compression ratio of 8.8:1, giving a power increase from
600 to nearly 1,000 h.p., and this was fitted into a Bernard fuselage of
the pursuit type; but it was never regarded as more than a stop-gap
measure to facilitate pilot training, and even this combination was not
yet ready for tests. For the Nieuport-Delage, with its much more
advanced airframe design and construction, there was no hope at all.

The French government had set aside the lakeside base at Hourtin,
in the Gironde, for training and acceptance trials, and the pilots
engaged to test the new machines were Florentin Bonnet for the
Bernard machines (he still held the world speed record for landplanes
in the Bernard-Ferbois V.2), and Sadi Lecointe for the Nieuport. On
6th August Florentin Bonnet, attempting a loop in a Nieuport 62
trainer immediately after take-off, crashed and was killed.

Whether this tragedy affected France's readiness to compete seems
doubtful; reports that Bonnet and Sadi Lecointe were to fly in the race
had been denied, the racing team being said to consist of young pilots
of the French naval air service. But within 48 hours of the accident the
French had withdrawn, giving the explanation that although machines
and engines were now ready, there was not enough time to give the
pilots adequate training.

The news from Santee Wharf, Annapolis, where Al Williams was
preparing to test his Mercury racer under conditions of absolute
secrecy, was inevitably sketchy. By mid-August he had got no further
than his preliminary taxying tests, but these, according to reports,
were satisfactory up to and beyond 100 m.p.h. Those who witnessed
them, however, were not so sure. On more than one occasion the propeller was damaged by spray as Williams throttled back at the end of
his taxying run, and it was not until he learnt to cut his switch at the
appropriate moment, so that the propeller stopped or windmilled, that
this danger was overcome. As with the S.6, however, all attempts to
take off proved abortive; the Mercury's floats sat low in the water, and
when taxying below 'hump' speeds there was the same tendency to
bury the left wing. The use of rudder and aileron to correct this tendency increased drag loads so sharply that the floats never came up on
the step. Eventually Williams discovered, more or less as a last re-

G

source, that by keeping the controls centralised the machine would eventually right itself; but he still could not get the plane off.

The water that was churned up in the course of these take-off attempts was so blinding for the pilot that Williams had to cover his goggles with a handkerchief until he had built up sufficient speed for the spray to clear the cockpit, but this dangerous procedure did not commend itself to the Navy Department when they heard about it. Further propeller damage frustrated at least one determined attempt at take-off, and a faulty gasoline feed was responsible for other failures. But at last, on 18th August, Williams finally lifted the Mercury into the air for a few hundred yards. The roar of the labouring Packard as it fought to keep the machine airborne was ominous, and Williams never got more than a few feet off the water. Then he was down again, defeated by the same old troubles—low gasoline pressure and another bent propeller.

It was clear to Williams that something was radically wrong, and when the engineering data was reviewed it was found that despite its nicely-proportioned appearance the Mercury was 400 lb too heavy. There was no way of saving this weight, and the only answer was to instal a more powerful engine. A new Packard X engine developing 1,300-1,500 h.p. was prepared, but there was no time to instal and test it before the destroyer that was to take the Mercury to England sailed. Williams planned to have the engine mounted on the way over and complete his test programme on the Solent, but at this point the Navy Department withdrew their support, David S. Ingalls, Assistant Secretary for Aeronautics, refusing Williams permission to compete. It was a bitter blow for Williams, who had sunk most of his personal capital in the venture.

* * *

By their decision to diversify, and because of their unbroken run of high-speed experience under racing conditions since 1926, the Italians seemed likely to be better placed than anyone, but the variety and complexity of their designs brought accompanying problems, and although the high-speed flight at Desenzano practised assiduously on the old Macchi 52s, they too had to wait until August for the delivery of the first of their new racers. They then had to contend with the sort of weather that, while an acknowledged hazard at Calshot, was not normally to be expected at Lake Garda. Initial tests with the Piaggio, with Dal Molin as pilot, revealed difficulties with the water-screw clutch, and this and the Savoia quickly established themselves as non-starters. There were mechanical troubles, too, with the Macchi 67, but by mid-August the Fiat C.29 had successfully completed its maiden flight. The new A.S.5 engine had run well on the test-bed, and after a basic fault in the float structure had been corrected there was no indication of trouble until, when about to alight after its second flight, the C.29 caught fire. The pilot, Francesco Agello, escaped, and the fire was quickly extinguished.

This setback came less than a month from the race, with only ten days to go before the team was due to pack up and leave for England. The Macchi 67, however, had meanwhile completed its first flight in the capable hands of Guiseppe Motta, the Italian second in command and first choice for what was expected to be Italy's fastest machine, and the C.29 was quickly repaired. The first flight was again entrusted to the courageous but diminutive Agello; he was the only member of the team who could fit without discomfort into the tiny cockpit.

Agello climbed in, taxied away from the lake shore, opened the throttle and began his take-off run, but the machine refused to unstick. He was towed back to the slipway, but no apparent fault was found, and half an hour later he went out again. His second attempt at taking off was again unsuccessful, but on his third attempt the plane left the water after a remarkably short run. It had risen to 50 feet, and travelled little more than a hundred yards, when it suddenly dipped forward and alighted heavily, wiping off the floats.

Motor boats and a patrol seaplane dashed to the spot, but at this point the lake was over 300 feet deep, and apart from a few fragments of fuselage and floats the machine had vanished. Something that looked like the body of the pilot was floating on the water, but this also disappeared. Soon afterwards the object was seen again, and it proved to be Agello. He was pulled on board one of the motor-boats and taken ashore, and after a medical examination it was found that, with the exception of a few scratches, he had escaped injury.

To the two existing non-starters—the Piaggio and the Savoia—now had to be added the C.29. A second machine of this type had been built, but there was no prospect of getting it ready and tested before the race, and in any case there were obviously serious faults that could only be ironed out over a period. That left the Maccchi 67, only one of which had so far been delivered and tested. Nevertheless General Balbo, on hearing that Agello was uninjured, ordered the trials to continue, and further flights were made in the Macchi 67 that afternoon.

After this the bad weather returned; but on Thursday 22nd August, in conditions of haze and an ill-defined horizon, Motta got off again in the M.67 for what was intended to be one of his last flights before leaving Lake Garda for Calshot. Indeed the advance guard of the Italian team had already reached the United Kingdom, and the un-packing of the cases containing the M.52R and an M.52 which was to be used for training had been begun that day. The 35-year-old Motta had joined the high-speed flight at Desenzano on its formation in April 1928, and he had flown all the Macchi racing types frequently. Now, practising high-speed runs on the machine which had always repre-sented Italy's best hope of victory, he had reached a speed of 362 m.p.h. when his machine dived steeply into the lake from a height of 300 feet. Unlike the more fortunate Agello, Motta was killed.

The cause of this accident is uncertain, but there are several possibilities. One report said that Motta stalled during a turn, much as Centurione and Borra had done. Another report suggested that the stall, if stall there was, was caused by the effect on the pilot of the dense smoke that the Isotta-Fraschini engine always emitted: this cleared the cockpit in straight and level flight but was apt to fog the windscreen and enter the cockpit during turns. Alternatively, condi-tions were said to have been much the same as when Sam Kinkead lost his life in the Solent. The Macchi company inclined towards a combina-tion of the first and third reasons; but special ventilating tubes to protect the pilot from the danger of noxious fumes were fitted in the cockpit of the other two M.67s.

Neither of these machines, however, was yet ready, and although work on them was expedited it became apparent that the last remaining hope of an effective Italian challenge, as in 1926, lay in a postponement. The Italian air attaché in London at once contacted the Royal Aero Club for their views, and to follow this up the Italian government made their own formal request for a 30-day postponement—or even 20 days if a month was too long—on the same day, giving bad weather and disorganisation following the loss of their leading pilot and machine as their reasons.

The Italian request was considered by the organising committee next day, 23rd August, and they were unanimous in concluding that the date could not be altered in any circumstances. They based their judgment solely on their interpretation of the rules. As organisers of the contest they held that they were bound by the regulations, which they had followed so far to the letter; under these regulations the date for the contest once fixed was unalterable. Not only did they have no

power to change it, but if such change were made, other competitors
(for example France, who had already withdrawn), would have the
right to feel aggrieved at an extension of time which, if given earlier,
might have enabled them to compete. This decision, which was taken
without any overt check being made on the state of British preparedness, was communicated to the Italian air attaché on the same day.

There were, in addition, many organisational reasons for rejecting
the request. And the race was an examination in timing and readiness
as well as in speed and skill. To give a challenger another few weeks to
get ready while the defender stood still or went stale might be to
present that challenger with the trophy—as the Americans had discovered at Hampton Roads. But the Air Ministry and the Royal Aero
Club took their stand on the basis of the regulations alone, and in this
they had the emphatic support of the F.A.I.

The reaction of the Italian Press was to urge the Italian government to withdraw, and reports appeared to the effect that they had
done so; but no authoritative statement was received in England. On
27th August the organising committee announced that the British
team would race over the course whether foreign competitors arrived
or not, so visitors were assured of a spectacle; but next day General
Balbo, announcing that Italy would take part in the race after all,
issued the following statement:

"The Italian team is going to England merely to perform a gesture
of chivalrous sportsmanship and in order to avoid the appearance that
an announcement of withdrawal would have of being a counter-reply to
the refusal to postpone the race.

"The probability of victory by our team, already hard pressed by the
very great delay of the building firms in delivering the machines and
the engines, is almost annulled by the death of Captain Motta. His
death not only deprives us of our best pilot, but has cost us the engine
and the machine which had been perfected for the best speed, and has
also meant a week's interruption in our programme.

"We thus present ourselves in London with two seaplanes, one of
them absolutely new, which has never touched water, and with two
perfectly new engines which have so far never been tested in flight.
We have to comfort us only the fact that we leave at the hangar at
Desenzano two new machines conceived on the boldest plans, on
which we place many hopes for the record for speed which we intend to
keep in the hands of our country."

*   *   *

Orlebar's first taxying tests in the S.6 at Calshot, as already recorded, were highly discouraging. "On each one I was deluged with quite three times as much spray as the old types had ever thrown up," he wrote afterwards, "and the machine . . . swung violently to port, digging her left float so deep into the water that the wing-tip seemed only an inch or two off the surface."[1] Mitchell, however, was reassuring, and he proposed that, as with the S.5, most of the fuel should be carried in the starboard float. As with Williams's Mercury, the dipping and swinging stopped as speed increased, and so did the sheet of spray that enveloped the cockpit; but when the floats started hydroplaning and the nose came down there was a tendency to porpoise, and when Orlebar eventually tried to take off the machine ploughed on and on. The forward pull on the stick was extremely strong, and although the machine showed occasional signs of getting off Orlebar dared not open right out owing to an apparent lack of back-elevator control. D'Arcy Greig had a try and ran for about $2\frac{1}{2}$ miles at take-off speed until the engine boiled, but the machine still wouldn't unstick.

The take-off technique in the old Glosters and the S.5 had been similar to that of the conventional landplane—holding the stick slightly forward and keeping it central and allowing the machine to fly itself off when it reached take-off speed. When Orlebar made his next attempt later that same day, 10th August, he decided to adopt the old seaplane technique of putting firm backward pressure on the stick when flying speed was reached and virtually hauling the machine off. The breeze had meanwhile stiffened and the water surface was more rippled, and this may have helped; but the technique proved successful and it was employed from then on. Orlebar's subsequent report was not uncritical, but once off the water the machine reacted beautifully and its behaviour in the air was exactly as forecast by Mitchell. Minor troubles such as vibration, tail-heaviness and stiffness of the aileron controls were cleared in the next few days, and the chief problem that remained was overheating; there was not enough radiator surface to get rid of all the heat generated at continuous full power. One answer was to fit extra patches of radiator to the floats, and Mitchell also found a way of cooling the inside surfaces of the wing radiators by means of air scoops.

Waghorn had his first flight in the S.6 on 19th August and Atcherley his first on the 20th. Each man got in another flight on the 21st. By this time the first Gloster VI was ready, but then the weather clamped

[1] *Schneider Trophy*, by Wg. Cdr. A. H. Orlebar, A.F.C. (Macdonald, 1933).

down and four vital days were lost. Thus at the time of the Italian request for a postponement only one new British machine had flown— and that had gone back to Supermarines for the fitting of additional radiators. The British were no further forward than the Italians, and indeed but for Motta's accident the two nations would have been in much the same position.

The British aircraft were nominally civil machines, and the Air Registration Board had granted a certificate of airworthiness on the basis of five hours' running time for each engine before overhaul, so after this period each engine had to be removed and taken back to Derby for stripping, repair and testing. To achieve this and still keep two serviceable S.6s at Calshot a special Phantom lorry was built with a cradle for the 'R' engine, to return time-expired engines to Derby quickly and deliver overhauled replacements. After every second round trip the brakes of the Phantom needed relining.

On 25th August the Gloster VI had its first brief air test and the second S.6—N.248—was also air-tested for the first time. Then the weather clamped again and for another four frustrating days nothing could be done. When flying was resumed the engine of the Gloster ran erratically, cutting out on the turns and even in level flight, while the first S.6 behaved alarmingly when it was given a full racing load of 124 gallons of fuel. In six attempts Waghorn failed to get airborne, and although he got off on the seventh it was obvious that, as with the Mercury, more power was needed. The only way to achieve it was by means of a small reduction in the pitch of the propeller, increasing the engine revolutions at take-off speeds; but although this proved effective it brought a corresponding increase in revolutions in the air, putting up fuel consumption (and therefore weight), and generating more heat. None of these increases could be tolerated, and the only way out of the dilemma was an unpalatable one—to fly with the engine slightly throttled down in the actual race.

Another problem with the S.6 was leakage from the wing radiators, which occurred after every flight. Wing flexing during the turns, straining the rivets and joints in the coolers, was the cause, and the engineers could find no remedy. It happened that D'Arcy Greig had been having radiator trouble in his Austin Seven, and he had stopped the leaks by pouring a patent sealing compound called Johnson's 'Neverleak' into the radiator. This somewhat desperate remedy was eventually tried with the S.6.

Experience with the Gloster VI was even more disheartening. The

faults in the petrol feed system persisted, and although the ground
team worked round the clock to trace and cure the trouble, and even
moved their beds into the hangars and snatched a few hours' sleep in
their overalls, they defied correction. On the test bench, and when
run up in the machines on the ground, the engines ran perfectly, but
every time they went into the air and the throttle was opened they
began popping. Three times in three days the whole fuel system was
changed, but the symptoms remained. The night before the race both
the Glosters had to be withdrawn.

No one was more disappointed than D'Arcy Greig, who because of his
superior experience to Stainforth was to have flown the Gloster in the
race. "Had Folland designed the Gloster VI for the Rolls engine
instead of the Napier," he said later, "I believe it would have walked
away with the contest."

The luck of weather and serviceability had favoured Waghorn, his
handling of the S.6—on the few occasions when he had been out in it—
had been impressive, and he was first choice for this machine. The
second S.6 was to be flown by Atcherley. Greig was more familiar than
anyone with the S.5, having attacked the record in it, and this combination would complete the team; but even Greig, who had been with the
high-speed flight for sixteen months, had compiled only a little more
than 11 hours' flying on all the racing machines put together. His plane,
N.219, was the one Worsley had flown at Venice, but with a geared
Lion of similar horse-power.

*   *   *

When the Italian pilots arrived at the R.A.F. station at Calshot, a
mile or so inland from the slipway, on Thursday 29th August, the
British team were in the middle of lunch. They expected the Italians to
join them—but the visitors had brought their own food supply and
their own chefs, and they were taking no chances on English cooking.
Under the command of Lieutenant-Colonel Mario Bernasconi, the
pilots consisted of Captain A. Canaveri, Lieutenants Giovanni Monti
and Remo Cadringher, Warrant Officer Tommaso Dal Molin and
Sergeant-Major Francesco Agello. The smartness and cut of their
uniforms made the R.A.F. men, whose uniforms were baggy with the
strain of a long summer, look shabby, and the strict discipline to which
they were subjected made them difficult at first to mix with. But the
high spirits and penchant for practical joking of Atcherley and Greig
soon broke the ice.

General Balbo arrived on 31st August to take overall charge of the team, and like the other Italians he had to submit to the pranks of Atcherley and Greig. Balbo's best snooker shots were apt to be aborted by the surreptitious addition of chewing gum to the tip of his cue, while Atcherley's aim with a small starting pistol, firing chewing-gum pellets, made bending down to play shove-ha'penny a vulnerable pastime. Another trick was to pull a handkerchief out of a pocket, and with it some small change. The polite Italians would rush to help, only for yet another chewing-gum pellet to find its mark. A dead porpoise washed up on the beach found its way, via the back seat of Atcherley's Bentley, into everyone's bed in turn; but the Italians, Balbo included, took it all in good part.

Another diversion for the Italians was the presence at Calshot—originally as a member of one of the motor-boat crews, but working temporarily now as secretary to Wing Commander Sydney Smith, the man in charge of race organisation—of Aircraftman T. E. Shaw (Lawrence of Arabia). Trenchard, visiting Calshot with other V.I.P.s shortly before the race, spotted Shaw talking to Lady Astor. "Keep your eye on that damned fellow," he told D'Arcy Greig. Soon afterwards Lawrence was observed in deep conversation with Balbo.

Six Italian machines were being erected—two Macchi 67s, the two Macchi 52s, and a Fiat C.29 and a Savoia 65, the two last-named being merely window dressing. The Italians used the old Macchi 52 for practice, and its soiled appearance, streaked with oil and exhaust smoke, contrasting strongly with the bright scarlet of their new machines, earned it the name of 'The Moor of Venice'. The first flight of an M.67 at Calshot was made by the tall, fair-haired Monti on 4th September; he got off safely in spite of being baulked on his take-off run by a motor-boat. He kept well away from Calshot to avoid close observation, but so far as could be seen he tried no high-speed runs. After about fifteen minutes he was down again with a broken stay-wire.

On 5th September, the day before the navigability tests, Dal Molin was out in the M.52R; this machine, which still held the world record, was to be the Italian third string. Water could be seen streaming from the floats as he took off, and although he alighted smoothly the plane started to heel over as he pulled up. Help was rushed out to him and he was towed in with a nasty list; he had apparently hit some debris on his take-off run. What the Italians thought of this and the interference experienced by Monti can be imagined; the busy waterway of the Solent came as a rude shock after the tranquillity of Lake Garda.

One of the Macchi 67s, numbered seven in the order of starting and to be flown in the race by Cadringher (the draw had included the American and French entries), had a three-bladed propeller, but when Cadringher tried to take off in it on 5th September he failed. Thus on the night before the navigability trials only one of the two new Macchis, No. 10, had flown at Calshot, and that for only about fifteen minutes. But the British machines had done little better. The second S.6 (N.248) and the S.5 (N.219) were undergoing repairs at Woolston up to 4th September, and there was only just time for Atcherley and Greig to get in a final run; while Waghorn, doing the final test on N.247 with a new engine and a full load, recovered from a nasty porpoising run only to misjudge his alighting and drift into a passing barge. As he saw the danger he leapt out onto a float and tried to ward the barge off, but he could not prevent it bumping into a wing-tip. Luckily the damage was slight.

The one thing that no one could fault in those last few days before the race was the weather—except that the pilots complained of the heat. The weatherman at Calshot had predicted that the first week of September would be fine, and he was right. He explained afterwards that it always was. On his somewhat empirical long-range forecast the date of the contest had been fixed.

* * *

The lack of flying time of both teams on the actual race machines made the navigability and seaworthiness tests of unusual interest. The cool mist of the early morning dispersed as the sun warmed the air, and it was another perfect day. The course for the tests was marked out in front of East Cowes, and the take-off and alighting area was swept clear of debris. Waghorn's machine, N.247, was due to be first away, and it was started up by Lovesey. After being launched from the pontoon Waghorn opened the throttle, and as he did so the engine coughed and spluttered and regurgitated, throwing out a hideous mixture of flame and smoke. It seemed impossible that it could clear itself, but a moment later it was running smoothly and away Waghorn went. He completed the tests without further trouble and then returned across the Solent to Calshot, where the machines were to tie up for the mooring-out test in a protected bay north of the Castle.

Next came Dal Molin in the Macchi 52R, followed by D'Arcy Greig in the S.5. Neither experienced any difficulty, but Cadringher, who was due to go next in the three-bladed Macchi 67 (No. 7), was not quite ready, so Monti in the other new Macchi (No. 10), took his place. He swung alarmingly at first, but his second take-off run was arrow-straight, and the machine behaved beautifully, looking stable on the water and speedy in the air. Then, as he came round for his first alighting, he was suddenly confronted by a huge warship steaming right across the landing lane. It was H.M.S. *Iron Duke,* flagship of the C-in-C Portsmouth, which had been ordered to take up its allotted position by noon. Monti avoided it and completed his tests correctly, but it was another black mark against the Solent.

Atcherley came next, keeping his S.6 running fast through the half-mile taxying test, and last came Cadringher. Flying a machine that had never been off the water before, not even in Italy, Cadringher accomplished the tests without fuss, and by two o'clock all the contestants were safely moored at Calshot.

Safely moored: that was how it seemed. But the starboard float of Atcherley's machine, N.248, was leaking; perhaps he had taxied too fast. After two hours the machine began to develop a pronounced list, and one of the ground-crew N.C.O.s went out in a dinghy to take a closer look. They couldn't stand by and do nothing if the machine was going to sink, but to touch it before the end of the mooring-out test meant disqualification, and there was more than three hours to go. Orlebar's reaction was to get Mitchell out of the Mess, where he was sleeping after working through the night on the final preparations, and together they watched the water-level creeping up the float. Mitchell estimated that the plane would float for another three hours, and his estimate proved about right. At the end of the six-hour period the plane had an ugly list, but it had not capsized, and after it had been hauled ashore the float was emptied out and repaired.

Both teams had thus come through the tests without serious mishap, and all that remained to be done was the final inspection, servicing, tuning-up and refuelling. Everyone who hadn't worked through the night had been up before dawn, and at eight o'clock the pilots left the sheds and went back to the Mess for supper and bed, leaving the mechanics with an hour or two's work to do before they followed suit.

There were no last-minute shocks for the Italians. Comparatively untested as their machines were, they had developed no snags during the day. It was the British who had narrowly escaped disaster. And it was the British for whom disaster was waiting. One of the Rolls-Royce mechanics, changing a sparking plug in Waghorn's machine, found a spot of white metal on the electrode and showed it to Moon.[1] Moon passed it without comment to Lovesey. Both men knew they were looking at swarf from a scored cylinder. The cause could only be piston failure. The cylinders were in blocks of six, so the whole block would have to be changed. The block was too heavy to be lifted by hand, the new block would have to be lowered into position absolutely truly, and it was a task for which the party at Calshot were hopelessly ill-equipped.

Under the race regulations the changing of an engine was not permitted after the navigability trials. The changing of parts of an engine was permissible, but would they be allowed to change a cylinder block? And how were they to do it? The answers decided upon were, first, that the engine would be useless as it was, so nothing would be lost by repairing it; and secondly Hives, the man in charge of the Rolls-Royce experimental department, knew that a party of his fitters had arrived in Southampton from Derby earlier that evening to see the race. He drove to the Crown Hotel in the town, where some of them were staying, and told them to "get cracking, there's a cylinder block needs changing". Rousing themselves after an evening on the town, and sorting out their shoes, which the wag of the party had switched around outside their bedroom doors, they reported for duty. With the help of the police the rest of the party were collected from various hotels, and at about 2 a.m. the job was begun.

Normally such a task would never have been attempted with the engine installed in the machine, but this time there was no alternative. The block would have to be lowered into position at an angle, and there was no overhead tackle to help. One extraordinary piece of luck was the presence of charge-hand fitter Jack Marsden, a member of the experimental team. There was a gudgeon pin which because of its location could not be knocked out with the right hand, and Marsden was left-handed.

It was daylight when the machine was pushed out on to the slipway in front of the Castle to test the engine. Lovesey got into the cockpit, and after warming up the engine he gave it a 20-minute run at full throttle. It ran perfectly, and it actually developed a few more revolutions than before.

The removal of the block had disclosed a partially seized piston and a badly scored cylinder, besides other incidental damage: how had it

---

[1] Flying officer T. H. Moon, technical officer appointed to the high-speed flight. The mechanic's name was J. S. ("Stan") Orme.

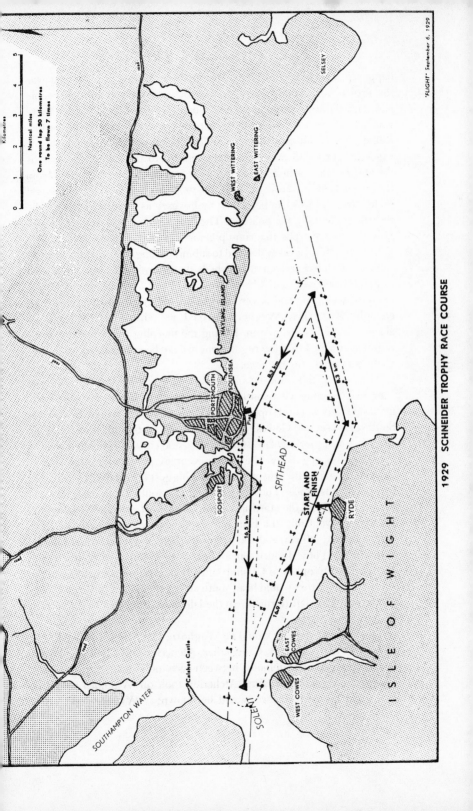

1929 SCHNEIDER TROPHY RACE COURSE

"FLIGHT" September 6, 1929

happened, and how could they prevent it happening again? That was
the problem that faced Lovesey. His diagnosis was that the trouble
had started during prolonged slow-running before take-off, when there
was not enough air velocity in the supercharger volute to drive the fuel
round. The result was that excess fuel which had accumulated in the
supercharger volute was delivered en masse to the cylinder as soon as
the engine was opened up. This excess fuel washed away the oil from
the cylinder walls, causing the pistons to 'pick-up' in the steel cylinders;
the evidence of this had been seen by Lovesey as Waghorn opened the
throttle on leaving the pontoon. The only counter was to give the engine the shortest possible run-up before take-off. Having made up his
mind about this, Lovesey decided to submit the engine to no further trial.

When Orlebar arrived at the sheds that morning he was astonished
to find himself confronted by a crowd of grimy, exhausted mechanics,
many of whom he had never seen before. He learned the story soon
enough. But when Waghorn arrived at ten o'clock the night's
alarums were kept from him. During the morning the Schneider committee confirmed that the regulations had not been infringed, so everything was ready for the race.

The course this time was quadrilateral, starting in front of Ryde
Pier and heading east-south-east for Seaview before turning east-
north-east to a point opposite Hayling Island, then north-west for
Southsea, west for Cowes, and finally back east-south-east for Ryde
Pier. It was a glorious late-summer day, and crowds estimated at over
a million congregated at the various vantage points along the Hampshire coast and on the Isle of Wight, the biggest crowd ever to assemble
for a Schneider race. The breeze, from the south-south-east, dictated
the positioning of the starting vessel, H.M.S. *Medea*, and Orlebar and
Bernasconi went out in a launch from Calshot after an early lunch to
settle the take-off run and the positions their pontoons would take up
beforehand. They decided on a spot at the mouth of Southampton
Water directly opposite Calshot; after taking off on a signal from the
Medea, competitors would head south across the Solent towards Cowes
before swinging left to run down the Isle of Wight coast to the start of
the circuit at Ryde.

The order of starting would be Waghorn, Dal Molin in the M.52R,
D'Arcy Greig in the S.5, Cadringher, Atcherley and Monti, and there
would be a gap of 15 minutes between each individual starting-signal.
This meant that by the time Atcherley took off Waghorn would be
down and his performance would be known; if Waghorn had safely

completed the course, Atcherley could go all out for a fast time. Waghorn's instructions were not to exceed an indicated engine temperature of 95 degrees centigrade; but if he got round successfully, Atcherley would be allowed to risk an engine temperature of 98 degrees. A brilliant flyer who was in great demand at air displays all over the world, Atcherley was confidently expected to break all records. But even he would be inhibited from using full throttle by the risk of excessive fuel consumption.

The Italian tactics were to send their two new machines off last on the principle that, uncertain as they were themselves of their likely performance, their opponents must know even less. They would thus endeavour to turn their lack of knowledge to account. Waghorn and Atcherley, aware that the Italians had exceeded 360 m.p.h. in practice runs and uncertain what they might achieve now, would have to push their new machines pretty well to the limit, and the very presence of the two M.67s might be sufficient to stampede them into trying just that bit too hard, straining their engines or running out of fuel. Dal Molin in the M.52R might then be left to fight it out with D'Arcy Greig in the S.5, and if that happened the Italians believed the modified M.52 would win.

To counteract this obvious danger Orlebar planned to delay Atcherley's start for almost the full 15 minutes that he was allowed. Thus, provided Cadringher went off to time, they would have nearly half an hour in which to assess the M.67's potential and brief Atcherley accordingly. It was a somewhat similar ploy to that practised by Ferrarin at Hampton Roads three years earlier.

Calshot was not one of the officially recommended vantage-points, but the beach, narrowed by the high tide, was packed with people, and they settled down to a grandstand view of one of the most exciting parts of the race—the actual take-off of the machines. They also had a good view of the Cowes turning-point across the water, the sharpest corner of the circuit. By 1.30 the four pontoons had been towed out to the starting-point—one for each of the British machines and a larger one carrying all three Italian entries—and at 1.40 the crew started filling N.247 with hot oil. At 1.50 Lovesey got into the cockpit, and three minutes later he started up, running the engine at full throttle for barely two minutes and being careful not to let it run too slowly from then on. Soon he was replaced by Waghorn, and at 1.59 the pontoon was towed into wind and Orlebar gave the signal to launch.

To Dick Waghorn the day seemed almost too good to be true. The previous day, which had been his birthday, had seemed incomparable, and yet today was unique, the sky of a deep blue rarely seen in England, with visibility amazingly clear. He absorbed all this as he sat in the cockpit on the pontoon. The butterflies in his stomach that had prevented him from eating any lunch had settled, and directly he was launched he pointed the nose of his machine 70 degrees to the right of the wind and began his take-off run.

Using right rudder to keep to the right of the wind, he ran along with the left wing inches from the water; this was the only way to prevent an uncontrollable swing to the left. Up to 30 m.p.h. the cockpit was enveloped in spray, and he kept his head down. Then, clear of the spray as he ran at 40-50 m.p.h. across wind, he began the trickiest manoeuvre of all—getting the plane into wind without letting the nose swing right round. As he applied left rudder the machine began to accelerate rapidly, and as he reached hump speed she came directly into wind. He had judged it nicely, and the machine took up a new position on the water, much lower forward. At 100 m.p.h. Waghorn lifted her off, and after bouncing lightly two or three times he was away. As the machine finally left the water the starting-gun went off.

The spectators at Calshot saw the plane climb steeply, swing off a little towards Cowes, and then sweep down in a dive as it disappeared towards the starting-line. Waghorn was making the most of the opportunity of a flying start. But the groups of shipping that had gathered inside and around the circuit during the morning, and especially immediately behind the destroyers on which the pylons were mounted, presented a confusing picture when viewed from the air. Waghorn located the Seaview turning all right, but the only isolated vessel in the neighbourhood of the turn off Hayling Island proved to be an oil tanker. He had lost the pylon against the background of shipping, and he had strayed off the circuit because of it. Fortunately he had gone outside the circuit not inside, so there was no risk of disqualification, but he had lost valuable time.

The Southsea pylon was clear, and he picked out the Cowes pylon correctly depite a flotilla of destroyers behind it. His temperature gauge was holding steady at 95 degrees, throttle slightly back, and as he flashed past the flags and bunting that bedecked Ryde Pier and punched the first hole in his lap counter he felt more sure of himself. The confusions of the circuit were falling into perspective and he knew that nothing would again be so unnerving as the kaleidoscope of shipping that had bewildered him first time round.

25 (a)   The troublesome Gloster VI. The liner in the background is the Mauretania

25 (b)   The British pilots, 1929. Left to right: Flt. Lt. D. D'Arcy A. Greig, Fg. Off. H. R. Waghorn, and Fg. Off. R. L. R. Atcherley

26 The three machines
which correctly completed
the quadrilateral 1929
course. Top, Waghorn's
S.6; centre, the S.5;
and bottom, the M.52R

27 Waghorn rounding one of the mark-boats during the 1929 race

28 (a)   The Macchi MC.72. This type still holds the world speed
record for propeller floatplanes

28 (b)   The reserve S.6B, 1931—and how Orlebar kept his feet dry

Already the loudspeakers were announcing his lap speed: 324 m.p.h. He had broken all previous speed records, yet his time was slower than anticipated, and the British team heard the figures without elation. With the diving start his circuit speed ought to have been several miles an hour faster. They did not realise how much he had lost through mistaking the distant Hayling Island turn. His second lap, however, showed a marked improvement—329 m.p.h.—and he settled down to some perfect cornering and wonderfully consistent piloting, confirmed by a third lap of 331·1—his best so far, and, as it proved, his best of the race.

By this time Dal Molin had taken off in the M.52R, and Waghorn, coming up to the Cowes turn towards the end of his third lap, was just in time to see the Italian diving for the starting-line. At Seaview he couldn't see him, but at the Hayling Island turn he could make out a speck just ahead, and by the Southsea turn he could see him clearly. The biggest thrill of the race so far came as Waghorn began to overtake him. The chase lasted right along the leg from Southsea to Cowes, with Dal Molin flattened on the water and Waghorn above him at 200 feet. Rounding the Cowes pylon the Italian was still a hundred yards ahead, but as they raced into the straight towards Ryde Waghorn tore past the Macchi and completed his fourth circuit before Dal Molin completed his first. The Macchi's speed for this lap, however, was 286 m.p.h., five miles an hour better than Webster's in the S.5 at Venice, so it looked as though Dal Molin might outpace Greig. But this could have only minor significance unless Waghorn faltered, and there was no sign of his doing so. His fourth lap was completed at 328 m.p.h. and his fifth at just under 330.

For Waghorn everything was going according to plan. The air in his cockpit was hot, but a stream of fresh air from a specially fitted ventilating pipe was cooling his face. The engine temperature was steady at 95 and he was still slightly throttled back, conserving his fuel. He was holding his height at 200 feet, which gave him a clear view of the course ahead.

Six times Waghorn pierced the lap counter as he passed Ryde Pier; now he headed for the Seaview turn for the last time. He knew he had flown a good race and given the Italians something to beat, and there was still Atcherley to come. But as he turned at Seaview and aimed for the pylon off Hayling Island his engine momentarily cut right out. It picked up at once but it gave him a horrible fright.

Seconds later the engine started missing badly and he knew that something was seriously wrong. He could hardly believe it, as he had followed his instructions punctiliously, but the symptoms suggested fuel starvation. He knew his margin was narrow, but it was surely not as critical as that. He pulled up to six, seven, eight hundred feet; perhaps if the engine cut out altogether he would be able to glide to the finish. He rounded the Hayling Island pylon, but the long straight from Southsea to Cowes seemed interminable, with the engine sputtering and only taking about half throttle all the way. Somehow he got to the Cowes turn, and ahead of him lay the final straight into the finish; but as he came round the pylon his engine stopped completely and he was forced to put down off Old Castle Point.

Shock, bewilderment, chagrin, despair—for the next few minutes Waghorn suffered all the agonies of self-condemnation and self-disgust. He would have been even more dejected, if that were possible, had he known that D'Arcy Greig had just completed his first lap at 284 m.p.h., two miles an hour slower than Dal Molin. Greig was flying the S.5 absolutely flat out but it wasn't going to be good enough.

Would the Rolls engineers ever believe that he had obeyed their instructions? Wouldn't they conclude that he had pushed the engine too hard? He knew how accurate their calculations had always been, and he was certain that the fault, if fault there was, must be his. He was still slumped miserably in the cockpit, dreading the inquest that he knew must follow, when the motor launch drew up alongside.

He couldn't understand their reaction. They were waving at him excitedly, full of animation and enthusiasm. What could have happened? Then from their shouted quips and chiding queries he knew. Like Webster at Venice he had become confused in his lap counting. He had been flying an extra lap!

Another man who had missed the first elation of Waghorn's successful flight was Lovesey. Exhausted by his efforts in the previous 48 hours, he had gone to sleep on one of the pontoons and would have fallen into the water but for the timely intervention of Orlebar.

Waghorn's average for the seven completed laps was 328·63 m.p.h. He had done exactly what had been expected of him, and he was towed back to Calshot in triumph. Meanwhile interest centred on the battle between the two old warhorses the M.52R and the S.5. With the new record set up by Waghorn this struggle lay principally in the realms of sentiment, but it was bitterly fought nevertheless. Neither Dal Molin nor Greig knew for certain whether Waghorn had finished, and both flew lap after lap at full throttle. The Italian's lap speeds were 286,

287, 285, 283, 283, 283, 282, and although Greig's were equally consistent he was still two miles an hour behind at the finish.

While these two machines were still in the circuit, the spotlight was turned on Italy's main challenge, opened up by Cadringher in the first Macchi 67. This was the decisive moment of the race. The speed of the new Macchis, uncorroborated as yet, was about to be revealed.

No one would have guessed, from Cadringher's take-off, that this was only his second flight in the machine. He crossed the Solent, turned east of Cowes, and sped down towards Ryde. Flattening low on the water, lower even than Dal Molin, who was still in the circuit ahead of him, he flashed across the starting-line, his engine exuding smoke and giving out a shrill, menacing scream.

Rounding the Hayling Island pylon Cadringher was just about the same distance behind Dal Molin as Waghorn had been when he overtook him near the end of his fourth lap; thus the long straight from Southsea to Cowes would afford spectators a thrilling comparison. Away went Dal Molin with Cadringher after him, but along the Hampshire coast the gap between the two machines hardly seemed to narrow, and coming round the Cowes mark boat Dal Molin was holding his lead. When Cadringher got to the turn he seemed to overshoot and swing wide, and for a time he was actually flying inland.

Cadringher was suffering from the old trouble in the M.67: exhaust fumes. The rotation of the propeller directed the smoke emitted by the stubby exhaust pipes into the windscreen on every turn to port, and on this left-hand circuit Cadringher was being continually half-blinded and half suffocated, despite the special ventilating tubes. This and a reduction in engine revolutions of 400 per minute which had been forced on the Italians by mechanical troubles accounted for a disappointing circuit speed of 284 m.p.h. Cadringher couldn't see the pylons, and soon he turned across the quadrilateral and alighted. The first of the new Macchis was out of the race.

For a short time Greig had the circuit to himself; and then, just as he was finishing, Atcherley began his take-off run in the second S.6. Whether Waghorn's time would be good enough to beat Monti remained uncertain, and it was up to Atcherley to improve on Waghorn's record and put Monti under as much pressure as possible.

By this time the wind had freshened and the surface was roughened by a considerable swell. Atcherley followed exactly the same take-off drill as Waghorn had done, but because of the changed conditions he began to porpoise badly. His goggles were showered with oily water, rendering them almost opaque, and as he fought to regain control he pushed them momentarily up over his forehead. Immediately he did so the force of the slipstream tore them off.

From this point on Atcherley had to keep his head well inside the cockpit, and this hampered his view. He completed the take-off safely, but approaching the starting-line he was over land, and in seeking a better line he ran dangerously close to the Seaview pylon. His time for his first lap reflected his haphazard course at the start; he was round in 6 minutes 9 seconds against Waghorn's first lap of 5'45". But as he adjusted himself to his sighting difficulties his lap speeds improved. 325 for his second lap was followed by 330 and then 332, the best lap of the race so far. Meanwhile the final drama was evolving as Monti took off in the second Macchi 67 and zoomed up higher than any of the previous competitors before diving for the starting-line.

Crossing the line right over the top of the pier pavilion, Monti entered the circuit just ahead of Atcherley and hurtled round the Seaview pylon and out towards the Hayling Island turn. Along the Hampshire coast he flew lower over the water than anyone, and he seemed to be going faster than Atcherley, who was tucked in behind him about 150 feet higher. They swept round the Cowes turn one after the other with Atcherley making the sharper turn, and then, flying a more southerly course than their predecessors, they crossed the pier well behind the pavilion. Monti's time, however, was disappointing, his greater speed an illusion born of his daring low flying. His lap time was 6 minutes 11 seconds. But Atcherley, too, had had a difficult first lap, and now he was breaking all records and threatening to overhaul Waghorn. Could Monti perhaps do the same?

The question was soon answered. Like Cadringher, Monti had been handicapped by fumes and a smoked-up windscreen, plus a similar drop in engine revolutions, and now, as he made for the Seaview turn, a broken water-joint spurted clouds of steam and a jet of boiling water over his arms and legs. Badly scalded, he managed to put the Macchi down safely; but the Italian challenge was over.

Atcherley's speed for his fifth lap had fallen to 328 m.p.h., but he finished strongly in 331 and 332. His overall average of 325·54 was not quite so good as Waghorn's, but he had set up new records over 50 and 100 kilometres and finished second in the race. There was, however, one final sensation to come. The judges ruled that Atcherley had passed inside the Seaview turn on his opening lap, and they announced his disqualification. His 50 and 100 kilometre records stood, but he forfeited second place to Dal Molin. Waghorn, though, was confirmed as the winner.

The minds of the entire British team went back to that climactic moment the previous evening when the speck of swarf was discovered on one of the plugs of Waghorn's machine. It had looked impossible then to locate the trouble and repair the engine in time. Indeed it would have been impossible but for the fortuitous presence in Southampton of the entire experimental team. Had they driven down from Derby on the morning of the race, as they easily might have done, the old Macchi 52R, so beautifully flown by Dal Molin, would have won the race for Italy.

Supermarines, Rolls-Royce, the fuel and oil companies, the instrument makers, the sparking plug manufacturers, the makers of many other aids and accessories, cashed in on the victory with big advertisement campaigns, but no one cared to reveal the debt that was owed to a certain popular sealing compound. After one fairly generous dose of Johnson's Neverleak there had been no more trouble with the radiators.

For the Italians the victory that had so nearly come their way had been too much even to hope for, and the dispiriting effect of many months of abortive effort were plain in Bernasconi's reaction to the question whether Italy would compete next time. "I don't know if we want a next time," he said. "The cost of taking part in this contest is simply staggering." General Balbo was less disillusioned. "We have obtained the results we expected," he said at the subsequent banquet, "but we have now finished playing our part as sportsmen. Tomorrow our work as competitors will begin."

Ramsay MacDonald, Prime Minister of Britain's new Labour government, although not officially on the toast list, finally responded to insistent demands for a speech. After paying a warm tribute to the spirit of the Italians in making a race of it, he too cast his thoughts forward to the next contest. "We are going to do our level best", he said, "to win again."

1931

at Calshot

"I can see nothing of value in it."

Marshal of the Royal Air Force Sir Hugh Trenchard

Hugh Trenchard relinquished his post as Chief of the British Air Staff at the end of 1929; and one of his last acts was to re-establish his earlier stand against the involvement of the R.A.F. in air racing. "I am frankly against this contest," he minuted the Secretary of State for Air on 10th September 1929, three days after Britain's victory at Calshot. "I can see nothing of value in it." High-speed machines, he said, would continue to be developed under scientific and research programmes, but the expense of the Schneider contest was out of all proportion to its value. The contest was bad from the Service viewpoint, bad from the viewpoint of efficiency, and bad for R.A.F. morale as a whole. But he did not explain why this should be so. The Air Member for Supply and Research, now Air Vice-Marshal Sir John Higgins, perhaps aware of this weakness, added a note on the preoccupation of his technical staff with the Schneider machines for months before each contest, and the minute was sent.

Having pressed the case for R.A.F. participation in 1927 on the basis of the material advantages that would accrue, Trenchard was excusing withdrawal chiefly on the grounds that the expenditure could no longer be justified by the rewards. This exactly paralleled the American disengagement of 1926-27. What was more difficult to explain was how a government department which had taken its original stand on the certain failure of private enterprise could now abandon the contest to that hitherto despised agency.

Flexibility, however—the changing of one's mind—had long been a convenient military canon; and the government needed little persuading. There was a growing realisation in both Britain and Italy that the burden even of a biennial contest was becoming excessive. Add to this the financial crisis in America, which was already aggravating Europe's own economic troubles, and the government's attitude looked logical and sensible and not inconsistent with that of its predecessor.

It had taken all the Air Council's powers of persuasion to enlist the support of the Conservative government in 1927, and the debt of hospitality had been fully discharged in 1929.

The final decision was taken at a Cabinet meeting on 25th September, and five days later the news was published in the form of an Air Ministry statement. A Royal Air Force team, it said, would not again be entered, leaving British participation to private enterprise under the auspices of the Royal Aero Club. Two main considerations had influenced the decision: first, government participation had given the contest a character out of tune with the intentions of the original donor, and second, although a much-needed impetus to development had been given by the entry of an R.A.F. team in the last two contests, sufficient data had been collected and the large expenditure of public money was no longer justifiable.

The British government thus followed the American example; but no American plane had got to the starting-line since that decision was taken, and in any case there was no guarantee that other countries would follow Britain's lead. Indeed by March 1930 the Air Ministry were well aware that both France and Italy were preparing, with government backing, for the next contest. So the 'gesture' ingredient of the policy had signally failed. A private backer for an American entry had also come forward, and Al Williams, due for a seagoing appointment, resigned his commission rather than miss the chance of competing.

Vickers-Supermarine and Rolls-Royce began discussions on the possibility of defending the trophy themselves at an early stage, and in March 1930 Supermarines wrote to the Air Ministry to say that they had set themselves the task of attaining another 25 m.p.h. round the course; would the development running required to produce the necessary increase in horse-power be acceptable as a normal charge against engine development? Supermarines made it clear that their plans were based on the assumption that the two existing S.6s would be loaned back to them for conversion and rebuilding for the race, and that pilots of the high-speed flight would be loaned to fly them, provided both machines and men were covered by insurance. The government's attitude, however, based on Air Ministry advice and expressed in answer to questions in the House of Commons that month, was that it would not be possible to lend either machines or pilots; the Air Council feared that such assistance might involve them still further. Taunted with the paradox of a Socialist government relying on private enterprise, the government held their ground. The Tories, in urging the State to assume full responsibility, were in no less paradoxical a position.

Trenchard, however, had now retired, and the attitude at the Air Ministry was rather less rigid. The development costs of the 'R' engine, it was thought, could probably be accepted, and the new Chief of the Air Staff, Sir John Salmond, was preserving an open mind about lending the S.6s. This meant a definite change of policy, which was subsequently endorsed by the government. Thus on 8th April 1930 the Air Ministry were able to agree to stand the cost of the engine development, and to lend the two S.6s, provided the cost of insurance and modifications was borne by private enterprise and provided the machines were returned after the race. R.A.F. pilots, however, would not be allowed to fly them, not even when on leave.

The Air Ministry were gradually getting themselves into much the same position as in 1925; by helping a private entry they would automatically bear some of the responsibility for failure. But the concessions granted were not enough. Insurance cover for competitive high-speed flying proved unobtainable, and long before the end of 1930 it had become apparent to both the Air Ministry and the Royal Aero Club that raising a worthwhile private entry for the 1931 contest, for reasons of finance, organisation and the training of pilots, was going to be a well-nigh impossible task.

Throughout the year a quarrel had been raging between the Royal Aero Club on the one hand and the Italian and French aero clubs on the other over the question of the sum to be deposited on entry. Britain, charged under the regulations with the responsibility for organising the race, was determined to protect herself from frivolous entries and last-minute withdrawals by increasing the forfeit, and to this end she proposed, at the F.A.I. conference in January 1930, that the guarantee per machine be increased to 200,000 fr. (about £1,600) and that the final entry date for the 1931 contest be brought forward to 31st July. The F.A.I. passed the first of these proposals but left a decision on the closing date for entries to the general conference in June. Another proposal passed at this meeting was that the watertightness and navigability tests should be replaced by a taking-off and alighting test to be carried out immediately prior to the race; this was principally designed to shorten the contest and take full advantage of a day's good weather.

The general conference of June 1930, apparently ignorant of the

reasons behind the decision taken in January, and under pressure from
Italy and France, ruled that the forfeit per machine be limited to
5,000 fr. (£50) provided entry was made by 31st July. This un-
constitutional decision was a complete *non sequitur*, but it was naturally
followed by three entries each on behalf of Italy and France at the
reduced rate. The Royal Aero Club, rightly regarding the January
ruling as irrevocable, refused to accept these entries, returning them to
the clubs concerned. Italy, accusing Britain of flouting the authority of
the F.A.I., then addressed her entries to the F.A.I. itself, offering at
the same time to organise the next contest in Italy without extracting
any forfeit for withdrawal of entries. This would have saved them
money, and they were not enamoured of the Solent anyway. In this
seeming impasse France eventually adopted the role of mediator, and
on 29th November a meeting of the international sporting commission
of the F.A.I. confirmed the January decision and set the final date of
entry as 31st December, a ruling that was accepted by all parties. It
was a satisfactory outcome for Britain, but the uncertainty of the previous months had been a powerful hindrance to progress, and the end
of 1930 approached with Britain not much further forward then when it
began.

The evident determination of Italy and France to enter the contest
and to build new machines meant that Britain must build afresh too;
and on 8th December a sub-committee of the Royal Aero Club estimated that the cost now involved, assuming the building of two new
machines with the necessary engines, was about £100,000. An earlier
estimate made by the Air Ministry had put the figure at not less than
£80,000. Could such a sum be raised by public subscription? Public
opinion, as ventilated in the Press, appeared to be strongly in favour of
an attempt to secure the trophy, but there was the danger that the
newspapers were using the situation as a stick to beat an unpopular
government with, and in any case £100,000 was a lot of money to
raise. When at the end of December the entries of Italy and France
were finally confirmed (no entry was received from America, Al
Williams's plans having again foundered), the Royal Aero Club made
strong representations to the Air Ministry for a reversal of the earlier
government decision.

All they got was bleak and absolute rejection. "The Government has
decided", said an Air Ministry statement of 15th January 1931, "that
in the present financial situation the expenditure of public money involved (not less than £80,000 if a Royal Air Force team were

organised) is not justified, and that their previous decision must be strictly adhered to; the defence of the trophy and all incidental expenditure must be left to the Royal Aero Club and private enterprise, and the Government should not give any assistance either direct or indirect, whether by the loan of pilots, aircraft, or other material, by the organisation of the race, the policing of the course, or in any other way." This was worse than going back to square one.

The committee of the Royal Aero Club met on 19th January to consider what further action they could take, and next day, suspecting perhaps that it was the shadow of Trenchard they were fighting as much as the government, they approached Lord Amulree, the Air Minister, personally and asked whether, if £80,000 were raised privately, the government would then undertake to defend the trophy. Lord Amulree consulted the Cabinet that evening, and the answer he got was that even in that case the government would do nothing. The bitterest opponent was Philip Snowden, Chancellor of the Exchequer, who went beyond his brief by demanding that the government take immediate action to "put an end to this pernicious form of rivalry" by approaching other governments to get them to abandon the race as well. All that emerged in the House, however, was that the government, their financial objections cut from under them, were falling back on the "reasons of policy and principle" that had been forgotten when the Air Ministry statement was made six days earlier.

The government were now subjected to a bitter and persistent attack in the Press and in Parliament, and through every available medium. Their refusal of support was castigated as a "major government blunder", and they were vilified as pacifist, defeatist, unenterprising, even anti-British. "When I went to the Air Ministry in 1922," wrote Sir Samuel Hoare in a letter to *The Times*, "the British aircraft industry was almost at its last gasp. Now, when every other industry is passing through a period of unprecedented depression, the export of our aircraft to foreign countries, already to be valued in many millions, is steadily rising. This change I mainly assign to the reputation that we have won for ourselves in foreign markets, and that we should not have won to the same degree without the resounding victories in the Schneider Cup race." Meanwhile the Society of British Aircraft Constructors was sending a circular letter to every Member of Parliament urging participation—and they backed up their appeal with a promise of £10,500 towards the expense of competing. It was their experience, they said, that "the British victories in the last two contests have given to British aviation and technique, both in aircraft and engines, a prestige in the minds of foreign buyers of aircraft that probably could not have been attained in any other way". To lose the trophy by default, they claimed, would be a serious blow to Britain's export trade. The London Chamber of Commerce weighed in with a circular to Members of Parliament in similar vein; and on the question of policy and principle the government were asked why, since the Italian and French entries had full State support, the British should hold themselves above other governments in this regard. Even the foreign Press was critical, one Italian newspaper describing official British attempts at self-justification as "quite puerile". The race, they said, had maintained its sporting character; it had encouraged a healthy and laudable rivalry; and it had technical and industrial importance.

On 26th January Ramsay MacDonald re-stated the government's position in the House. He complained of the failure of the Royal Aero Club to make their position clear many months earlier, and he pointed out that even now there was no guarantee that the necessary funds could be raised. In all the circumstances, he said, the government could find no justification for reversing their previous decision. So the door seemed finally shut. Asked to receive a deputation, however, the Prime Minister, with characteristic ambivalence, faltered. He wished he had been sent a deputation six months ago; but he would be glad to receive one now if any good could be done by such a course.

To the Royal Aero Club and the Air Council alike, this looked like the thin end of the wedge. One was hopeful, the other apprehensive. The government's attitude, urged the Air Council, should be absolutely rigid, and if any concession had to be made for political reasons it should be confined to the loan of existing machines. In any case it was now so late that the prospects of victory were greatly reduced, and it would be better for the Royal Aero Club to bear the odium of defeat than the R.A.F.

Although one or two newspapers got very near the truth, the Air Council's attitude was not known to the public, so they were also escaping the odium of popular disapproval. Few people realised that the R.A.F. chiefs fully endorsed the government's persistent refusals, and stories of Air Council recalcitrance, and of internal R.A.F. jealousies and discord over selection, were laughed out of court.

On Tuesday evening 27th January MacDonald received a deputation consisting of five Members of Parliament, led by Commander O. Locker-Lampson, who had asked for the meeting, and Sir Philip

Sassoon, Chairman of the Royal Aero Club. In refuting the charge of dilatoriness, Sassoon pointed out that the quarrel over the entry guarantees had lasted throughout 1930 and that until a valid challenge was received little progress could be made; nevertheless the engine and airframe manufacturers had laid tentative plans. The Prime Minister asked the deputation not to press for a final decision then, but he agreed to reconsider the matter, and he promised that if a question was asked in the House on 29th January he would make a statement.

The Royal Aero Club had so far received promises of financial support totalling £22,000, which was a long way short of the target. But while MacDonald was reviewing his position he received a telegram which seemed likely to settle the financial question once and for all. "To prevent the Socialist Government being spoilsports," it read, "Lady Houston will be responsible for all extra expenses necessary beyond what Sir Philip Sassoon says can be found, so that Great Britain can take part in the race for the Schneider Trophy." The signature was that of Lucy Houston.

At a Cabinet meeting on the morning of 28th January, J. H. Thomas and Lord Amulree were detailed to leave at once for the Air Ministry to take part in a consultation with representatives of Vickers-Supermarine and Rolls-Royce; also attending was the Chief of the Air Staff, who had arranged the meeting. The questions to which the government needed the answers were: was it possible to provide the machines; did Britain still have a chance of winning; and what would be the effect on the aircraft industry, according to whether Britain won or lost? The answers given by the manufacturers were that, if Britain surrendered its chance of victory, large orders for the reconditioning of machines abroad which Britain might otherwise have expected to receive would be lost, most probably to Italy, who were already a serious competitor; they believed that the industry was as well prepared as in 1929; and they thought there was a good sporting chance of victory. The representatives of the construction firms were then asked to withdraw, and the ministers pressed Sir John Salmond for his personal opinion. "On balance," said Salmond, "I'm bound to come to the view that Britain ought to take part in the race." Thus, after all the long months of repudiations, the final affirmative was spoken by the R.A.F.[1]

Next day, 29th January, MacDonald made his promised statement in the House. There was, he still maintained, no certainty that the funds could be raised; but "although the government are strongly

[1] Cabinet Papers.

averse from perpetuating these contests between rival government teams, they are so interested in the race that they are prepared under the circumstances once again to authorise the defence of the trophy by the Royal Air Force, and the provision of assistance as in 1929, provided that a definite undertaking is given immediately that the necessary funds will be made available from private sources." It was a resounding victory for Press and public opinion, in which the Royal Aero Club had played a notable part.

Lucy Houston, eccentric widow of a millionaire shipping magnate, had meanwhile been in touch with the Royal Aero Club, and the guarantee sought by MacDonald was forthcoming next day. "The supremacy of English airmen can only be upheld by their entrance for the Schneider Trophy," she cabled MacDonald, "and as I consider this of supreme importance and to show that I am not to be daunted I will guarantee the whole amount one hundred thousand pounds that you consider necessary and I know I can confidently rely on the kindly help and co-operation of all who will rejoice if England wins." There were disparaging inferences to be drawn even from this, but MacDonald refused to take offence. He acknowledged the message gratefully, and passed the offer on to the Royal Aero Club.

The Socialist government's alleged lack of patriotism, enterprise and imagination, and Lady Houston's public-spirited gesture of defiance, have become fabled. But the truth is that although, as Snowden's outburst shows, some members of the Cabinet were emotionally opposed to any form of international competition, on the advice they were receiving, and with the economic crisis that was developing, the government were acting logically, while Lucy Houston was doing the right thing for the wrong reasons, even if her heart was in the right place. She had all the strengths and weaknesses of the diehard jingoistic Tory, and although one need not doubt her patriotism, she hated the Socialists and rejoiced in the chance to snub them with her money. This is the text of a message she sent at the time to the Press Association:

"When the Socialist Government gave the paltry excuse that they could not afford the expenses necessary for England's airmen to participate in the race for the Schneider Trophy, my blood boiled with indignation, for I know that every true Briton would rather sell his last shirt than admit that England could not afford to defend herself before all comers.

"I am proud to say I inherit the spirit of my forefathers, who considered one Englishman equal to any three foreigners, but this Government is trying to instil into us the poisonous doctrine that we are a third-rate Power, and doing their best to make us so.

"England has always been first in peace, first in war, first in courage and first in beauty. Are we now going to take a back seat? No, most emphatically, no. We are not worms to be trampled under the heel of Socialism, but true Britons, with a heart for any fate, except the slavery of Socialism."

There was much more from her in the newspapers in this vein.

To their eternal credit the government stood all this and much other calumny and abuse without ever seeking to blame their air advisers. Yet these air advisers, from Trenchard down, never came forward to defend the government, not even in after years.

*   *   *

"The contest is only postponed." That had been General Balbo's theme at the 1929 banquet, and the Italians soon got to work to turn their rhetoric into reality. On 22nd October 1929 a meeting was held under the aegis of the Italian government with Colonel Bernasconi, captain of the 1929 team, in the chair, at which plans were discussed with leading Italian engineers for the construction of new machines for the 1931 contest. But meanwhile an investigation ordered by Balbo into the failures of 1929 had concluded that the distribution of work amongst several companies had been a mistake; resources were scattered and the benefit of past experience was not made available to all. Thus Fiats and Savoia-Marchetti had both chosen design solutions which Macchis had already found impracticable. It was clear that a project combining Macchi airframe and Fiat engine was the only viable one, and after the frustrations of 1929 both companies were keen to work together again. Fiats put up a project for a new engine with contra-rotating propellers, and this idea was at once fastened on by Castoldi, who had asked for windtunnel experiments of this type of propulsion as far back as 1921. The advantages lay in the vast improvement that would result in gyroscopic balance (cancelling out the torque problem on take-off and in the turns), and in the absorption of power.

Of the four types of machine prepared for 1929, further development of the Piaggio-Pegna was abandoned after a discouraging series of tests, and the history of the Fiat C.29, too, resulted in its discontinuance. The second machine never flew. The Savoia-Marchetti 65 was persevered with; but during an attempt on the world speed record on 18th January 1930 it crashed into Lake Garda, killing the only successful Schneider pilot still in training at Desenzano, Dal Molin. He had reputedly been overcome by fumes. That left only the Macchi 67, and a reversion to the policy of putting all their eggs into one basket, as in 1926-27, was more or less forced on the Italians.

It was inevitable that Castoldi should seek to improve on his 1929 design, and the revolutionary new Fiat engine gave him full scope. Wings and tailplane of his new machine, labelled Macchi-Castoldi 72, were similar to the M.67, but the fuselage had to be longer to accommodate the new supercharged A.S.6 engine, and the stubby cigar-shape of earlier Macchi-Castoldi designs disappeared altogether.[1] The whole of the wing, which was made of duralumin, was covered with flat tube radiators to help solve the cooling problem, and the forward and centre portions of the fuselage were also metal, wood being used only for the tail. The supercession of the three-banked Isotta-Fraschini allowed a considerable reduction in frontal area.

A second course for high-speed pilots under Mario Bernasconi was started at Desenzano; ten new pilots were posted in, and of the survivors of the 1929 team Monti and Agello elected to stay on. Most of the training in 1930 and the first half of 1931 was done on the old Macchi 52.

The revolutionary nature of the new engine design inevitably brought unforeseen problems, and although the Italians were determined to compete if at all possible, they could hardly afford to risk the public indignities of breakdown and failure a second time. Thus General Balbo, during the presentation of the air estimates in the Italian Chamber on 29th April 1931, cast the first doubts on Italian participation. "At the present stage of things I cannot affirm with certainty that we shall take part this year," he said. "We mean first of all to make sure of our preparation." The efficiency of the pilots could be counted on, he said, but this time the machines would have to pass searching tests before being sent to England. "I know the discouraging difficulties the industrialists have to overcome," continued Balbo, and

---

[1] The A.S.6., designed again by Tranquillo Zerbi, was virtually two 12-cylinder V-type 1,500 h.p. engines bolted back to back, the crankshaft of each engine being connected to the reduction gear, from which two airscrew shafts, one inside the other, ran forward to the airscrews within the vee of the front group of cylinders. The cylinders themselves, of pure steel, were independent of each other and easily replaced. The engine was designed as a single unit with a single induction system, but the only mechanical connection between the two separate banks was the throttle lever.

he made special reference to the engines. Balbo expounded the enlightened view, remarkable under a Fascist dictatorship, that the contest called for the development of a sporting sense capable of accepting defeat with a good grace and without taking the consequences too tragically. But with France also competing, Italy would only take part if she were sure of doing well.

The first MC.72 arrived at Desenzano in June 1931, and the pilot chosen for the initial tests was Giovanni Monti. The take-off, shorn of the torque problem, was perfect, but the plane flew for no more than two minutes before faulty carburation forced Monti to alight. Further flights disclosed a functional carburettor defect which was especially troublesome approaching full power, when there was danger of backfiring. Even so, speeds of up to 375 m.p.h. were registered, though the engine was often running irregularly, there were cooling problems, and the propellers were rarely rotating in phase.

At the end of July notification was received in London that the Italian advance party would arrive at Calshot on 12th August and the main contingent, with the new racers, on the 26th, so Italian intentions seemed firm. But on 2nd August the Italian plans were thrown into tragic disarray. Captain Monti, throttling down after take-off and aiming to overfly the base at Desenzano so as to demonstrate the erratic behaviour of the engine carburation for those on the ground, crashed into the lake. "I saw the aircraft pitch up slightly, then nose downwards, spin for a quarter of a turn, and then dive into the water," wrote Muzio Macchi recently.[1] An investigation was carried out by the Italian Air Force, and afterwards Muzio Macchi asked Colonel Bernasconi the result. He was told that the two contra-rotating propellers had touched following a bearing failure. "I was not entirely convinced", he says, "by this theory."

For the moment the Italian plans remained unchanged; but there were reminders that the decision promised by Balbo in his speech of 29th April had not yet been finally made. The Italians might still withdraw, and indeed by mid-August there were persistent rumours that they intended to do so. The four remaining pilots chosen for the team— Lieutenants Stanislao Bellini, Ariosto Neri and Pietro Scapinelli, and Warrant Officer Agello—were flying the second MC.72, and a third machine was being prepared, but Balbo was insisting on personally witnessing further trials before making up his mind.

Balbo's visit to Desenzano was arranged for 20th August, but the

[1] From Signor Macchi's answers to the author's questionnaire.

weather closed in and his visit was cancelled, and it was not until the
23rd that he could be sent for and trials proceeded with. Neri was at the
controls, and everything seems to have gone well, but many more tests
were needed, and further flights were planned for the following day
with an alternative pilot in the cockpit. Again the weather clamped,
and Balbo's decision was postponed from day to day. The only firm
news in this period came on 28th August, when it was reported that
fishermen on Lake Garda had recovered the body of Giovanni Monti.

* * *

After their failure to make good their entry for the 1929 contest, the
French continued their preparations with the 1931 race in mind.
Criticism of the government and aircraft industry for its failure to keep
pace with other European nations intensified, and a diagnosis of
fragmentation resulted early in 1930 in the uniting of the stronger
firms under government pressure into two separate inter-dependent
groups. The policy remained to enter the Schneider contest and to
attack the world speed record, but it was realised that the gap in
practical experience and expertise resulting from the years of non-
participation would be even more difficult to bridge.

Provisional orders for new machines were again placed by the French
Air Ministry with the Bernard and Nieuport companies, and the
Dewoitine company, founded in 1922 for the construction of metal aircraft, also received a provisional order for two machines. The new
designs were all planned in the orthodox low-wing wire-braced monoplane style, nothing revolutionary being attempted, but speeds in the
region of 390-400 m.p.h. were hoped for. Testing of the 1929 machines,
which would now be used for training, was to go forward. The 1931
machines were to be designed around new engines built by Lorraine,
Renault and Farman; the Hispano-Suiza engines already ordered
would power the 1929 machines when these were ready.[1] Pending the
final executive decisions, however, none of these new orders was confirmed.

The Hourtin base remained at the disposal of the constructors for
trials, and on 15th November 1929 Antoine Paillard, who had succeeded Bonnet as chief test pilot to the Bernard company, flew the
stop-gap 1929 machine fitted with the boosted Hispano-Suiza engine

[1] Both the Lorraine and the Renault engines were planned as 12-cylinder
V-types of an exceptionally low weight-power ratio, each expected to develop
about 2,300 h.p.; the Farman was to be an 18-cylinder T.

H

for the first time. This plane, intended for use as a training machine, was designated HV.41. Further development of these 1929 types, however (HV.40, HV.41 and HV.42), was diverted into another stop-gap machine, the Bernard HV.120, which was almost identical to the HV.42 except that its dimensions varied slightly and it employed wing surface radiators instead of the external type. This machine, produced as an interim measure while the design of the new 1931 type went forward, was powered by the long-awaited 18-cylinder Hispano-Suiza, and the first flights were successfully completed by Paillard at Hourtin in March 1930.

Nieuport-Delage were not so far advanced, and all the 1931 machines were still on the drawing-board. Indeed the final order for both airframes and engines was delayed until December 1930. French procrastination over the entry fees very probably contributed to this delay, and confirmation of the French entries was actually left until the last possible day, 31st December 1930; but immediately afterwards they announced the appointment of three pilots to form and train a high-speed flight.

Under the leadership of Captain Amanrich, twelve pilots from the fighter units of the Armée de l'Air were selected for preliminary training, all of whom would be flying seaplanes for the first time. By mid-February the flight had been established at Étang de Berre, a lagoon on the Côte d'Azur near Marseilles, where it was expected that the weather would be better than at Hourtin and the water surface smoother, despite the mistral. The contest machines were not expected to be ready before the summer, and for several months the only fast seaplane available at Berre was the HV.41. The Bernard 120, powered by a geared Hispano-Suiza 1,500 h.p. engine, was still undergoing tests in the hands of Antoine Paillard, and a second Bernard 120, fitted with a direct-drive engine, was not yet ready for testing. Flight tests of the 1929-type Nieuport-Delage, designated ND 450, had meanwhile begun at Hourtin under Sadi Lecointe.

At this vital stage in the preparations test pilot Antoine Paillard fell ill. His precise, accurate observations were greatly valued by the Bernard company, and there was no one immediately available to replace him. On 15th June he died of peritonitis at the age of 34; but this setback was followed by a denial by the secretary of the French Aero Club that France was about to withdraw. She was doing her best, he said, to be ready, though successful preparations would obviously form an essential prerequisite to entry.

Paillard was eventually replaced, and by July most of the pilots at Berre had flown one or other of the Bernard 120s. By this time it was apparent that French representation at Calshot would almost certainly be confined to the re-vamped machines originally intended for 1929, and since these machines had a top speed of not more than about 320 m.p.h. it was decided to modify them by reducing the wing area, sacrificing control and safety for speed. The second Bernard 120 was therefore returned to the makers, but tests continued with the first machine in the hands of Lieutenant de Vaisseau Bougault, a well-known long-distance flyer and one of the best qualified pilots in the flight.

One of the most intractable problems with the Bernard 120, as with nearly all high-speed machines of the era, stemmed from the lack of a variable pitch propeller. Several propellers of different diameter were tried, with various pitch settings, but the combination of sufficient power at take-off with a high rate of efficiency at speed proved elusive. Increasing the propeller diameter only aggravated the problem, as the spray set up by the bow-wave damaged the blades. A three-bladed metal propeller was tried, but this too proved unsatisfactory.

There was another serious setback on 24th July when the first ND 450, having been returned to the makers for overhaul, crashed into the Seine. The pilot, Fernand Lasne, escaped serious injury, but the plane would need rebuilding. And six days later, on 30th July, came tragedy. The geared Bernard 120 crashed into the lagoon at Berre during trials and the pilot, Lieutenant Bougault, was killed. Reports said that the propeller, presumably damaged on take-off, had broken up in the air; another report blamed a fractured engine casing. But the conclusion of the official commission of enquiry set up after the accident was that a plug had worked loose and penetrated the windscreen, killing the pilot. Bougault's death was an especially severe blow as he was the only Service pilot fully competent to fly the type, geared or ungeared.

Not surprisingly, this incident infected the high-speed flight with an atmosphere of pessimism and gloom. Trials at Berre were suspended, and the long training programme seemed likely to prove completely abortive. The second ND 450 had not yet been tested by Sadi Lecointe, and with Paillard and Bougault dead there was no one to fly the modified Bernard 120 in the race. Although this machine in its original form had completed 27 flights without mishap, its wings were being shortened by three feet, and this would make it more difficult to fly. The wing area of the surviving Nieuport-Delage was also being reduced, and its wing loading would be correspondingly increased. In the time available the only pilots with any chance of becoming proficient on these modified machines were the test pilots themselves.

Throughout 1931 it had been rumoured that Sadi Lecointe, a veteran of 40 whose pilot's licence antedated that of Maurice Prévost, would fly the Nieuport-Delage at Calshot. This rumour had been emphatically denied, and indeed while the high-speed flight was in full training at Berre it probably had no substance. Now it stood out as the only hope. Another well-known French aviator, Jean Assolant, came forward to volunteer to take over the flight testing of the second Bernard 120 and to fly it in the actual race, and thus it was that despite the long period of training of Service fighter pilots at Berre, two civilian pilots were nominated to fly the French entries at Calshot.

On 9th August the French Air Minister, now M. J. L. Dumesnil, after visiting the seaplane base at Étang de Berre to see the situation for himself, said he would decide within the next few days whether or not France would compete. The only machine at Berre with any chance of taking part was the direct-drive Bernard 120, the Nieuport being still at Hourtin in the Gironde. Neither of these modified machines had yet been flown. It seemed improbable that France would take part, but transport arrangements were put back to allow a later departure date and a final decision was postponed from day to day. The news from Rome was equally discouraging, but speculation as to what competition Britain would have to face kept public interest titillated.

Further airscrew problems dogged the Bernard 120, though Jean Assolant eventually made several promising high-speed runs at Étang de Berre; but the machine had not yet undergone the kind of stamina test it would need to prove its fitness for the Schneider. And at Hourtin, Sadi Lecointe was experiencing similar thrust problems with the Nieuport-Delage. It was not until the last days of August that he hauled it off the water for the first time, but he still maintained or affected an optimistic outlook. "Today an important step was taken in France's preparations," said the Paris correspondent of a London newspaper on 1st September. "M. Sadi Lecointe, her greatest high-speed pilot, made two flights in the Nieuport-Hispano plane which has been tuning up for several weeks at Hourtin. . . . He was delighted with these trials, and intends to press the plane to the limits of its speed possibilities without delay, possibly today." The race, however, was only eleven days away, the plane showed signs of directional instability, and the longest of Sadi Lecointe's two flights had been ten minutes.

* * *

When Ramsay MacDonald bowed to the pressure of public opinion, Britain had just over seven months in which to get ready, less than any of the competing teams. But unlike their challengers they were building on a foundation of success. On 31st January a meeting was held at the Air Ministry which was attended by A. F. Sidgreaves, Managing Director of Rolls-Royce, and Sidgreaves promised an increase in power from the 'R' engine of not less than 400 h.p. Since time was too short to allow the design and construction of an entirely new type of seaplane, the task facing Vickers-Supermarine was mainly restricted to altering the existing S.6 design to accommodate the improved engine power; in addition, the change in the regulations requiring a fully loaded take-off and alighting directly before the race meant improving the water qualities, since extra fuel would have to be carried, and a fully loaded alighting had never been contemplated before except in emergency. Two new seaplanes were ordered, designated S.6B, and the two 1929 machines were to be similarly modified and styled S.6A.

As a result of experience with the 1929 machines, and following extensive experiment and research, improvements were made to the oil, water and fuel systems, and to the floats and the controls. The efficiency of the oil coolers was increased by about 40% to cope with the increased horse-power, and the dissipation of water heat was improved by covering the top surface of the floats with radiators. Considerably more fuel was again carried in the starboard float than in the port float to offset the enormous engine torque, and the air resistance and take-off characteristics of the floats, following tests with models, were improved.

Finally there was the problem of control: aileron flutter had been experienced on the S.5s when the controls became slack, and when the high-speed flight began practice in 1931, rudder vibration on one of the S.6s nearly led to disaster. Orlebar was flying the machine at the time, and Lovesey, who had been with him on the pontoon before take-off, was watching the flight. Climbing at full throttle, Orlebar noticed a nasty vibration, but when he eased back the throttle it stopped. After a minute or so he opened up again, and he was doing about 350 m.p.h. at 300 feet, turning to keep over the Solent, when the vibration suddenly returned, in far more violent form. The rudder bar forced his feet alternately backwards and forwards, the stick moved fore and aft in his hand, and he realised he was encountering tail flutter. He slammed back the throttle but the vibration continued. Lovesey, watching from the pontoon, guessed what was happening: the whole plane and its

outlines were blurred. Orlebar was down to about 50 feet and preparing for a crash when the flutter ceased abruptly and he alighted
straight ahead. All the control wires had been stretched and the fuselage
was badly buckled in front of the tail; only the immense strength of the
construction had prevented the tail from breaking off.

The threat of control flutter in the new machines, with their greater
speeds, was an even more serious one, and Mitchell at once set to work
to establish the cause and find a cure. His remedy was to fit mass-
balancing weights to the rudder (and the ailerons, as a precaution) and
to stiffen the fuselage.[1] It was during this period that he realised what
an advantage it would be if he could fly, and Lovesey, who had flown
his own Moth for some years, persuaded him to train for his pilot's
licence, which he afterwards gained.

At Derby the requirements were equally clear. First they had to
increase the power output of the 'R' engine from 1,900 to 2,300 h.p.,
at the same time giving increased power for take-off with the heavier
load that would have to be lifted; and second they had to reduce the
fuel and oil consumption to lessen the load for the two take-offs and the
practically fully-loaded alighting. There were setbacks at first, but both
requirements were eventually met.[2] Meanwhile Rod Banks mixed
another of his fuel cocktails (which this time contained 10% alcohol) to
give extra power and a better fuel consumption.[3]

[1] Another control problem stemmed from the rigid form of construction which
made the normal method of adjusting the rigging to obtain slight modifications in
trim impossible. Under Mitchell's direction, duralumin strips about an inch wide
were built into the trailing edges of the control surfaces, and these strips, adequately
stiff in flight, were easy to bend on the ground with an adjustable spanner. Manipu-
lated by an amount determined by experiment, these strips helped to keep the
machines properly trimmed without any action by the pilot.

[2] By increasing the engine speed, the supercharger gear ratio, and the size of the
air intake, the power output was duly increased, but the resultant rise in oil and fuel
consumption was astronomic. The use of two grooved scraper rings per piston,
however, one at the bottom of the skirt and one at the top, and a deeper sump,
helped to achieve a dramatic cut in the oil consumption. Losses through the crankcase breathers, too, were eliminated.

[3] Trouble with exhaust valves had been experienced in 1929, and the fuel consumption had had to be set rather rich to avoid valve failure; if a valve or plug over-
heated and pre-ignition occurred the result was an almost immediate connecting
rod or piston failure. Sodium-cooled valves had been developed in America, and
Banks, who was about to cross the Atlantic for his firm, was given a drawing of the
'R' exhaust valve by Hives and asked to have some salt-filled valves made up to
pattern. He brought them back on his return, and when tried on the test-bed they
stayed almost black whereas the standard valves glowed a bright red. Further sets
were then designed and produced at Derby, giving a valuable saving in fuel consumption without fear of pre-ignition or valve failure.

All parts of the engine had to be strengthened to absorb the increased stresses of the higher power output—showing how accurate the stress calculations had been for the previous race—and the same searching examination of a 60-minute run at full throttle was set. By the end of April the first experimental engines were lasting about twenty minutes before some kind of failure occurred, and by mid-July the period had been extended to half an hour. This was long enough for the initial taxying, water-handling and brief flight trials at Calshot, and the delivery of practice engines began. Testing at Derby went on day and night this time, under the same conditions as in 1929, though this time the simulated airflow was raised to a maximum of 400 m.p.h. The uproar penetrated for miles around, especially at night, and the nerve-racked citizens of Derby cried out in protest. All the tact and diplomacy of the Mayor was required to soothe them, but in the end patriotism won and the tests were allowed to continue. At last, on 12th August, exactly a month before the race, the engine passed its test, running at 3,200 revs for a full hour and giving 2,350 horse-power.

Air Ministry policy in 1929 had been to field an entirely fresh team, and they would have preferred to do so now, but the short time available for preparation forced them to take advantage of the experience available. Atcherley and Greig had been posted overseas, and Waghorn was apparently not considered, but Orlebar was chosen again to lead the team, to his great delight, and Stainforth was also retained. The other pilots chosen were Flight Lieutenants J. N. Boothman, F. W. Long and E. J. L. Hope, Lieutenant R. L. Brinton of the Fleet Air Arm, and Flying Officers H. H. Leech and L. S. Snaith. They assembled at Felixstowe—some of them were already stationed there—in March, and moved to Calshot in May. Soon afterwards, with not enough aircraft of the racing type to keep them all occupied, Brinton and Leech were released.

The first setback came with the buckling of the fuselage caused by rudder oscillation in N.247; this machine and N.248 were duly modified to incorporate the remedy devised by Mitchell. An accident caused by the wash of a huge liner capsized N.248 and resulted in a cracked eardrum and a posting for "Freddie" Hope, and following this misfortune Jerry Brinton was recalled. Then came the delivery, on 21st July, of S.1595, the first of the new S.6Bs.

"When I first took her out," wrote Orlebar, "she gave a very good imitation of a kitten chasing its tail. I had many attempts to take off, but each time she swung so violently that I had to stop. Eventually, I did once get her going fast enough to overcome the swing, but only by starting from almost directly down wind; she then swung left, completely round, until she was well out of the wind again to the left, and was careering straight at Calshot Castle without room to clear it, so that I had to stop again." Orlebar tried again two days later, and at one point he thought he was going to get off. But the swinging was as violent as ever, and this time he collided with a barge, damaging the radiators. That meant a wing-change and a whole week's delay.

This at least gave time for experiment and reflection. Possible causes were increased torque, the greater weight of the machine (for which there could be no cure), and the choice of propeller. The latter was of reduced diameter—8'6" from tip to tip against 9'6" in the previous race —and to absorb the power more efficiently at high speed the blades had been set at a bigger angle. Eventually the first two possibilities were eliminated and the fault was traced to the propeller. The blades of these fixed-pitch propellers had always been virtually stalled at take-off speeds and this had been a recurring problem.

Of the six airscrew blanks that had been ordered by Fairey-Reeds for the race, two were already forged to the 8'6" design and had to be scrapped. A third was partly finished but could be converted to about 8'10", but this was not enough. The remaining blanks were reforged at the tips to obtain 9'6". Meanwhile one of the 1929 airscrews, damaged at the tips and unusable at its full diameter, was cut down to 9'1½" as an experiment. It gave sufficient power for take-off, with a controllable amount of swing, and from that point on it became first choice for the race.

The second S.6B was delivered on 11th August, the first fine day for over a week, and it was flown next day. But then for five more days the wind blew too strongly for water-work in the racers. When at last practice was again possible, late on 18th August, it was Britain's turn for the kind of tragedy that had already marred the preparations of Italy and France. Jerry Brinton, whose disappointment at being released from the flight had only been equalled by his joy at returning, was a victim of the longitudinal instability that was always a danger in these floatplanes at the moment of take-off. As he sat in the cockpit of N.247 with the engine running, about to attempt his first take-off in an S.6, Orlebar, who was with him on the pontoon, gave him a final run through, reminding him of the crucial point of the take-off, the moment when the nose-up attitude was so pronounced that it was the hardest thing in the world to resist the impulse to let the stick go forward. It *had* to be resisted. "If you get into trouble," said Orlebar, "close the throttle and keep the stick right back."

Brinton did a short run to get the feel of the swing and the early porpoising, then began his take-off. Orlebar timed the run, which was smooth and well executed, and he had stopped the stop-watch and begun to relax when the tail of the S.6 went up a little and the machine sank back on the water. It jumped off at a steeper angle, fell again and hit more heavily this time, then bounced to thirty feet before nosing forward and plunging in. The floats were torn off and the machine turned over.

There was a fast tide running, and all efforts to swim or clamber down the fuselage to the cockpit were defeated in the next few minutes. Eventually the rescuers were reduced to towing the submerged wreck back to Calshot for the crane there to lift it clear. It was some consolation to learn later that Brinton must have been killed instantly, having broken his neck in the crash.

N.248 was still being repaired following Hope's mishap, and now N.247 was a twisted mass of metal which only complete rebuilding would reclaim. Of the two S.6Bs, one had completed less than 90 minutes' flying and the other less than an hour. But in spite of all these setbacks, Britain was still reasonably well placed to defend the trophy.

* * *

The Italian and French experience had run so much in parallel that sooner or later they were bound to reach the stage of consulting each other and considering what bilateral action they might take to effect a postponement; the only surprising thing was that they had not got together before. On the morning of 3rd September, after discussions in Paris and Rome aimed at presenting a united front, the Italian air attaché in London called on the secretary of the Royal Aero Club and informed him that unless a postponement of at least six months was granted they would find it impossible to compete. A few minutes later the French air attaché, accompanied by the secretary of the French Aero Club, made a similar call. Both deputations explained that bad weather, bad luck and the loss of pilots and aircraft had made the request unavoidable, for the safety of their pilots and the reputation of their countries. They dwelt on the unsatisfactory nature of a walk-over, even for the defending nation, and they pointed to provisions which they believed they had found in the regulations covering just such a postponement. If no competitor appeared, neither challenger nor

H 2

defender, the race could be annulled and held at a later date. Such a provision certainly existed, and the French delegation suggested that an approach to the F.A.I. should be made; but to bring about such a situation by collusion, however expedient, smacked to some of sophistry.

The following communiqué was issued simultaneously by the French and Italian Air Ministries later that day:

"The French and Italian high-speed flights up to the last minute have neglected no effort in order to assure their participation in the Schneider Trophy contest. In spite of the eagerness of test pilots and those entrusted with the high-speed machines, engineers and constructors, to be ready for the race, bad accidents and exceptionally unfavourable weather conditions have made it impossible to bring the machines to the desired degree of perfection. In these conditions the French and Italian Ministers of Air, after consultation, have come to the common decision that due care for the safety of the pilots and the reputation of their countries' products do not permit them to enter machines which have been prevented by circumstances from being completely ready. General Balbo and M. Dumesnil express their unqualified admiration for the works accomplished by their respective pilots and technical experts, but consider it their duty to beg the Royal Aero Club of Italy and the Aero Club of France to request the Royal Aero Club of Britain to postpone this great international competition until next summer. Meanwhile they have both given orders that the research and experimental works now in progress should be continued without interruption."

The Royal Aero Club replied to both clubs without hesitation. They pointed out that the rules of the contest did not allow of any postponement except from day to day; to approach the F.A.I. would be equivalent to the Royal Aero Club's proclaiming itself unable to compete on 12th September, which was not the case. And there were other considerations. All the elaborate preparations necessitated by the conditions governing the contest had been made, and a very large expenditure had been incurred by all concerned. The Club still hoped that the challengers would be able to compete, and they stressed the great disappointment that would be felt by the British public if the Italian and French teams withdrew.

Insinuations from abroad that the British situation was equally precarious were indignantly denied at Calshot, and on the evening of 4th September it was announced that even if there were no opposition the race organisation would go forward and the British team would carry out its programme. This could conceivably have been no more than a posture to persuade the challengers not to withdraw, and as the names of the French and Italian teams were handed in to the Royal Aero Club on the same day it looked as though both countries were keeping their options open; but on 5th September official confirmation was sought and received by the Air Ministry that neither country would compete.

* * *

After Jerry Brinton's death on 18th August the weather at Calshot had again closed in, giving few opportunities for flying, and from 26th August up to the time of the withdrawal of the challengers flying was not possible at all, except for some circuit familiarisation on hack machines. Nevertheless there was complete confidence that the new racers would be ready. The S.6A that had been crashed by Hope, N.248, had been reconditioned, and it flew again on 6th September, while the two S.6Bs, which had been modified meanwhile to bring the centre of gravity forward, flew again on the same day. They proved to be free from the instability that had earlier been characteristic in the turns, and there was also a great improvement on take-off. Bearing Brinton's crash in mind Orlebar ordered his pilots to keep the stick hard back when they got into the air whatever happened, until the nose attempted with increasing speed to come up higher still. The machine was then "hanging on the propeller", but the angle of attack was not excessive and there was still plenty of lift. No one had any more trouble with longitudinal instability at the point of take-off from then on, not even with a full load. "If only we had known that sooner!" wrote Orlebar.

There remained one persistent problem—trouble with the engines due to the eroding action of the fuel cocktail on the compound which sealed the fuel tanks and fuel pipes. This compound when loosened polluted the fuel and clogged the filters, causing persistent cutting out of the engines in flight, and no one could think of a remedy. But Mitchell, who thrived on adversity and was nervous when nothing went wrong, sat down in his office and worked it out. Suddenly his face relaxed into a broad grin. The actual joints, he had found, were un-affected—it was the excess compound which was coming adrift. "You'll just have to bloody-well fly them", he told Boothman, "until all that stuff comes off." And this is what they did.

The Air Ministry attitude was amplified in a statement issued on

8th September, in which they outlined the plan that would be adopted for the fly-over. One of the two S.6Bs would fly round the course and attempt to beat the existing Schneider record and the 100-kilometre record as well; if this machine failed an attempt would be made by the surviving S.6A, followed by the second S.6B. This meant that if the first S.6B failed, the S.6A would try to make sure of winning the contest, and if it succeeded the second S.6B would try to set up a record for the course.

The weakness of this plan as a spectacle was that if the first S.6B completed the course successfully neither of the other machines would fly. It was not perhaps to be expected that the three British machines would be allowed to race against each other; but the considerations of private enterprise and public interest that had confirmed the Royal Aero Club in their refusal to agree to a postponement still applied. Something was needed to inject excitement and tension into the occasion and to draw the crowd, and short of a race between the three machines the best way of providing it seemed to lie in an independent attempt on the absolute world speed record. At first the Air Ministry resisted: they could visualise the contest turning into an air display. But in this final clash of principles with the Royal Aero Club they eventually gave way. Assuming that S.1595 completed the Schneider course and qualified as the winner, S.1596 would be freed for an attempt on the record. This range of possibilities offered the certainty of an attractive spectacle.

After the lottery of the selection process and all the months of training, it now seemed likely that only two pilots would be required to fly on the actual day. Choosing these pilots placed Orlebar in a dilemma. Evaluating his men in order of merit was an unenviable task, yet he was the only man qualified to do it. Eventually the order was decided on seniority with the flight. George Stainforth, the man who had been left out in 1929, was given first choice, and the dilemma was thus transferred to him.

To win the Schneider contest was an honour without parallel, and to win the final race and secure the trophy would be a historic achievement. But this was neither a contest nor a race. Satisfying though victory might be, it demanded, in this instance, no exceptional skill from the pilot. But to get the last ounce of speed out of the S.6B and put the record out of contemporary reach—that surely was the choice that any adventurous mind must make. After some hesitation, George Stainforth plumped for the record.

In 1929 Stainforth had chosen to fly the Gloster VI—and chosen

29 (a)   Lady Houston at Calshot, 1931

29 (b)   R. J. Mitchell with Sir Henry Royce

29 (c)   The British team, 1931. Left to right: Flt. Lt. G. H. Stainforth, Flt. Lt. J. N. Boothman, Sqdn. Ldr. A. H. Orlebar, Flt. Lt. F. W. Long, and Fg. Off. L. S. Snaith

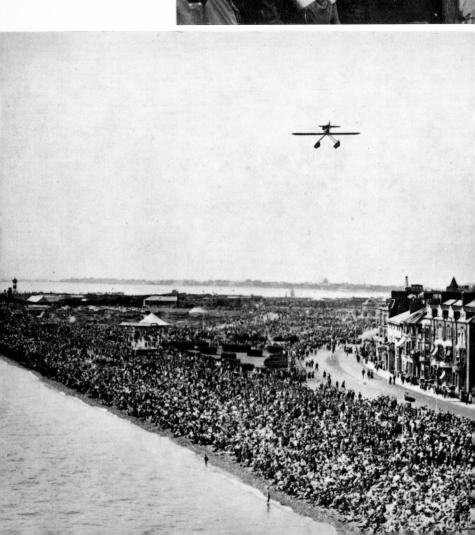

30 (a) Flt. Lt. J. N. Boothman being chaired after the victory that won the Trophy outright for Great Britain, and (b) the crowd on Southsea beach watching the fly-round

wrong. Now his ambition was to become the first man to exceed 400 miles an hour in a timed run. A limiting factor, however, was that the engines installed in the contest machines were designed to stay a course of 217 miles; a specially boosted sprint engine would give more speed over a short distance. In any case, whereas the carving of one's name on the Schneider Trophy was ineradicable, speed records were ephemeral. Had Stainforth again chosen wrong?

According to the same criterion of seniority, the remaining pilots comprised John Boothman, Frank Long and Leonard Snaith in that order. Responsibility for the fly-over thus fell to Boothman. Long would stand by to fly the second S.6B in the race in case of need, leaving the 'safe' machine, N.248, to Snaith.

Born in 1901, John Boothman had spent many holidays as a youth in France, and he spoke French fluently; thus at the age of 16, turned down by the British forces because of his age, he joined the French Red Cross as an ambulance driver and was sent out to Salonica. But the British authorities eventually caught up with him, and he was on his way home when the Armistice was signed. He joined the R.A.F. in 1921.

Two days before the race the Italians, anxious to make an attempt on the world speed record as a counter to Britain's impending capture of the trophy although still plagued by cooling and fuel feed problems, lost their second MC.72: the pilot, Bellini, was reputedly trying to exceed a speed of 394 m.p.h. previously registered by Neri. After a number of successful runs he overflew the Desenzano base, throttled back, then opened up again and turned left towards the lake. He crossed the water at very high speed in his fastest run yet, but then flew straight into rising ground on the far side. The impact was terrific, the aircraft was completely demolished, and the engines fell into the lake.

The reason for the crash was determined in poignant fashion by the discovery of a burned sleeve from Bellini's uniform three kilo-metres from the point of impact; obviously the Macchi had blown up in mid-air. Examination of the engines later confirmed that a particularly violent back-fire had provoked an explosion in the carburettor air intake, setting fire to the gravity tank behind it. "After this accident," says Muzio Macchi, "all test flying was stopped, and all hopes of an attempt on the record were abandoned."

Meanwhile the financial crisis that had beset Britain throughout the year had culminated in the formation of a National government under MacDonald and, on the eve of the race, a drastic and disagreeable budget from Philip Snowden. A total of over two million permanently unemployed was convincing evidence of Britain's tottering economy; yet she was the one nation which had successfully prepared for the race, and it was a tragedy that she was going to be denied one. Interest in the occasion, however, was scarcely diminished. In a period of deep national depression it was something in which patriotic hearts could rejoice. The very speeds themselves were magnetic to a public addicted to outdoor sensation. These speeds, beyond all other human experience though they were, still lay within the scope of popular imagination, and the thrill of witnessing a display of unprecedented pace and power, something that no other nation in the world could even challenge, drew another vast crowd to the Southampton area on the day of the contest.

There was a consciousness, too, of history being made. The contest that had spanned almost the entire history of competitive flying—a history which the majority had seen unfold—was about to end. That end might not be mourned, but neither would it be forgotten. Britain, short of some unaccountable blunder, would be the outright winner, and even if the final victory might seem inglorious it was none the less deserved, and the glory was there.

All that was now needed to turn the promised spectacle into fiasco was bad weather. After a week of Indian summer, Saturday morning, 12th September, dawned reasonably fine, but the forecasters were predicting a deterioration after midday. The fly-over was due to begin at noon, and the story everywhere, along the Hampshire coast and on the Isle of Wight, was of jammed car parks, packed grandstands, and crowded beaches and vantage-points. Everyone seemed to have studied the Schneider course—triangular this year—and the three-kilometre speed course to be flown by Stainforth, and to have chosen their places accordingly.

The machines were launched early and were soon out on their pontoons, ready to be towed into position for take-off. The towing had in fact already started when Orlebar returned from an examination of water conditions and ordered the pontoons back. There was a strong wind and a heavy sea, and it was too rough for floatplanes. At eleven o'clock it began to rain, and as the squally weather continued it became a day for mackintoshes and umbrellas on land and oilskins at sea.

At one o'clock the fly-over was put off until next day, and the crowds stoically dispersed, dried themselves out, and returned in even greater numbers on the Sunday. The patient multitude was rewarded by a perfect September day, and by eleven o'clock the beaches were filled from end to end, sea- and sun-bathing and family picnics relieving the monotony of waiting. The air was crystal clear after the squalls of yesterday, and by midday the visibility had risen to 15 miles. From Southsea beach Boothman's progress would be visible right round the course.

The starting- and finishing-line was again drawn in front of Ryde Pier, the course leading down past Seaview as before to the first pylon, erected on a destroyer anchored off St. Helen's Point. But the next leg extended right across the Solent and beyond Hayling Island to a pylon situated on the coast itself at West Wittering, just east of Chichester Harbour. Then came the longest leg, 14 miles along the Hampshire coast from West Wittering past Southsea and Gosport to a point midway between Cowes and Lee-on-Solent, marked again by a pylon on a destroyer. Then back past Ryde Pier to Seaview.

At midday Boothman took a slow hack round for a final look at the course. The pontoons had already been towed out and anchored off Cowes, where the take-off area was marked out alongside the starting-vessel. Considerations of shipping and tides—and perhaps a strong protest from the Lord's Day Observance Society—had dictated a starting-time of one o'clock. Shortly before one, the loudspeakers along the seashore bellowed the news that flying was about to begin, and the vantage-points thickened dramatically as people poured out of restaurants, hotels and cafés and scurried to the promenades and beaches.

There was a gentle northerly wind and a nice chop on the water, but the swell out in Chichester Bay, a hangover from the previous day, still looked unpleasant, not at all suitable for a forced alighting. Nevertheless with some misgivings Orlebar ordered the fly-round to start. Lovesey was there, as in 1929, to start up the engine and make a final check, and just after one o'clock the S.6B was launched from the pontoon. As Boothman opened the throttle the starting-gun went off.

The tension now was almost worse than in 1929, when everything had been subservient to the thrill of the race. This moment represented the culmination of six years of research, design and development, of trials and tests, triumphs and tragedies, by the Air Ministry, by Supermarines, by Napiers, by Rolls-Royce, by Glosters, and by countless others. It was the climax of a decade—yet how easily it could turn into bathos. To be beaten by superior forces might provoke criticism, but failure today would attract ridicule. And the possibility of failure, as all the team knew, was real enough.

Because of the risk of writing off the machines before the contest, the fully-loaded alighting that Boothman must accomplish had never been practised. And the longest flight yet put up by one of the S.6Bs was 27 minutes. S.1595 would have to keep going for considerably longer than that to complete the course.

As Boothman began his lone, unchallenged endeavour, there were many people present who thought of the Italians, and the wonderful courage displayed by their pilots in 1929. The bond that linked the two nations through the Schneider Trophy went deeper than mere sentiment; they shared a rare emotion, the love of enemy for enemy. Since the last contest Monti and Dal Molin had died, and now Bellini, lost in the eternal struggle to cross new frontiers. Britain too had suffered losses. Dick Waghorn, the winning pilot in 1929, had been killed testing a Hawker Horsley at Farnborough, and the death of Brinton was still a sharp memory.

These thoughts, and absorption with the task in hand, kept the crowd silent as Boothman began his take-off run. A northerly wind was blowing down Southampton Water, and he followed the usual drill of aiming well to the right of the wind, with full right rudder and stick hard back, head well forward for the first few seconds to shield his goggles, using rudder control as soon as it became effective. Once on the 'step' and into wind he swung the nose slightly either way to get a view straight ahead, kept the control column hard back, and got off nicely without porpoising in 36 seconds. He turned to port and climbed away towards the Needles, and after one or two turns to get the feel of the controls he throttled back and began his approach for the alighting.

Poor vision in the S.6B dead ahead forced him to approach across wind before choosing a line into wind clear of obstruction and keeping to it. He kept his speed steady at 160 m.p.h. throughout the approach. After flattening out he knew the plane would "float" for at least a mile, and he held the machine in the air for as long as possible, tense and anxious. The touchdown when it came was perfect.

That was the first hazard over. The regulations required him to be on the water for two minutes, and with the time taken in pulling up he needed to taxi for little more than a minute before he opened the throttle again to take off for the contest proper. As he accelerated he began to take a hammering from his own wash, and he dragged the stick back into his stomach to prevent porpoising. This time he took fractionally longer to get off.

He carried straight on up Southampton Water before turning over

1931 SCHNEIDER TROPHY RACE COURSE

Royal Aero Club of the United Kingdom, 1931.

Kilometres

0 1 2 3 4 5

Nautical miles

One round lap 50 kilometres
To be flown 7 times

WEST WITTERING
EAST WITTERING

HAYLING ISLAND
SOUTHSEA

PORTSMOUTH

Pier

GOSPORT

SPITHEAD

START AND FINISH

RYDE
Pier

Calshot Castle

PRELIMINARY
TRIAL AREA

SOUTHAMPTON WATER

SOLENT

WEST COWES
EAST COWES

ISLE OF WIGHT

the eastern shore and heading back south, cutting across the course inside the Cowes pylon before diving from 800 feet for the starting-line with the throttle fully open. His instructions were to run no risk of fouling the pylons, and he took the first turn beyond Seaview in the wide 80-degree bank that they had practised. Another mandatory instruction was that he was not to exceed an engine water temperature of 95 degrees centigrade. As he sped across the long stretch of open water towards West Wittering his eye registered an indicated air speed of 378 m.p.h. at 3,200 revs, and his engine temperature was steady at 88 degrees, so he kept the throttle wide open.

After turning at West Wittering, within sight of Henry Royce's home and the beach where the 'R' engine had been born, he gave the crowd their fill of sensation as he thundered over their heads along the Hampshire coast. This is what they had been waiting for—the tiny machine winging towards them, its huge floats apparently treading the air, a glimpse of the pilot in his open cockpit as he passed with an ear-splitting roar overhead, and then the accentuated silence as the sound receded and the machine dissolved into a distant speck. Then Boothman was rounding the western pylon and running in to complete his first lap.

The air speed indicator in the S.6B was overreading, and the loud-speakers announced a lap speed of 343 m.p.h. This was lower than had been hoped for, but Orlebar and Lovesey, watching from the pontoon, felt it was just about satisfactory. If Boothman failed to beat Wag-horn's 1929 average of 328·63 by a substantial margin it had been agreed that Orlebar would be free to order Long and Snaith, waiting on their pontoons now with mixed feelings, to follow. Boothman's success would mean, for them, no take-off.

Hugging the Hampshire coast for the second time, Boothman watched his temperature gauge rise rapidly. He eased back the throttle to 3,100 revs, the indicated air speed dropped to 360, and the water temperature settled at 95 degrees. He carried on at this throttle setting and his lap speeds dropped, to 342 on his second lap and 340 on his third. His fourth lap fell below 340, and on this circuit he was so disturbed by a series of air bumps off Southsea that next time round he flew out to sea to try to avoid them and had to swing wide to round the Cowes pylon, and he didn't get back into his proper line until he was past Ryde Pier. Even so his fifth and sixth laps were steady at just under 340.

The S.6B was beginning to fly badly left-wing low, probably due to the change of trim as fuel was consumed. And as Boothman finished his sixth lap he saw the Royal Aero Club headquarters ship *Homeric* exude a puff of black smoke which he thought might be a signal to say he had completed the course. Had he miscounted, as Webster and Waghorn had done before him, and would he be forced down for lack of fuel? He decided to trust his lap counter; and then he saw the water temperature rising again. He throttled back gradually to 3,000 revs until he rounded the Cowes pylon for the last time, then opened the throttle wide for the final exhilarating run towards Ryde Pier. The puff of smoke had been an irrelevance, and he completed his seventh lap at 337·7 m.p.h., giving an overall average of 340·08. It was just about enough, and as he passed the finishing-line the entire concourse of shipping broke into a cacophony of hooting and whistling which almost drowned the cheers of the crowd. He had been airborne for 47 minutes in all.

While the second S.6B was being prepared for the record attempt, Snaith entertained the crowd with a thrilling exhibition of stunting in a Fairey Firefly, and at four o'clock Stainforth was ready. His four high-speed runs of three kilometres each, flown off Lee on Solent, two with the wind and two against, broke all previous records with an average of 379·05 miles per hour and sent the crowd home happy.

Not so happy, however, were the makers of the engines. They had prepared a sprint engine specially for an all-out record attempt, but it had not been ready for the day of the Schneider. Orders to clear Calshot to make way for the return of R.A.F. flying-boat squadrons had already been given, and the break-up of the high-speed flight had begun. But Rolls-Royce were determined to be the first engine-makers to contribute to a record in excess of 400 m.p.h., and they persisted. Eventually, following the personal intercession of Sir Henry Royce, the Air Ministry relented. There were further setbacks to come, the worst being when the machine originally allotted for the record cartwheeled on alighting and sank. But on 29th September, flying S.1595 with the new sprint engine and a special fuel, Stainforth became the first man to exceed 400 on a measured run when he set up a new world record of 407·5 miles an hour.

Conclusion

EVALUATION of the impact of the Schneider contest on the development of aviation would be a study in itself, beyond the scope of these pages, which purport to do no more than tell the story of the races. The same might be said of any attempt at assessing the contest's influence on the campaigns and battles of World War II. Yet significant pointers may perhaps be suggested. Extravagant claims are no better than wild denunciations, but in this case they were certainly more numerous. "I can see nothing of value in it," wrote Trenchard; but the consensus of opinion was against him. His contention that high-speed research could operate as effectively in a vacuum was not shared by his contemporaries, and indeed it contradicted the very arguments he had employed to persuade the British government to back the race in the first place. "The importance of the spur which a fixed definite date of such a contest provides cannot easily be overrated," said *Flight*. And the impetus came in an era dominated by the notorious ten-year rule, under which Britain was not to expect to have to fight a major war within ten years, and at a time when little research for its own sake could be afforded.

The Schneider racers were far from ideal as vehicles through which the general development of landplanes might be accelerated; but nevertheless they fulfilled this function. In an article in *Aeronautical Engineering* entitled 'Racing Seaplanes and Their Influence on Design' which appeared on 25th December 1929, R. J. Mitchell stated his view. Information and experience gained in the development of racing aircraft, he believed, had a pronounced influence on the design of both military and civil types. "During the last ten years," he wrote, "there has been an almost constant increase in speed in our racing types. To maintain this steady increase very definite progress has been essential year by year. It has been necessary to increase the aerodynamic efficiency and the power-to-weight ratios of our machines; to reduce the consumption and the frontal areas of our engines; to devise new methods of construction; and to develop the use of new materials. The results obtained in the form of speed have been a direct and absolute indication of our progress in aeronautical development." And of the improvements in engine design he wrote: "It is quite safe to say that the engine used in this year's winning S.6 machine . . . would have taken at least three times as long to produce under normal processes of development had it not been for the spur of international competition. There is little doubt that this intensive engine development will have a very pronounced effect on our aircraft during the next few years."

A. F. Sidgreaves, Managing Director of Rolls-Royce, was of a similar opinion, and after the 1931 contest he issued this statement:

"As a result of the test this year all the main components of these engines have undergone a definite improvement, and in consequence the life of the standard engine in service will be much longer than it would otherwise have been.

"From the development point of view the Schneider Trophy Contest is almost an economy because it saves so much time in arriving at certain technical improvements. It is not too much to say that research for the Schneider Trophy Contest over the past two years is what our aero-engine department would otherwise have taken six to ten years to learn. . . .

"For the last few years Britain's supremacy in the manufacture of aircraft is generally recognised, and is due to the experience and knowledge gained in contests such as that for the Schneider Trophy."

The opinions of these men, as interested parties, may not have been unprejudiced, and a less partial view may be that of Air Vice-Marshal Hugh Dowding, Air Member for Supply and Research at the time of the last contest. Dowding was strongly opposed to international competitions like the Schneider on both technical and moral grounds; technical because of the peculiarities of the seaplanes, and moral because "I do not think we ought, in peacetime, to call upon service pilots to take such risks in the course of their duty. . . ." (Dowding's concern for his pilots was no retrospective pose: this is taken from a minute he wrote to the Chief of the Air Staff on 27th October 1931.) "In my opinion," he wrote, "it is a regrettable circumstance that we should have been forced by international competition to construct and fly aircraft with stalling speeds in the neighbourhood of 110 m.p.h." Further efforts, he urged, should start from the basis of a maximum landing speed of about 75 m.p.h., concentrating on getting the highest possible top speed with this limitation. If that were achieved the advantage of the seaplane, with its unrestricted space for take-off and alighting, would disappear. But Dowding greatly valued the reservoir of expertise that had been built up. "What I wanted", he said many years later, "was to invite private tenders from two firms to cash in on the experience that had been gained in aircraft construction and engine progress so that we could order two of the fastest machines which it was possible to build with no restriction except landing speed. . . ."[1] The result, added Dowding, was the emergence of the Hurricane and the Spitfire.

Of equal importance to the individual experience gained was the welding together of design teams and even groups of companies in a common enterprise, something difficult to achieve in peacetime. Dowding was one of the first to see that a natural outlet for this already harnessed energy and skill was the high performance fighter.

When the Air Ministry issued Specification F7/30, Mitchell advised his company to tender, and work was started in 1932; but the machine he produced, which first appeared in 1934 and was unofficially called the Spitfire, was not accepted. The specification, which called for a low landing speed and a short landing run, was too restrictive, besides being insufficiently advanced to produce an aircraft of really high performance. However, although only the prototype was built, further valuable lessons were learnt; and Mitchell, during convalescence in Austria after a serious operation, is said to have become so perturbed by German militarism that on his return he persuaded Vickers-Supermarine to let him go ahead and design a fighter as a private venture, unhampered by official specifications. The weakness of Britain's air defences he either knew or surmised, and he was confident that by utilising all the experience gained with his racing seaplanes he could produce a fighter so superior to anything then known that the government would be certain to award his firm a contract. This was the real genesis of the Spitfire. The prototype, powered by the new Rolls-Royce Merlin, which was developed from the experience gained with the 'R' racing engine, flew for the first time on 5th March 1936. Mitchell died in the following year at the age of 42, but the shape of Britain's air defences was by that time firmly delineated.

Just as the Curtiss racers set the pattern for the pursuit-type military aeroplane of the 1920s, so Mitchell's Schneider machines set the pattern for the 1930s. Other countries, including Germany, inevitably benefited from Mitchell's work, but for Britain the progress was vital. Mitchell's achievement was not only to produce the fastest of the high-speed aeroplanes of his time; they were also the safest.

Everyone closely connected with the races in the countries concerned has testified to the enormous technological advances that were made race by race, and the Americans certainly lived to regret that they

[1] *Dowding and the Battle of Britain*, by Robert Wright (Macdonald, 1969).

hadn't competed for a few more years. To these advantages, so far as Britain was concerned, must be added the imponderables of prestige, air-mindedness, readiness, and self-confidence, plus the knowledge that if the aircraft industry and the Royal Air Force put their minds to it they were a formidable combination.

The history of the Spitfire, and of the Merlin engine for that matter, is another story, indeed two more stories, but their contribution to the Allied war effort was immense. And there were many incidental and peripheral advantages, of which supercharging and fuel development are interesting examples. The design and development of the type of blower used in the 'R' engine bore unforeseen fruit some years later when Frank Whittle's first successful jet engine embodied a unit of this basic type. And the special fuel development work of Rod Banks, and the complementary development which arose from it, was to play a dramatic part at a crisis point in the Second World War. Without the Schneider contest it is unlikely that this fuel development would have taken place, as it had no general service or commercial use; but at the time of the Normandy landings and the threat from the German flying bomb, the potential was remembered and a similar fuel was developed at the R.A.E. which gave Mustangs and Spitfires another 30 m.p.h. at low level.

A modern view of Mitchell's designs for the Schneider contest was presented by Sir George Edwards, Chairman and Managing Director of the British Aircraft Corporation, in 1968. "There can be no doubt", he wrote, "that the boldness of these designs and the passion for engineering detail which they displayed made a profound impact on aeronautical design and set the scene for the successful generation of British fighters which were so decisive in saving Britain from defeat in later years. If the industry had been limited during these inter-war years to design studies alone and had not been able to translate ideas into hardware by actually building aeroplanes, it is certain that such successful fighters as the Spitfire and the Hurricane would not have emerged."

* * *

The Italians did not give up their efforts to regain the world speed record, but it was not until Rod Banks went to Italy to assist Fiats with their fuel problems that they succeeded. Banks's first task was to find out why the engine carburation system 'fired back' during flight; the Italians were still plagued by this fault. He found that while Fiats had tried the forward facing or ram air intake originated by Rolls-Royce, which made use of the forward air speed of the aircraft to increase the pressure on the inlet side of the supercharger, they had only fitted this intake in the aeroplane itself, not on the test-bed.[1] During testing, without the forward airflow (which Rolls-Royce had taken care to simulate), there was the normal differential pressure across the carburettor; but with the forward air intake at a pressure equivalent to an air speed of up to 400 m.p.h., this differential was reduced and consequently the mixture weakened off. The result was the back-firing which had often fractured the induction system and supercharger casing; and since the supercharger was driven by the rear engine, there was a considerable length of pipe involved and the ensuing explosion could be of great violence, often causing a fire. Herein lay the cause of most of the Italian frustrations and tragedies of 1931.

Banks deduced all this from his experience with Rolls-Royce at Derby, and he persuaded Fiats to install an engine and blower in their test house to simulate flight conditions.[2] He also convinced them of the value of a 60-minute run at full throttle. The flight engines were duly modified, check-tested, and returned to Desenzano, no further trouble was experienced, and in April 1933 the Italians regained the record, the successful pilot being the diminutive Agello. Eighteen months later, on 23rd October 1934, Agello set up a new record of 440·68 m.p.h. which still stands for propeller seaplanes.

Trenchard's assertion that the Schneider race was bad for his pilots is not borne out by their subsequent careers; all those who took part and survived long enough reached air rank. Among wartime casualties were George Stainforth, killed in action in the Middle East in 1942 at the age of 43, and 'Freddie' Hope, of the original 1931 team, also killed in action. Orlebar died in 1943, and the years have inevitably taken toll of others, among them Boothman, Worsley, Schofield and, more recently, Atcherley.

But of all the Schneider contenders, no nation produced more courageous pilots or suffered more tragic losses than Italy, and of their high speed pilots nearly all were subsequently "caduto per incidento di

---

[1] From a lecture by Air Commodore F. R. Banks, published in *The Aeronautical Journal*, Vol. 72, No. 687, March 1968, and from a personal interview with Banks.

[2] According to Muzio Macchi, Fiats found and rectified the air intake problem without waiting for Banks' advice. The Fiat position is that after the first tests an auxiliary engine was indeed used to simulate the airflow, but that the solution was not found until transparent panels were fitted in the carburettor, so that the behaviour of the fuel could be seen.

volo"—killed in an air crash. Centurione, Motta, Dal Molin, Monti, Bellini; to this list were subsequently added Neri in 1932, Macchi test pilot Sartori in 1933, de Briganti in 1937, Bacula in 1938, Ferrarin in 1941, Scapinelli in the same year, and Agello in 1942. Yet the oldest, de Bernardi, survived them all. The story of his end is as poignant as it is fitting. He had become a stunt pilot, and in April 1959, at the age of 67, after thrilling the crowds at a Rome air display with a magnificent demonstration of aerobatics, he suffered a heart attack. He made a perfect approach and landing, taxied in, lined up his machine on the tarmac, and applied his parking brakes. The engine, however, was still ticking over. Eventually one of the mechanics climbed in to see why he hadn't switched off. Although the circumstances were different, de Bernardi, like so many of his contemporaries, had died in his cockpit.

APPENDIX I   SUMMARY OF RACES*   1913 AT MONACO

28 laps of 10 kilometres each (280 kms)

RACE NO.	PILOT	REPRESENTING	AIRCRAFT	ENGINE	SPEED/REMARKS
19	Maurice Prévost	France	Deperdussin	160 h.p. Gnome	45.75 m.p.h. (True average 61 m.p.h.)
2	Roland Garros	France	Morane-Saulnier	80 h.p. Gnome	Completed course: average about 60 m.p.h. but delayed start spoiled time
5	Charles Weymann	U.S.A.	Nieuport	100 h.p. Gnome	Retired on 25th lap
6	Dr. Gabriel Espanet	France	Nieuport	100 h.p. Gnome	Retired on 8th lap

* Only those machines which can be said to have "come under starter's orders" are included in this Summary.

1914 AT MONACO *28 laps of 10 kilometres each (280 kms)*

RACE NO.	PILOT	REPRESENTING	AIRCRAFT	ENGINE	SPEED/REMARKS
3	Howard Pixton	G.B.	Sopwith Tabloid	100 h.p. Gnome Monosoupape	86·78 m.p.h.
7	Ernest Burri	Switzerland	F.B.A.	100 h.p. Gnome Monosoupape	51 m.p.h.
6	*Pierre Levasseur	France	Nieuport	160 h.p. Gnome	Retired on 18th lap
5	Dr. Gabriel Espanet	France	Nieuport	160 h.p. Gnome	Retired on 17th lap
—	Lord Carbery	G.B.	Deperdussin	160 h.p. Le Rhone	Retired on 3rd lap
—	Maurice Prévost	France	Deperdussin	200 h.p. Gnome	Retired with engine failure
—	Roland Garros	France	Morane-Saulnier	160 h.p. Gnome	Withdrew
1	Charles Weymann	U.S.A.	Nieuport	160 h.p. Le Rhone	Withdrew
—	William Thaw	U.S.A.	Deperdussin	160 h.p. Le Rhone	Withdrew

1919 AT BOURNEMOUTH

10 laps of 20 nautical miles each (200 n.m.)

RACE NO.	PILOT	REPRESENTING	AIRCRAFT	ENGINE	SPEED/REMARKS
7	*Sgt. Guido Jannello	Italy	Savoia S.13	250 h.p. Isotta-Fraschini	Completed 11 incorrect laps
5	Basil D. Hobbs	G.B.	Supermarine Sea Lion	450 h.p. Napier Lion	Crashed at end of 1st lap
1	Vincent Nicholl	G.B.	Fairey IIIA	450 h.p. Napier Lion	Retired on 1st lap
3	Harry Hawker	G.B.	Sopwith	450 h.p. Cosmos Jupiter	Retired on 1st lap
2	Lt. Jean Casale	France	Nieuport 29-C-1	300 h.p. Hispano-Suiza	Did not start
6	Sadi Lecointe	France	Spad-Herbémont	340 h.p. Hispano-Suiza	Did not start

* Race declared void, but right to stage next contest awarded to Italy.

1920 AT VENICE *10 laps of 37·117 kilometres each* (371·17 kms)

RACE NO.	PILOT	REPRESENTING	AIRCRAFT	ENGINE	SPEED/REMARKS
7	Lt. Luigi Bologna	Italy	Savoia S.12	550 h.p. Ansaldo	107·22 m.p.h.

1921 AT VENICE *16 laps of 24·6 kilometres each* (393·6 kms)

RACE NO.	PILOT	REPRESENTING	AIRCRAFT	ENGINE	SPEED/REMARKS
1	Giovanni de Briganti	Italy	Macchi M.7	250 h.p. Isotta-Fraschini	117·9 m.p.h.
14	Piero Corgnolino	Italy	Macchi M.7	250 h.p. Isotta-Fraschini	Ran out of fuel on last lap
4	Arturo Zanetti	Italy	Macchi M.19	680 h.p Fiat	Did 141 m.p.h. on early lap but later caught fire
5	Sadi Lecointe	France	Nieuport-Delage	300 h.p. Hispano-Suiza	Failed navigability test

1922 AT NAPLES *13 laps of 28·5 kilometres each* (370·5 kms)

RACE NO.	PILOT	REPRESENTING	AIRCRAFT	ENGINE	SPEED/REMARKS
14	Henri Biard	G.B.	Supermarine Sea Lion II	450 h.p. Napier Lion	145·7 m.p.h.
8	Alessandro Passaleva	Italy	Savoia S.51	300 h.p. Hispano-Suiza	143·5 m.p.h.
9	Arturo Zanetti	Italy	Macchi M.17	260 h.p. Isotta-Fraschini	133 m.p.h.
10	Piero Corgnolino	Italy	Macchi M.7	260 h.p. Isotta-Fraschini	123·7 m.p.h.

1923 AT COWES

5 laps of 37·2 nautical miles each (186 n.m.)

RACE NO.	PILOT	REPRESENTING	AIRCRAFT	ENGINE	SPEED/REMARKS
4	Lt. David Rittenhouse	U.S.A.	Curtiss CR-3	465 h.p. Curtiss D-12	177·38 m.p.h.
3	Lt. Rutledge Irvine	U.S.A.	Curtiss CR-3	465 h.p. Curtiss D-12	173·46 m.p.h.
7	Henri Biard	G.B.	Supermarine Sea Lion III	550 h.p. Napier Lion	157·17 m.p.h.
9	Lt. de Vaisseau Hurel	France	C.A.M.S. 38	360 h.p. Hispano-Suiza	Retired after 1 lap.
10	Lt. Pelletier d'Oisy	France	C.A.M.S. 36	360 h.p. Hispano-Suiza	Damaged in collision —did not start
6	R. W. Kenworthy	G.B.	Blackburn Pellet	Napier Lion (probably 550 h.p.)	Crashed during navigability trials
11	J. Duhamel	France	Latham L.1	Two 400 h.p. Lorraine-Dietrich engines mounted in tande	Did not start— engine failure
5	Lt. Frank Wead	U.S.A.	Navy TR-3A	300 h.p. Wright	Withdrawn

1925 AT BALTIMORE

7 laps of 50 kilometres each (350 kms)

RACE NO.	PILOT	REPRESENTING	AIRCRAFT	ENGINE	SPEED/REMARKS
3	Lt. James H. Doolittle	U.S.A.	Curtiss R3C-2	600 h.p. Curtiss V-1400	232·57 m.p.h.
5	Hubert Broad	G.B.	Gloster III	700 h.p. Napier Lion	199·17 m.p.h.
7	Giovanni de Briganti	Italy	Macchi M.33	435 h.p. Curtiss D-12	168·44 m.p.h.
2	Lt. George T. Cuddihy	U.S.A.	Curtiss R3C-2	600 h.p. Curtiss V-1400	Retired on final lap
1	Lt. Ralph A. Ofstie	U.S.A.	Curtiss R3C-2	600 h.p. Curtiss V-1400	Retired on 6th lap
4	Henri Biard	G.B.	Supermarine S.4	700 h.p. Napier Lion	Crashed on navigability trials
4*	H. J. L. Hinkler	G.B.	Gloster III	700 h.p. Napier Lion	Crashed on navigability trials
8	Riccardo Morselli	Italy	Macchi M.33	435 h.p. Curtiss D-12	Withdrawn through engine trouble

* substituted after Biard's crash in the S.4

1926 AT HAMPTON ROADS *7 laps of 50 kilometres each (350 kms)*

RACE NO.	PILOT	REPRESENTING	AIRCRAFT	ENGINE	SPEED/REMARKS
5	Major Mario de Bernardi	Italy	Macchi M.39	800 h.p. Fiat A.S.2	246·50 m.p.h.
6	Lt. Frank C. Schilt	U.S.A.	Curtiss R3C-2	600 h.p. Curtiss V-1400	231·36 m.p.h.
1	Lt. Adriano Bacula	Italy	Macchi M.39	800 h.p. Fiat A.S.2	218 m.p.h.
2	*Lt. William G. Tomlinson	U.S.A.	Curtiss Hawk	435 h.p. Curtiss D-12	137 m.p.h.
4	Lt. George T. Cuddihy	U.S.A.	Curtiss R3C-4	700 h.p. Curtiss V-1550	Retired on final lap
3	Captain Arturo Ferrarin	Italy	Macchi M.39	800 h.p. Fiat A.S.2	Retired on 4th lap
2	*Lt. William G. Tomlinson	U.S.A.	Curtiss R3C-3	700 h.p. Packard 1A-V-1500	Crashed during navigability trials. Tomlinson transferred to Curtiss Hawk

1927 AT VENICE *7 laps of 50 kilometres each (350 kms)*

RACE NO.	PILOT	REPRESENTING	AIRCRAFT	ENGINE	SPEED/REMARKS
4	Flt. Lt. S. N. Webster	G.B.	Supermarine S.5	875 h.p. Napier Lion (geared)	281·65 m.p.h.
6	Flt. Lt. O. E. Worsley	G.B.	Supermarine S.5	875 h.p. Napier Lion (ungeared)	273·07 m.p.h.
5	Capt. Federico Guazzetti	Italy	Macchi M.52	800 h.p. Fiat A.S.2	Retired on 6th lap
1	Flt. Lt. S. M. Kinkead	G.B.	Gloster IV B	875 h.p. Napier Lion (geared)	Retired after completing 5 laps
2	Major Mario de Bernardi	Italy	Macchi M.52	1000 h.p. Fiat A.S.3	Retired on 2nd lap
7	Captain Arturo Ferrarin	Italy	Macchi M.52	1000 h.p. Fiat A.S.3	Retired on 1st lap

1929 AT CALSHOT

7 laps of 50 kilometres each (350 kms)

RACE NO.	PILOT	REPRESENTING	AIRCRAFT	ENGINE	SPEED/REMARKS
2	Fg. Off. H. R. Waghorn	G.B.	Supermarine S.6	1900 h.p. Rolls-Royce 'R'	328·63 m.p.h.
4	Wt. Off. T. Dal Molin	Italy	Macchi M.52R	1000 h.p. A.S.3	284·20 m.p.h.
5	Flt. D. D'Arcy A. Greig	G.B.	Supermarine S.5	875 h.p. Napier Lion	282·11 m.p.h.
7	Lt. Remo Cadringher	Italy	Macchi M.67	1800 Isotta-Fraschini	Retired on 2nd lap
10	Lt. Giovanni Monti	Italy	Macchi M.67	1800 h.p. Isotta-Fraschini	Retired on 2nd lap
8	Fg. Off. R. L. R. Atcherley	G.B.	Supermarine S.6	1900 h.p. Rolls-Royce 'R'	325·54 m.p.h.—but disqualified for cutting a pylon

1931 AT CALSHOT

7 laps of 50 kilometres each (350 kms)

RACE NO.	PILOT	REPRESENTING	AIRCRAFT	ENGINE	SPEED/REMARKS
1	Flt. Lt. J. N. Boothman	G.B.	Supermarine S.6B	2350 h.p. Rolls-Royce 'R'	340·08 m.p.h.

No challenger. Flt. Lt. Boothman flew round the course alone to win the Trophy outright.

APPENDIX II

TABLE OF DIMENSIONS OF PRINCIPAL AIRCRAFT

Figures issued and reported vary considerably but those given are as accurate as possible. Wing-span measurements for biplanes refer to top plane only.

YEAR	AIRCRAFT	MAX ENGINE POWER	POWER TO WEIGHT RATIO (h.p. per lb.)	DIMENSIONS			WEIGHT		WING LOADING (lbs per sq. foot)
				WING SPAN	FUSELAGE LENGTH	WING SURFACE (sq. feet)	EMPTY	GROSS	
1913	DEPERDUSSIN	160	·33	44'3"	29'6"	301	2095	2646	8·8
	NIEUPORT	100	N/K	39'7"	28'7"	242	1323	1874	7·7
1914	SOPWITH	100	·40	25'6"	20'	237	992	1433	6
1919	SAVOIA S.13	265	N/K	26'6"	27'2"	211	1609	2072	9·8
1920	SAVOIA S.12	550	N/K	38'4"	32'10"	495	N/K	4784	9·6

1921	M.7 (bis)	250	N/K	25'2"	22'2"	255	1720	2382	9.4
1922	SEA LION II	450	N/K	31'10"	27'6"	N/K	2381	3163	9
	S.51	300	N/K	32'9"	30'4"	247·5	1716	2376	9·6
1923	CR-3	465	·66	22'8"	25'	148	2119	2747	18·5
	SEA LION III	550	·62	N/K¹	N/K	285	2403	3230	11·3
1925	R3C-2	600	·94	22'	20'2"	144	2134	2738	19
	GLOSTER III	700	·96	20'	26'10"	152	2028	2687	17·7
	M.33	435	·79	32'10"	27'4"	161	2073	2777	17
	S.4	700	·96	30'7"	26'7"	139	2600	3191	23
1926	M.39	800	1·12	30'4"	22'	156	2865	3548	22·7
	R3C-4	700	N/K	22'	20'	144	Not known. Said to be similar to R3C-2		28
	R3C-3	700	N/K	22'	20'	144			
1927	S.5 (geared)	875	1·29	26'9"	24'3"	115	2680	3242	

258

	GLOSTER IVB (geared)	875	1·12	22′5″	26′4″	139	2300	3085	22
1929	M.52	1000	1·43	29′5″	23′4″	151	2622	3340	22
	S.6	1900	1·54	30′	26′10″	145	4471	5771	40
	GLOSTER VI	1320	2·05	22′6″	26′3″	129	2292	2997	23
	M.67	1800	1·74	29′5″	23′5″	152	3890	4740	31
	M.52 R	1000	1·47	25′9″	23′4″	117	2578	3261	27·9
1931	S.6B	2350	2·03	30′	28′10″	145	4590	6086	42
	MC.72	2400	2·03	30′8″	28′3″	166	5510	6407	38·6

[1] Wing span known to have been less than Sea Lion II.

Sources

Sources

Lists of books consulted, lectures, articles and papers specifically referred to, aviation magazines studied, and societies, companies and individuals who have helped with my researches, are appended. My grateful thanks are due to all who have helped me so generously; but I must particularly mention Hank Kavelaars, of Rijswijk, Holland, and Tom Foxworth, of New York, who made their own wide researches on this subject fully available to me and who were unstinting in their help and advice.   RALPH BARKER

Books

Flight Without Formulae, by A. C. Kermode (Pitman, 1960).

Aviation of Today, Its History and Development, by J. L. Nayler and E. Ower (Warne, 1930).

Aviation: Its Technical Development, by J. L. Nayler and E. Ower (Owen, 1965).

British Racing and Record Aircraft, by Peter Lewis (Putnam, 1971).

Empire of the Air, by Viscount Templewood (Collins, 1957).

Swifter than Eagles, by John Laffin (Blackwood, 1964).

Trenchard, by Andrew Boyle (Collins, 1962).

A History of Marine Aviation, by John Killen (Muller, 1969).

Aeromarine Origins, by H. F. King (Putman, 1966).

British Flying Boats and Amphibians, by G. R. Duval (Putnam, 1966).

The Aeroplane: an Historical Survey of its Origins and Development, by C. H. Gibbs-Smith (H.M.S.O., 1960).

Avro Aircraft since 1908, by A. J. Jackson (Putnam, 1965).

Blackburn Aircraft since 1909, by A. J. Jackson (Putnam, 1968).

Hawker Aircraft since 1920, by Francis K. Mason (Putnam, 1961).

Take-off Into Greatness, by Grover Loening (Putnam New York, 1968).

Testing Time, by Constance Babington Smith (Cassell, 1961).

Lady Houston, D.B.E., by J. Wentworth Day (Wingate, 1958).

Lucy Houston, D.B.E., by Warner Allen (Constable, 1947).

Spitfire—The Story of a Famous Fighter, by Bruce Robertson (Harleyford, 1960).

The Great Air Races, by Don Vorderman (Doubleday, 1969).

War in the Air, Volume 1, by Sir Walter Raleigh (O.U.P., 1922 and 1969).

Wings, by Henri Biard (Hurst and Blackett, 1934).

The High Speed and Other Flights, by H. M. Schofield (Hamilton, 1932).

Schneider Trophy, by Wing Commander A. H. Orlebar (MacDonald, 1933).

Dowding and the Battle of Britain, by Robert Wright (Macdonald, 1969).

A Pride of Unicorns, by John Pudney (Oldbourne, 1960).

British Seaplanes Triumph in the International Schneider Trophy Contest, 1913-1931, by Ellison Hawks (Real Photographs, 1945).

Racing Planes and Air Races, Volumes I and II, by Reed Kinert (Aero Publishers Inc., Fallbrook, California, 1967).

Lectures, Articles and Papers

The Centenary Journal of the Royal Aeronautical Society, 1866-1966 (many articles and reminiscences).

My First Ten Years in Aviation, by Sir Thomas Sopwith (*Journal of the Royal Aeronautical Society*, Volume 65, No. 604, April 1961).

The Rotary Engine, by Norman Hall Warren (Air BP 41).

Fifty Years of Engineering Learning, by Air Commodore F. R. Banks (*Journal of the Royal Aeronautical Society*, Volume 72, No. 687, March 1968).

Milestones and Memories from 50 Years of Aero Engine Development, by A. C. Lovesey (11th Sir Henry Royce Memorial Lecture, Royal Aeronautical Society, 7th November 1966).

The Two Rs, 1904-1954: A Commemorative History of Rolls-Royce Aero Engines (*Flight*, 7th May 1954).

Sir Henry Royce, Bart: Lecture by Ivan Evernden, (*Journal of the Royal Aeronautical Society*, Volume 60, No. 552, December 1956).

The "R" Engine—a private paper by A. C. Lovesey.

The "R" Engine, by C. W. Morton (*Rolls-Royce News*, 29th April 1959).

R. J. Mitchell, Aircraft Designer, by Joe Smith (*The Aeroplane*, 29th January 1954).

Reginald Mitchell, 1895-1937, by Dr. Gordon Mitchell (R.A.F. Souvenir Book, 1966).

The Sopwith Tabloid, by John W. R. Taylor (*Model Aircraft*, December 1964).

From Sopwith Aviation to Hawker Siddeley Aviation, Lecture by John Crampton to Royal Aeronautical Society Historical Group, 19th January 1971.

The Royal Aero Club Gazette—Diamond Jubilee Year Book—1901 to 1961.

Various Aircraft Year Books published by the National Aeronautic Association, Washington, D.C.

The Curtiss R-6 Racer, by Thomas G. Foxworth (*Journal of the American Air Historical Society*, Summer 1970).

The Curtiss R2C Racers, by Thomas G. Foxworth (*Journal of the American Air Historical Society*, Spring 1966).

The Mystery Racers, Parts I and II (*Journal of the American Air Historical Society*, 1967).

The Supermarine S.4—S.6B, by C. F. Andrews and W. G. Cox (Profile Publications No. 39, 1965).

The Schneider Trophy, 1929, by Flight Lieutenant H. R. D. Waghorn (*Journal of the Royal Aeronautical Society*, Volume 34, No. 233, May 1930).

Glosters and the Schneider Trophy, by Basil Fielding (*Royal Aircraft Establishment News*, Volume 21, No. 11, November 1968).

Aeronautical Research Committee—1927 Schneider Trophy Contest—Collected Reports on British High-Speed Aircraft (H.M.S.O.).

Aeronautical Research Committee—Collected Reports on British High-Speed Aircraft for the 1931 Schneider Trophy Contest (H.M.S.O.).

The Schneider Trophy Seaplane—Some Notes on the Special Features of the S.6B—Prepared by the design staff of Supermarines under R. J. Mitchell (*Aircraft Engineering*, October 1931).

Aircraft Described No. 147, the Bernard V.2, by J. H. Robinson (*Aero Modeller*, January 1966).

The Schneider International Seaplane Contest, 1913-1931—Synopsis of a Lecture by W. G. Cox (*The Halton Magazine*, Volume XXV, No. 2, Summer 1962).

The Story of the Schneider Trophy Race, 1913 to 1931, by Henry R. Palmer (1962 Supplement to *This Was Air Travel*, Superior Publishing Company, Seattle).

Ali Nuove, Rome—Special Edition of 28th March 1959.

Il Reparto Alta Velocita, 1934-1954

Fiat Aviation 1908-1962 (Fiat Monograph No. 1).

Personal Biographies of Aviators (Musée de l'Air).

Fuel Problems of the 1931 Schneider Trophy Contest (Ethyl Export Corporation).

Group Captain Snaith Retires (unsigned article in *Royal Aircraft Establishment News*, Volume 21, No. 10, October 1968).

Cabinet Papers (Public Record Office).

Air Ministry Files covering the period (Public Record Office).

Technical Aspects of the Schneider Trophy Races—Lecture by Dr. Ing. Ermanno Bazzocchi to Royal Aeronautical Society branches at Coventry and Southampton, 17th and 18th March 1971.

Newspapers and Magazines

Flight	L'Aérophile
Aeroplane	L'Air
Aeronautics	Ala d'Italia
Aero and Hydro	Aeronautica
The Aero	Rivista Aeronautica
Aviation	Aircraft Illustrated
Flying	The Times
Aero Digest	New York Times
L'Aéronautique	Bournemouth Echo

The United States Works Progress Administration Bibliography of Aeronautics (Parts 5, 6 and 7—Seaplanes, Flying-Boats and Amphibians), compiled from the Index of Aeronautics of the Institute of Aeronautical Sciences (1938), lists many articles and papers in aviation magazines and journals on matters relating to the races.

Research Assistance

H. C. Kavelaars, of Rijswijk, Holland, who made his comprehensive albums of Schneider Trophy material available to me, and who helped in many other ways.

Thomas G. Foxworth, of New York, to whom I am indebted for much material on American participation.

The Royal Aeronautical Society Library.

Air Historical Branch, Ministry of Defence (Air).

Library, Ministry of Defence (Air).

Imperial War Museum.

British Museum Newspaper Library.

National Aeronautic Association (Washington, D.C.).

Royal Aeronautical Society (Coventry Branch).

Musée de l'Air.

Air Attaché, Italian Embassy, London.

Muzio Macchi, whose answers to my lengthy questionnaire cleared up many ambiguities on Italian participation.

Aeronautica Macchi, and especially Dr. Ing. Ermanno Bazzocchi and
Dr. Ing. Guilio C. Valdonio.

Divisione Aviazione, Fiat.

Dr. Ing. Franco Bugada, of Milan.

Giorgio Apostolo, of Milan.

Aurelio Piavani, for his translations of Italian documents.

Rolls-Royce, and especially C. W. Morton.

Hawker-Siddeley Aviation.

J. H. Robinson.

Bruce Robertson.

Leslie Hunt.

R. W. Elliott.

John Blake, Royal Aero Club.

Chaz Bowyer.

Alan Clifton.

M. Louis Meurillon and M. Jean Liron, whose researches into French
Schneider aircraft were an invaluable source.

Mervyn and Marie-Thérèse Mills.

R. N. Dorey, formerly of Rolls-Royce.

B. S. Shenstone.

Derek N. James.

W. Woolston.

National Air and Space Museum, Smithsonian Institution.

Interviews and Correspondence

Personal interviews and correspondence with the following produced
much valuable material:

Sir Thomas Sopwith

Lt. Gen. James H. Doolittle, U.S.A.F.

Air Vice-Marshal S. N. Webster

Air Vice-Marshal F. W. Long

Air Commodore D. D'Arcy A. Greig

Air Commodore F. R. Banks

Air Commodore Sydney Smith

Wing Commander T. H. Moon

Captain Hubert Broad

A. C. Lovesey

Mrs. A. H. Orlebar

The late R. W. Kenworthy

Mrs. Kenworthy

Index